Hindi Cinema

Hindi Cinema
An Insider's View

Anil Saari

with an Introduction by
Partha Chatterjee

OXFORD
UNIVERSITY PRESS

YMCA Library Building, Jai Singh Road, New Delhi 110 001

Oxford University Press is a department of the University of Oxford.
It furthers the University's objective of excellence in research,
scholarship, and education by publishing worldwide in

Oxford New York

Auckland Cape Town Dar es Salaam Hong Kong Karachi Kuala Lumpur
Madrid Melbourne Mexico City Nairobi New Delhi Shanghai Taipei Toronto

With offices in
Argentina Austria Brazil Chile Czech Republic France Greece Guatemala
Hungary Italy Japan Poland Portugal Singapore South Korea Switzerland
Thailand Turkey Ukraine Vietnam

Oxford is a registered trademark of Oxford University Press
in the UK and in certain other countries

Published in India by Oxford University Press, New Delhi

ISBN 13: 978-019-569584-7
ISBN 10: 019-569584-4

Typeset in GoudyOlSt BT 11/14.2
by Excellent Laser Typesetters, Pitampura, Delhi 110 034
Printed at Roopak Printers, Delhi 110 032
Published by Oxford University Press
YMCA Library Building, Jai Singh Road, New Delhi 110 001

Contents

Perspectives on
Indian Cinema

The Makers of
Popular Cinema

Introduction

Hindi cinema's enormous reach across India and around the world is a subject of keen interest for cineastes these days. Its pot-pourri of ingredients—not the least its moorings in melodrama, which in turn is often bolstered by crude comedy and gratuitous sub-plots, and of course the fights, songs, and dances—is both a source of exasperation and wonder for new converts. In the Indian filmgoer's mind, it is an equivalent of the Nautanki, a variety entertainment in the folk tradition, which has fed off folk tales and epics like the Ramayana and the Mahabharata even when dealing with contemporary issues, and was therefore hugely popular with people of all classes in northern India well before the advent of cinema.

Even the science-oriented non-resident Indian population in Silicon Valley, California, sees commercial Hindi films on weekends to relax. As escapist entertainment and stress busters, they are second to none.

The poet, dramatist, journalist, and film aficionado, Anil Saari, was Hindi cinema's most enthusiastic advocate more than thirty years ago. Blessed with both a sharp critical faculty and brashness which stayed with him until his death in 2005, Anil was able to see many virtues in Hindi films, which in the eyes of other critics and intellectuals, mostly Western-educated, were nothing but crass mass entertainment—an opiate for a teeming population that was largely illiterate and impoverished. The money, according to cynical film distributors, at a time when Anil was cutting his teeth in film criticism, came from 'C' grade film centres in small towns and semi-rural India. He and Hamiduddin Mehmood were the two serious film critics from the 1970s who understood why commercial Hindi cinema was so overwhelmingly popular with audiences all over India. But the more overt champion of the 'Bumbaiya phillum' was Anil, for he had, through study and instinct, understood what made it tick.

In his seminal essay 'The Dynamics of Tradition and Modernity in Hindi Cinema', he observed:

On the one hand, its format violates the Aristotelian concept of the three unities of time, space, and action. On the other, it cannot be completely designated as a modern variation of a well-preserved folk tradition. It is influenced both by the world that confronts it—the Euro-American world— and the world of the vigorous traditions of Indian folk theatre. The two worlds impinge on the Indian's psyche and never allow him to escape from the psychological parameters of being a villager.

His early years in the industrial city of Kanpur in Uttar Pradesh perhaps contributed to the shaping of his sensibilities. He did his schooling and undergraduate studies there. Anil's father, Arjun Arora, was co-founder of the Communist Party of India (CPI) in UP and an active, highly regarded trade union leader. His mother, Raj Arora, was a doctor by training. This early exposure to the realities of the world gave him insights that not many of his tribe were privy to:

Yet it must constantly borrow from the affluent alien's film culture. For the Euro-American civilization of today is like a pot of gold at the end of the rainbow for the Indian whose psyche lies in the shadow of a long, callous history of economic disparities; a psyche that tries to preserve itself and its shell of flesh and bones from the wretched sea of poverty that exists all around it. The dividing line is so thin and fragile that consciousness can only lead each man to conceive of himself as an oasis in the desert. [from 'The Dynamics of Tradition and Modernity in Hindi Cinema']

It is to this escape from poverty and from the boredom of the humdrum reality of daily life that Hindi cinema has addressed itself with great dedication (without sounding ironic or patronizing) for the last forty-five years or more. It did, without really intending to (the Hindi film producer was first of all interested in profit and, only as an afterthought, in plaudits), affirm the status quo and strengthen the hands of all exploitative political parties, while on screen it preached what can be called a 'refracted egalitarianism' leavened with religion. Anil understood this aspect of Hindi cinema very well. His own politics, despite stout protestations to the contrary, was firmly progressive and evinced deep social commitment. He was, more than almost any other critic of his time or since, aware of the role that cinema would play in the building of an emerging democracy. India, after all, attained freedom in 1947. For him, entertainment and an awareness of socio-economic realities could go hand in hand as the vigorous, perceptive plays of Bertolt Brecht had proved in Europe. He was a great admirer of the poet–playwright who had escaped from Hitler's Germany and survived Senator McCarthy's Red witch hunt during his exile in Hollywood in the late 1940s through sheer cunning, literary genius not withstanding.

Anil had perhaps secretly hoped that Hindi cinema would produce its own Brecht whose awareness of life's inequities and its attendant politics would permeate the sensibilities of the market. But that did not happen, for the historical conditions were wanting. He observes, not without a certain regret:

[The] overall conservative framework of values is also stressed at the very end of the film. Its main purpose is to reassure the mass audience that the status quo shall be maintained; that they are not being confronted with the possibility and the trauma of a total upheaval in society which is a fairly frightening thing for the average Indian who cannot think beyond survival. It is a psychological obstacle that has drowned successive attempts at an Indian revolution. [from 'The Compelling World of Hindi Films']

He was alive to the possibilities of cinema, particularly Indian cinema, and the creative energies that emanated from it despite the financial and distribution obstacles in its path. Since Hindi films had the largest market and hence also the largest financial outlay, the burden on it to come good at the box office was also the heaviest. Despite such odds, talented directors, technicians, and actors emerged at regular intervals. Entertaining and sometimes enlightening films continued to be made. Of all the film-makers who contributed to the growth of Hindi films in the 1950s, Anil was most drawn to Guru Dutt, whose knowledge of Hindi and Urdu was at best sketchy but who nevertheless had a knack for attracting some of the best talent around him—scriptwriter Abrar Alvi, cinematographer V.K. Murthy, composers O.P. Nayyar and S.D. Burman, not to forget fine actors like Waheeda Rehman, Meena Kumari, Mala Sinha, Rehman, and Johnny Walker.

Guru Dutt made deeply-felt films of a pessimistic nature, where individuals were trapped by social conventions and the debilitating politics that emerged from it. Of course, he maintained in his work the outward forms of the commercial Hindi film of his day, had melodious songs which he filmed with grace and fluidity, and obligatory comic scenes to provide relief to the melodrama so integral to the plot. But within these limitations, he was able to make remarkably perceptive films. Anil was the first Indian critic to recognize Guru Dutt's cinematic gifts and to put them in the proper artistic perspective. He was also able to point out before any of his peers that Raj Kapoor's cinema was built around the songs in his films and that each song took the narrative forward. Raj Kapoor's socialist intent emerged through his Everyman character modelled on Chaplin's tramp, resulting in his astonishing popularity in the Soviet Union and even in certain Latin American countries! The melodious songs in his films composed by the Shanker–Jaikishen duo and simple storylines dealing with poor people trying to get by in a ruthless world, contributed to the success of his films.

The structures within which Hindi cinema functions and the place of poetry, or rather its use within it, are considered very seriously by Anil. He was acutely aware of the evolving language, grammar, and syntax of Hindi cinema and thus observed:

Mainstream Indian cinema has a long history of association between poets, the poetic tradition, and the making of films. This is so because the sprawling patchwork of fragmented episodes that structure the Indian film is anchored, kept in place, and united thematically by the philosophical world view that the film subscribes to and expostulates. [from 'The Use of Poetry in Hindi Cinema']

He further elaborates in the same piece: 'Both in Indian folk theatre and in mainstream Indian films, the outline of the philosophical world view is, therefore, written out and delineated not through the events of the plot but directly addressed to the audience through poetic invocations, songs and chants.'

The unenviable position of the scriptwriter in Hindi films, despite the presence of such literary stalwarts in the last seventy years as Saadat Hasan Manto, Ismat Chughtai, Krishan Chander, Rajinder Singh Bedi, Abrar Alvi, Rahi Masoom Raza, and Gulzar had not escaped Anil's attention. They were poorly paid and had to work under severe constraints. He felt the blame lay on both sides. The writers were not aware of what was required of them, given a film's final destination in the market place. The producers and directors were not aware of the difference that good writing could make to raise the quality of their films. It was, and continues to be, a Catch-22 situation.

Bad writing or not, Hindi films reach a large audience and are being appreciated for reasons more sociological than artistic. In a review of *Kabhi Alvida Naa Kehna* directed by Karan Johar, in the serious British magazine on cinema, *Sight and Sound*, Naman Rama Chandran, a critic of Indian origin, has the gall to suggest that in the not very distant future, the mushy films of Karan Johar will be taken as seriously as the melodramas of Douglas Sirk, the Hollywood master of the 1940s and 1950s.

Impetuous as Anil may have been on certain occasions, he would have thought twice before making such rash statements. A year before he passed away, he saw a film by Sabeeha Sumer, a young Pakistani director from Karachi. Her *Khamosh Pani* ('Silent Waters') affected him so deeply that he saw it six times during its run in Delhi. He recommended it to as many people as he possibly could and called it 'the best film from the sub-continent in the last twenty years'. This was in 2005. Whether *Khamosh Pani* was all that he said it was is a moot point but one thing is certain that it is indeed a deeply moving film about a Sikh woman who stays on in Pakistan after the partition, having been rescued by a neighbour who marries her and leaves her a widow some years later. In a bitter irony of fate, her young son becomes a fundamentalist.

The troubles of the unfortunate woman left their mark on Anil and though he may have somewhat exaggerated the film's cinematic qualities, he was right about the sincerity of its intentions and its deep humanity. *Khamosh Pani*'s greatest strength was its rootedness and that gave it a resonance, a ring of truth. Anil responded to all these traits in the film wholeheartedly. He was at that time diagnosed with cancer and fighting it with all he had. It was necessary for him even more than before, to find something that contained within it the seeds of truth, an essentialness capable of standing up to the most rigorous intellectual cross-examination.

It was this seeking that often led him up blind alleys but, equally, it put him, perhaps more than any contemporary critic claiming knowledge of cinema or an allegiance to it, in a unique position— that of an individual capable of prescience even while watching the humblest of films. He was, many a time, rewarded because of his patience. Watching Khyentse Korbu's *The Cup* with him was without doubt a pleasurable experience. This film, directed by an ordained Buddhist monk from Bhutan, had the simplicity and beauty of birdsong. As we came out of the auditorium at India International Centre in Delhi, both of us exclaimed in unison, 'Why can't we make such films in India?' He knew of course that making such a simple, beautiful, and profound film was not of the volition of a film-maker. He needed to have a kind of innocence, a natural receptivity to life's experiences and offerings, apart from qualities like hard work, discipline, and talent. These were the virtues that the young Satyajit Ray possessed when he made the Apu trilogy (*Pather Panchali*, *Aparajito*, and *Apur Sansar*, all based on Bibhuti Bhushan Bandopadhyay's Bengali novel *Pather Panchali*).

Anil recognized Ray's great artistry in these films, and perhaps fond memories of them prevented him from being disrespectful towards him, especially when comparing him with Ritwik Ghatak, a director he admired almost with the same passion as he did Guru Dutt. He felt Ray, in his latter years, was busy trying to be faithful to the tenets of a particular genre, while Ghatak regarded the story as a vehicle to find the cinematic form to the film he was engaged in. Though he respected Ray for his consistency and the undeniably high calibre of his cinema, it was the so called 'outsiders' Ghatak and Guru Dutt who caught his fancy. Ray, in his eyes, was the universally admired classicist, whereas Ghatak and Guru Dutt were iconoclasts who were destined to have troubled lives on and off the screen. He preferred the sweat and tears of struggle in an artiste's endeavours to the lucidity and the whiff of certitude that comes with predictable success.

His interest in Hindi films was not confined to their content and presentation. He was also intrigued by the way they were financed and exhibited. The stable sources of finance disappeared with the well-known production companies. After the collapse of studios like Prabhat, Bombay Talkies, Ranjeet Moviestone, Imperial, and Filmistan, soon after the partition of India in 1947, freelancers, mostly of the fly-by-night type, came into film production in Bombay in the hope of making a killing. People with disposable but unaccounted money became investors in Hindi films with the desire of making more!

Thus he explains Hindi cinema's persistence despite its unpredictable performance at the box office, the occasional hit or superhit being an exception, in this way:

Why there has not been a slump in feature film production in the country is that finance—often from new sources—is still readily available for commercial films; recession or no recession. As filmwallahs rightly believe, there will always be people ready to invest money in popular commercial films because the Indian film industry is one of the few avenues open to the medium or small-scale investor to convert his black money funds into legitimate money. Film financing remains one of the best means to invest black money and reap 'white' money returns. [*from* 'Black Money as the Mainstay of Hindi Cinema']

The situation, one may add, has not changed all that much. The small fry are now big fish in the game. Adlabs, a reputed film-processing and printing laboratory and production house was bought out by the Ambanis, the richest industrial family in India. It also has a very large interest in a chain of state-of-the-art multiplexes (with exorbitant ticket prices). Thus, at one go, the company now controls all the stages of film production—the actual making of the film through all its stages, its distribution on completion, and finally its showing to a paying public, that is production, distribution, and exhibition.

However, the small players, especially in towns and mofussil areas, will not be pushed out so easily. The economic growth has in the main benefited metropolitan cities, and the 10 per cent of population that comprises the elite. The multiplexes are for them because only they have the purchasing power to visit them regularly. For the rest, more conventional, perhaps less shabby than before, environs will have to suffice.

True, the makeshift and/or the travelling film theatre with its aura of romance, rickety film projectors, and tattered or patched up screens has made way for the portable video projector, and cumbersome cans of 35 mm film have been replaced by the VCD, and now increasingly, the DVD. But what Anil wrote so movingly about small, often improvised film theatres, or rather screening places, has not changed essentially. They continue to be an important source of revenue and will be so for some time to come, at least till a more equitable, economically just social order comes into being in India.

Then, as it is now, it was audiences who patronized rudimentary exhibition facilities, which made Hindi cinema a financially viable proposition. This explains the continuous falling back on the age-old epics for story material and mixing with it prevalent consumerist trends and the superficial emulation of social values. Though this also suggests a new way of storytelling which, in reality, has never been more than old wine in a new bottle. Similarly, the expansion of the market—what with the NRI populations across the world, the coming of video technology, and the sale of a film's music/songs—has not affected the character or spirit of the average commercial Hindi film fundamentally. The runaway successes of Sanjay Leela Bhansali's *Devdas* and *Black* and Kunal Kohli's *Fanaa* in recent years, despite their florid, melodramatic credentials, with audiences at home and abroad, of course of Indo-Pak origin, need no elaboration. Their lack of sophistication is invariably seen as mark of sincerity.

Anil was critical of Bhansali's *Devdas* and Bhansali's desire to earn immortality through it by investing every shot with frenetic energy with little thought or real feeling. His essay on the film shows him to be genuinely alive to the aesthetics and craft of film-making. He demolishes Bhansali without malice and with some erudition. At the beginning of his essay, Anil observes:

There is an axiom of literary criticism, expounded by the American scholar Yvor Winters, that should be posted at every film school in the world. Winters insisted that all poetry should make sense in terms of the living experience; even a poem written by T.S. Eliot or Gerard Manley Hopkins, he declared. [*from* 'What Went Wrong with Bhansali's *Devdas*?']

In continuation of his argument, and in defence of his critiquing *Devdas*, he says,

Sanjay Leela Bhansali's interpretation of Sarat Chandra's *Devdas* too thus emanates from his obvious desire to transform the novel into a cinematic narrative poem. Yet, as so often happens in Indian cinema when the director aims to create 'a poem on celluloid', the basic premises of aesthetic communication become blurred. [*from* 'What Went Wrong with Bhansali's *Devdas*?']

This *Devdas*, in colour and bursting at the seams with lurid melodrama, made quite a lot of money for its producer Bharat Shah, a diamond merchant. A film, especially an outright commercial one, invariably reflects, however crudely, the world around it. It is in the end a visual chronicle of the history of a country, city, culture in a given moment in time. Popular cinema willy-nilly is a vehicle for the depiction of a culture through the behaviour of characters enacting a story on screen.

The psyche of a nation, if at all there is such a thing, can also surely be conveyed with subtlety and imagination through films that are not in the outright commercial mould. The films of Satyajit Ray and Ritwik Ghatak in Bengal and Adoor Gopalakrishnan, G. Aravindan, and John Abraham in Kerala also depicted many complexities of life with clarity, beauty, and integrity. They have been, in a sense, the cultural ambassadors of Indian cinema abroad. Anil, however, was not satisfied with their performance at home because they failed to reach the 'all India' audience which patronized and sustained commercial cinema.

The fact that Satyajit Ray—who apart from being a great artistic success, was also the most commercially successful director in Bengali cinema[*]—was not able to find a large audience at the national level rankled with Anil. Why he felt this way is difficult to guess. He may have felt disappointed because none of the Indian art film-makers were able to communicate with an expansive viewership like the Hollywood masters from the 1920s, 1930s, and 1940s—Charlie Chaplin, John Ford, and, in his latter years, Alfred Hitchcock being some of the names that come to mind.

He was not convinced of the genuineness of the parallel cinema movement in the 1970s, and felt that although commercial Hindi cinema absorbed certain narrative techniques from it much to its benefit, the reverse had not happened in making the so-called

---

[*] A fact brought home to me by Tarun Mazumdar, one of Bengal's most successful commercial film-makers.

serious films more gripping and therefore audience-friendly. He never shook off the Leftist humanist values imbibed in his formative years, although his vision broadened as he went along and his curiosity about the world stayed with him till the end. The feeling that an artist must communicate with the largest number of people possible never quite left him. Immediately after his postgraduation from Kirori Mal College, Delhi University, he produced, along with painter J. Swaminathan of Leftist persuasion, who took a more credulous, even mystical path soon after, and Rajesh Mehra, a cynic and artist of considerable talent, an art magazine called *Contra 66*. Anil threw himself into the venture wholeheartedly, supervising the printing and publishing, apart from looking at proofs, raising funds, and writing art criticism.

Contra 66 ceased publication after a year but not before making a splash in the art world. It could not reach out to the larger audience that thirty years ago was yet far away from when the proliferation of galleries and buyers was to happen due to an economic upsurge, albeit of a limited nature, and when many artists for the first time since Independence could reap the fruits of their labour.

It was in the late 1960s—1968 to be precise—that he took to film criticism while retaining a keen interest in the other arts. In order to meet his filial obligations, he also worked at *Screen* of the *Indian Express* group of newspapers, *India Today*, *Sunday*, and *Hindustan Times*. He single-handedly brought out an issue of *Sunday* on India's defence policy and practice. He proved to be an astute political journalist, but he gave that up and returned to film criticism and wrote passionately every week about the latest commercial releases of Hindi and Hollywood films. His knowledge of world cinema continued to be augmented by his regular attendance at Delhi Film Society screenings and international film festivals.

Anil was a bilingual poet who wrote in English and Hindi. His favourite poet, Kabir, a leading poet of the Bhakti movement in northern India in the fifteenth century, wrote about complex existential problems in the most clear yet poetically-charged language. In his own poetry, and perhaps unconsciously, in his prose including film criticism, Anil wished to emulate Kabir and like him always strove to get to the heart of the matter.

While generally the most balanced and astute of observes, Anil could sometimes be led astray by his deeply held convictions. His anti-colonialism, for example, is patently visible when he says:

We have also made the mistake of concentrating on Europe for opening up a market for the art film. This has been at the cost of pushing away younger directors from the traditional overseas markets for the Indian film which is mainly in the post-colonial countries of Asia and Africa. (*from* 'Indian Goof-ups at International Film Festivals')

The trouble with this argument is that the average Indian art film was a dull, boring affair either full of platitudes or, worse still, philosophical ramblings leading nowhere. The market for such productions, then as now, was practically non-existent. Though they did win kudos at obscure film festivals abroad, no distributor worth his salt would touch them because for him the bottom line was always box-office success.

Anil was also generous and perceptive about actresses from Hindi cinema's past. His observation: 'Waheeda Rehman and Nutan were the angels of black-and-white cinema, their faces so eloquently expressive, their eyes so full of depth, in the play of light and shade' (*from* 'Golden Girls of a Golden Era') is certainly unusual but it stands up to scrutiny despite its overt romantic subjectivity. In the same essay he quotes the noted film lyricist and Urdu poet Sahir Ludhianvi on Meena Kumari, another major actress from the 1950s and 1960s: 'She was an artiste with a rare talent,' said Sahir 'with the soul of a poet which she had to sacrifice. Her youth was spent in depicting the various tragedies that befall Indian women, with no time to think of her own tragedy.'

Anil turns away from romantic allusions to hard reality when he discusses the social implications of the change in business mores caused by the crumbling of joint family structures that brought about the clash between tradition and modernity in the two decades following Independence in 1947. This led to a change in the status of women, although they were still at a major dis- advantage vis-à-vis men. It is the pain of being disadvantaged that was reflected in the visage of actresses like Suraiyya, Nalini Jayant, Meena Kumari, Madhubala, Geeta Bali, and even Nutan and Waheeda Rehman. But this had its benefits because they went on to play some of the meatiest parts in Hindi cinema. No mean achievement this, considering that there were star actors like Ashok Kumar, Raj Kapoor, Dilip Kumar, and Dev Anand, not to speak of eloquent character artistes like Motilal and Balraj Sahni, to pit their talents against.

Despite Anil's preoccupation with Indian films, particularly Hindi films, his knowledge of world cinema was vast. That, and his wide reading in literature—Indian and Western—philosophy, and sociology, gave his film criticism credibility. He was always at pains to be fair in his essays and reviews without curbing his enthusiasm for the burgeoning possibilities of the medium itself. He was intrigued by the various forms of narrative cinema, parti- cularly of the popular variety, and how much it had changed in its narrative strategies over the years without in any essential way changing in its core.

His insights were informed by his keen interest in politics and history, national and international affairs, and the almost imperceptible changes that come about in the behaviour of individuals and groups caught in a scientific and historical flux. He was from time to time able to record in his film essays these seismic changes, often so slight as to be overlooked, in a language that was clear enough to be understood and appreciated by a reasonably intelligent newspaper reader.

Long before scholars from the School of Oriental and African Studies led by sociologist Rachel Dwyer discovered the 'hidden possibilities' of Hindi cinema, Anil Saari paved the way. He dwelt on social and historical facts rooted in everyday life that led to a rich cinematic interpretation of reality in Hindi cinema. That, perhaps, was his major achievement as a film critic.

Delhi   PARTHA CHATTERJEE
November 2008   Film-maker and Critic

The Aesthetic Foundations
of the Hindi Formula Film

The Dynamics of Tradition
and Modernity in Hindi Cinema

Why has Hindi cinema failed to shed its over-the-top emotionalism and digressive narrative form? Is the Indian film-maker as much of a survivalist as the average Indian? The perennial question of aesthetics in popular cinema is addressed in order to understand the psyche of the average film-maker and his audience.

The 'popular Hindi film'—also known as the box-office formula film and the commercial film—is a genre in itself in international cinema. It is a genre that defies easy categorization.

On the one hand, its format violates the Aristotelian concept of the three unities of time, space, and action. On the other, it cannot be completely designated as a modern variation of a well-preserved folk tradition. It is influenced both by the world that confronts it—the Euro-American world—and the world of the vigorous traditions of Indian folk theatre. The two worlds impinge on the Indian's psyche and never allow him to escape from the psychological parameters of being a villager.

Existing in a no-man's land, the popular Indian film or, as may be a more appropriate definition in aesthetic terms, the Indian pop film, is an eclectic, assimilative, imitative, and plagiaristic creature that is constantly rebelling against its influences—Hollywood and European cinema and traditional Indian aesthetics and lifestyles.

Everything that it borrows from the Euro-American film scene it distorts and caricatures; in the manner of the village actor for whom nothing is sacred save the presence that the human body may command in a folk-theatre arena.

Yet it must constantly borrow from the affluent alien's film culture. For the Euro-American civilization of today is like a pot of gold at the end of the rainbow for the Indian whose psyche lies in the shadow of a long, callous history of economic disparities; a psyche that tries to preserve itself and its shell of flesh and bones from the wretched sea of poverty that exists all around it. The dividing line is so thin and fragile that consciousness can only lead each man to conceive of himself as an oasis in the desert.

The Indian pop film is the most sustained articulation of the pressures of the Euro-American lifestyle on the contemporary Indian's mind. Because the objects of modern technology—from the bicycle, the train, and the automobile to the massive and intricately designed factories—are so photogenic in appearance and so cinematically powerful in their physical-ness, the face of the technological world has always been intrinsic to cinema as a counterpoint to the timeless images of elemental life: the river, the lake, and the sea, the pretty flowers and trees. By counterposing images of technology with images of nature, cinema probes the human animal's relationships with the environment. Now merging into it, now dominating it, we hear and see the love song or the car ride in the rain or the lovers standing atop a dam or a cable car. The camera zooms in on the stars and fills the silver screen with their handsome bodies and their sentiment-suffused faces. The Bhakra-Nangal complex and the valley in the Alps are reduced to little more than studio backdrops.

For the Indian pop film-maker and his audience, the objects of technology are not merely cinematic motifs that mirror individuals in action, in a relationship with their environment. They are also the motifs of an elusive, largely inaccessible paradise on earth. This is what you could be doing, says the film-maker when he shows his lead players driving a car or carousing in a swimming pool, instead of pushing your way into an overcrowded city bus, cycling down a narrow, bumpy unending village track, or splashing in a village pond or a temple tank.

However, even as the film-makers give us this message, even as we lap it up, it is clear that this is a dream that can only be realized by a minority of the 8 million-odd Indians who fill some 9000 good, bad, and temporary cinema theatres every day of the year. Modern technology's gadget paradise on earth becomes a dream that can only be dreamt and scarcely pursued.

Nature's images of eternal life, on the other hand, belong to a world whose history has been one of uncertainty and travail, of poverty and extreme economic disparities, of feudal tyrannies and a monotonous routine. It is a world closed to technology, except in the bits and pieces that the rich landlords or big farmers 'import' from the city. The ecological monotony of village India lends itself, like a telepathic momentum, to the large-scale migration of peasants to urban centres and the urban young leaving India for England, Europe, and North America.

As the popular Indian film constantly posits it, ever since India became independent on 15 August 1947, modern technological aspirations have been interlocked with a largely feudal pastoral reality. The former injects a desire for change into the latter, which in turn colours the former with conservative dimensions of survival and consolidation.

Post-Independence industrialization in India, as in most other Third World countries, has been haphazard, restricted to regional pockets, and has had little effect on traditional socio-economics. Since twentieth-century industrialization in a society like India's is not the result of a self-propelling industrial (or technological) revolution but a process of change by grafting, much in the manner of a middle-class family that saves every penny it can to purchase possessions and properties that shall finally enable it to rise above its economic class, no clear demarcations between social mores, cultural values, and lifestyle can be made. Realism becomes impossible as style in the arts.

This amorphous social background provides the basis of the confusing format of the Indian pop film. Popular cinema is the most alert medium of communication in Indian society, because it is consistently concerned with preserving its enormous popularity. The demands of popular appeal see to it that the medium does not depart from the essence of the social situation. If mass media have the ability to introduce the common folk to new directions in life, the Indian experience also emphasizes the fact that mass media cannot depart too dramatically from life as it is—awkward and undefined. Mass media cannot introduce a greater rationality than that which already exists within society. Indeed, in many ways, the media must place itself on the lowest level at which certain mores and values are commonly accepted.

Such a role came naturally to the Indian pop film. It has never conceived of itself in aggressive terms. Even today, when its presence invades every city and town and a number of villages, it does not dare to assert itself as the dominating culture in the country. On the other hand, it has always been defensive and clamouring for social responsibility. This defensive posture of the most powerful and widespread communications media is the result of a 'living tradition' of contradictions in Indian society.

The feudal division of court culture and folk culture has, in India, become enmeshed within the idealistic culture espoused by the Indian religious order. In most parts of India, artistic activity is an intrinsic element of religious rituals and ceremonies. Over the centuries, these religious rituals have assumed an identity that makes the artistic activity merely a concretization of the philosophic essence of the ritual. The temples were not merely the schools of dance and music, they also made dance and music subservient to religious and philosophic ideals. This, in turn, fostered dogmas about the arts, about the grammar of their form, and about their social role.

This elitism in the arts coincided with the elitist categorization of society under the caste system. Certain types of music and dance were, like certain types of people, commendable, socially acceptable, and worthy of patronage. Other types of arts and people were 'untouchable'. These unrespectable arts came to include all those cultural forms that were not part of the religious framework or, as it turned out, art not patronized by at the court. These were the arts of the poor, far removed from the direct influences of court and temple.

The popularity of cinema in India is not accidental. It became a symbol of industrialization and of the new world society, as India sought to transform itself and enter the twentieth century. Indeed, the cinema theatre became the new temple. In the tradition of religious-cultural events such as the Ram Lila—the dramatic enactment of the story of the Ramayana—Janamashtami—the celebration of the birth of Lord Krishna—and other festivals such as Holi and Diwali, cinema gave a sense of the collective to a people bred as ciphers in a tight-knit community living in the very heart of industrialization, its sprawling cities, and its dehumanizing effects.

Cinema not only became the new arena of folk theatre, it went further and introduced a new religious pantheon of gods, goddesses, and priests. It destroyed the old and made common people look at themselves, rather than at superior beings. In many ways, the history of the Indian feature film—from its inception in 1912—is a history of rediscovery, by the Indian city, of folk theatre. The forbidden culture of a colloquial, iconoclastic, slangy version of the epics that the folk performers had created was now brought into the open and housed in palace-like edifices in the very centre of the rich minority's city. Admission was not only cheap, it was open to all who could pay for a cinema ticket. The film became an agent of liberation from the dogmatic, idealistic world of morality and religion and from the deprivations of poverty.

The Indian pop film is the only cultural outlet that Indian people have which accepts the great contradictions of Indian society within one format—the idealistic and the immoral, the ascetic and the hedonistic, the rags and the riches, the brave and the ludicrous. As against the caste system, religious elitism and sectarianism, and the concepts of art and culture in the court and among the ruling elite which divide various aspects of life and separate people on to different levels—in the way the Hindu joint family imposes definite stereotype roles on family members—the Indian pop film is willing to incorporate an innumerable number of people, details, motifs, facets, and events from everyday life in order to create a world view as close to and comprehensive as real life, no matter how chaotic that is.

Like the Hindu epics, whose familiar stories reawaken the hopes of a hopeless people, the Indian pop film has evolved a rationale of its own. Thus one film is like another. Each film confirms once again the world as it is and has been and is likely to remain. The very hopelessness created by poverty and social immobility demands that the world and the attractions of the world remain as they are. That, indeed, is how it is for the average Indian who is not a member of the ruling elite.

Yet there is also the human instinct for change, the desire to enlarge one's personality and one's presence, to transform oneself. Overriding that instinct is also the fear that a tidal change may sweep the small man aside and drown him. Ordinary Indians are people living on the border of extinction, surviving against odds all the time; they are a people who are too frightened to change lest they destroy even the little that preserves them presently. Therefore, the symbol of change must be one of make-believe.

Out of this tension between aspiration and fear has emerged the Indian pop film. It is an agent of liberation and also an agent of extreme conservatism. It is a show-piece of 'the sweet life' and of the wretched, a compound of clean, moral values enshrined by the family and the social framework and, on the other hand, of debauchery and hedonism, erotica and sensuousness.

This is the first 'formula' of the Indian pop film. The first precondition that the film must live up to if it is to be acceptable as a mass medium for those who feel 'deprived' or victimized by society. Each film must deal with as comprehensive a picture of the whole world as possible. For the cinema story is not about individual men and women but about situations common to a large audience. It is a cinema that must articulate collective dreams that the social system does not easily approve the articulation of; a cinema that must also confront the people with what they want out of life.

The need for a comprehensive world view imposes a highly stylized and formal format that in its broad outlines is symbolic, suggestive, and allegorical of the total world view of life on the Indian scene. Indian film-makers, most of whom have quickly shed any pretensions to art that they might have started with, and who work like hard-boiled businessmen dealing in an entertainment medium with heavy allegorical references, have evolved a list of ingredients that they consider acceptable to the mass audience. These elements can be seen in film after film, thereby provoking the label of 'the formula film'. Yet, because life is in a constant state of flux, the formulas are shuffled and recast from time to time.

The Indian pop film's relationship to trends and fashion in society is clearly discernible in the way the various formula ingredients are discovered and discarded. Essentially the Indian pop film is concerned with reflecting or portraying the human animal in an environment he is conscious of, does not have, but can acquire. It makes itself attractive by offering entertainment novelties that are not commonly available. The cabaret dance sequence of the Indian pop film stepped-in during the mid-1950s when big city hotels launched nightspots with women dancers and crooners. During the 1950s, however, the simulated cabaret dance in the pop film (for example, Nadira's dance in Raj Kapur's *Shree 420*) was located in a private club and not in a regular nightspot. It was only during the early 1960s, when nightclubs sprouted all over the metropolis, that the cabaret dance sequence came into its own. Throughout the 1960s and the 1970s, the cabaret dance sequence of the Hindi

pop film (which has been the forerunner and the dominant sub-
genre of the Indian pop film circuit) was a necessary requirement
for each and every film. It was only when it had become jaded and
commonplace that it began to be cut out of the show. It was no
longer a novelty for the audience.

This casual, stock-taker's attitude about the film's ingredients is
primarily a result of the fact that the images of contemporary reality
shown in the Indian pop film are the details within the rigid
framework of the 'film as an epic' about the contradictions and
categorization in Indian life. Within that rigid framework, these
details are constituted by the pop film's reflections of the way its
audience lives or desires to live. Every serious producer of Indian
pop films wishes to present these details as originally as possible.
The framework, however, remains the same.

The Indian pop film has evolved a highly individualistic format
for its purpose that is episodic in structure. Each episode is, in a
way, complete in itself with its own cathartic climax. The various
ingredients can, therefore, be cinematically unrelated to each
other—as, for instance, through flaws in continuity—without
disturbing the overall framework of the film.

The episodic structure is convenient both for simulating a
comprehensive world view and for keeping up with the times. It
also helps to make the Indian pop film a more engaging mass
medium than any other. The very looseness and imperfection of
the episodic structure makes it possible for a pop film to incorporate
the most recent happenings in Indian society and to give shape to
the very 'latest' objects of technology, fashions in daily living, and
social trends and events. This is largely done not in visual but in
verbal terms, with a strong satirical dimension, in order to
incorporate comment and reaction. Very often the pop film turns
out to be the first among the mass media to locate and comment
upon new social trends. This is because newspapers and magazines
in India are fairly elitist and rarely express the common man's
perspective. And when they do express his perspective, it is only

in terms of deflating his ego. Highly derivative of the mass media and fashions in Europe and North America, Indian newspapers and magazines coerce their readers to imitate things that are being done abroad. The Indian pop film, on the other hand, reduces objects and fashions from the Euro-American civilization into caricatures adorned with the shape, colours, and awkwardness of the Indian urban landscape. It reduces the 'foreign', 'alien', and inaccessible to a motley shape, an object of parody rather than one which could make the film-goer feel inferior.

Since radio and TV are didactic and propagandist organs controlled by the government, they do not have a mass-audience of their own at cultural level. Radio and TV cater primarily to the needs of political information and developmental instruction. At a cultural level, their programmes are divided into three sections. A major chunk of radio and TV time is devoted to classical music and dance. This is derived from temple and court art and does not command a mass audience because of its rarified and dogmatic aesthetics. A second need is rather 'educational', 'morally uplifting', or 'intellectual' in tone. Programmes fulfilling it could be on the life of a great Indian, a poet, or a saint. The third (and by far the most popular) chunk of radio and TV time is consumed by programmes that include the replaying of songs from films and from plays that are close to the pop film, in content and approach, if not totally derivative of it.

In the period after India's Independence in 1947, the Indian pop film has become gradually aware that it is the communication medium that is willing to reflect the point of view and perspective of that vast section of the population which is not part of the ruling elite. Pop film-makers have also realized that their fortunes lie in striking a rapport with the commonest of the common. The films, therefore, are constantly engaged in discovering this rapport. Such an effort, of course, requires an amorphous structure in the film so that all kinds of unrelated and even contrary attitudes, views, and visuals can be inserted in order to coincide with the various attitudes and perspectives that may be prevailing within one given audience in one given theatre.

The audience itself is an extremely diverse one. Not only does it reside in a vast kaleidoscope of regions with strong local cultures, it also comes from varied socio-economic levels in such regions.

The Indian pop film in the Hindi language is the one that is taken to most parts of the country. Moreover, being the dominant forerunner of the Indian pop film, this sub-genre has coped with this variegated audience by incorporating certain elements from the various regions of the country. These elements have been done over in a slapstick machine and reintroduced as minor formula details in the genre.

All this makes for a format that is not inhibited by a need to be perfect and complete in itself, a format that is malleable and given to additions and deletions. Such an imperfect structure is also required to contain and balance the strong streak of irreverence and iconoclasm that the Indian pop film inherits from folk theatre that entertains even as it sublimates the most violent tensions of protest in the minds of the audiences.

The spiritual needs of the larger part of the Indian people today, the contradictions which exist between their lives and the lives of the rich minority, the desire to escape from the purist aesthetics of the priests and the intellectuals of the court (the ruling elite), the need for hope in a hopeless and unchanging society, the need to get away from reality—all this leads to the rhythms of imperfection on which the Indian pop film thrives as an agent of liberation and of conservation; juxtaposing the obscene with the pious, and the inane with the brilliant. They are not so much films as revues of everyday emotions under the shadow of the great, eternal passions—blood and wealth, conflict and achievement, music and hedonism, sentiment and frailty, romance and ruthlessness.

In creating the make-believe pictures for such a world of situations and representative figures, the Hindi film follows a style of dressing up its people, its objects, and its backdrops which is completely different from that in the Euro-American film. Indian film-makers plagiarize Hollywood; but everything that they plagiarize, they distort and caricature to prevent a straight imitation of life in the West.

In the sustained and long campaign of distorting what it imitates, the Indian pop film may be said to be against a mindless mimicry of another culture. The Indian pop film's consistent espousal of chauvinism in cultural matters supplements such an interpretation of this sustained caricature of things foreign. It must also be kept in mind that for the vast majority of the Indian population, a life of Western manners and mores is simply not possible at the physical level. The cost of dressing up as a modern man is a hundred times more than most Indians can afford. It is only the upper class and middle-class minority that can afford to indulge in such a façade. By caricaturing the objects of an alien culture, which seems to the poor Indian to be the culture of an alien paradise on earth, the pop film makes it unreal and, at the unconscious level, even irrelevant and unnecessary. It revels in showing the beautiful as gross and ugly and the simple and the ascetic as dignified. It helps a man to see everything that can possibly be included in the film without really desiring it. This may be an anti-revolutionary approach, as radicals and Marxists in India insist in their criticism of the Indian pop film, but it is definitely a useful crutch in evolving an ideology for survival. In the confused terrain in which the Indian pop film exists, there are no clear directions into the process of industrialization—the dividing line between the haves and the have-nots is so vast that an element of conservatism is dominant. As long as the common Indian continues to have the psychology of the survivalist, the Indian pop film can change its broad framework only at the risk of losing its audience.

Saari, Anil, 'The Dynamics of Tradition and Modernity in Hindi Cinema', in The Hindi Film: Agent and Re-Agent of Cultural Change, *edited by Beatrix Pfleiderer and Lothar Lutze, New Delhi: Manohar, 1985.*

* * *

The Use of Poetry in Hindi Cinema

The various strands of story and philosophical content are held together by the poetry of the songs. Whatever be the merit of the film, the songs continue to be remembered well after the film has faded away.

It is not the poetry articulated in the Indian film, but the structure and the layout plan of our films that pose problems of comprehension and understanding from the point of view of film aesthetics as manifest in our cinema.

Very little work has been done on the structure of the Indian film. Through the 1970s, some of us attempted to focus on the unique sociological reverberations set off by the films and their interaction with a mass audience. It was in that period, about two decades ago, that Kumar Shahani wrote on several occasions about the concept of fragmentation, which underlies the structure of the Indian film. During his visits to India, the English film director Lindsay Anderson spoke repeatedly about the epic aspects of the Indian film's structure. At the Film Institute, Pune, Professor Satish Bahadur dwelt at length on the sociological roots of film content. And in film reviews and articles in the media week after week as a film critic, I peddled the line that the structural aesthetics of the Indian film could best be understood by an academic comparison of it with the different genres of Indian folk theatre. From this source emanates the seemingly chaotic structural flow of the Indian film.

Certainly, the structure of the Indian film is fragmentary and episodic. It has illusions of epic grandeur; it is as topical and sociological in parts as a news feature and in parts as traditional as the widest known social orthodoxies. It is also accepted that its structure is closer to the essentials of folk theatre than to the Aristotelian ideal of the unities of time and space.

However, a living, throbbing, prospering, and dynamic communications industry cannot be easily categorized. Its inputs are constantly multiplying, its influence emanating from more and more distant terrains. And there is, perhaps, a tendency to thrive creatively in the chaos. Thus, over the last five decades, we have seen musical and thematic incorporations of contemporary folk elements from Central Asia and West Asia, as well as Europe and America. These elements were absorbed through a unique form of improvisation, which has been taken from the living craft of Indian folk theatre performers.

As Lalu Ram, the nationally famous folk actor from Chhattisgarh, enlightened this writer in the early 1970s, the tradition of improvisation is an intrinsic element in the folk actor's performance. Within the parameters of the play's traditional format, leading folk theatre actors will improvise their own cues to launch forth their sallies and their commentaries on the contemporary world. That is why, for instance, in 1971, under the guidance of poet Niaz Haider and stage director Habib Tanvir, the Chhattisgarh Natak Mandali working with Habib Tanvir's Naya Theatre could reshape a traditional Chhattisgarhi folk play into a political drama encapsulating the exciting political battle being fought within the Congress Party.

It is this inclination and this ability for improvisation within the arena of a somewhat rigid and a somewhat ancient dramaturgy that we can observe the folk theatre artist performing, in his own manner, like the classical Indian musician. Expanding the individual performer's sweep over matters of a more contemporary dimension, utilizing and exploiting the space in the pauses between the various fragments of the epic folk play.

Of course, the voice of the creative folk artist is sharply distinct from the intellectual idiom of the classical Indian musician. It may even seem that their creative sensibilities belong to different creative processes. But, perhaps, these differences only boil down to the creative idiom employed than the impulses of creative expression. This, certainly, is my contention for what it is worth.

We may understand something of the structure of the Indian film if we analyse it in relation with the performance of an Indian folk play. We could perhaps visualize it in term of three parallel lines—the first could stand for the aesthetics of traditional epic theatre; the second for the variations and improvisations in the epic tradition to make it conform to a living folk theatre's requirements for a rural or semi-rural audience; the third would run parallel to folk theatre, be at one remove from the traditional aesthetics of Indian epic theatre, but develop its creative possibilities in a very urban milieu.

A proposition I would like to venture at this stage is that, perhaps, in the structural chaos of the mainstream Indian film we have also been witness to the somewhat haphazard formation of a very urban, Indian, folk form of communication. Because of its urban characteristics, it borrows both from the Indian tradition of folk theatre as well as from the European and American traditions of the revue, vaudeville, and the night-club act. Because it is an urban folk form of communication still in the throes of a transitional journey to discover its academic identity, the Indian film can be wholly eclectic in its improvisation, borrowing from the most unusual sources from time to time.

The eclectic nature of the mainstream Indian film, in many ways, runs parallel to the eclectic characteristics of what is known as the Indian parallel cinema. Both respond to influences from abroad and both derive much of their form and content from traditional Indian sources. The creative processes in which these inputs are incorporated seem to differ largely because the sources of influence of each—both those in India and from abroad—seem different from the other. But the creative process itself is perhaps not as different as we often assume. It will not seem different if the creative process of imbibing influence is seen as an interaction between ideas and intellectual values and the recreation of these abstractions through a cinematic visualization of human behaviour and the human condition as a whole.

To this complex, diffused, and structural terrain is closely linked that dimension of poetry which provides graphic illustration of the bonds between the literary sensibility and the cinematic engineering involved in the construction of Indian films.

Mainstream Indian cinema has a long history of association between poets, the poetic tradition, and the making of films. This is so because the sprawling patchwork of fragmented episodes that structure the Indian film are anchored, kept in place, and united thematically by the philosophical world view that the film subscribes to and expostulates.

It is the philosophical world view that provides the necessary unifying integrity to the episodic mass. In the Indian film, the concept of a compact plot or a properly worked-out theme becomes untenable because of the frequent eruptions of sub-plots and entertainment distractions. These seem to be an intrinsic characteristic of the Indian film. That could be why Indian film-makers, and the audience in its majority, do not demand a logical cohesion of the narrative.

Instead, the effective communication of the film-maker's intent is realized through the suggestion or articulation of a tapestry of philosophical views, comments, and perspectives—about the behaviour of man, the inexorable processes of emotional impulses, the laws of survival, and the indomitability of the human spirit.

As per the tenets of narrative logic the scenes and the sequences exist in themselves for their own emotional impact, rather than as segments of a chain of events building up to a conclusive climax. The logic of credibility behind each individual scene or sequence stems from the conviction it carries as a segment of the tapestry of emotions and feelings arranged in the philosophic world view chosen by the film-maker. That, perhaps, is why the structure of the Indian film is a structure of the orchestration of moods, rather than a plot. Instead of the concept of the larger plot, which incorporates sub-plots, we might see the structure of the Indian film with more clarity if we analyse the larger mood espoused, along with the sub-moods incorporated within the parabola of the larger mood.

In the conventional occidental fiction film, the evocation of the cinematic mood is technically created to heighten and give validity to the sequence of events in the film's plot. In the conventional Indian film the façade of the plot line is only the device to communicate the larger mood that the film wishes to convey.

This, to my mind, seems the essential feature in the Indian film's approach to the denouement of the theme through the main plot and sub-plots. In the occidental tradition, the denouement follows the strict demands of providing a logical and cohesive development to the sequence of events encapsulated in the fictional film.

This difference of approach between Euro-American and Indian cinema may be the result of a simple historical fact. In Europe, and later in North America, the novel exercised a seminal influence on the structure of the other narrative arts, such as theatre and the allied performing arts such as opera and the ballet. The novel's concept of an integrated storyline was to greatly influence the structure of all narrative arts in Europe and thereafter in North America.

On the other hand, the structural essentials of the novel have not yet permeated or been absorbed by the other narrative arts here to the extent of rearranging their structural foundations. That is why the structure of Indian folk theatre survives along traditional lines, instead of succumbing to the seductions of the novel's plot line in the same manner that European folk theatre forms did during the last two hundred years or so.

Both in Indian folk theatre and in mainstream Indian films, the outline of the philosophical mood and the philosophical world view is, therefore, written out and delineated not through the events of the plot, but directly addressed to the audience through poetic invocations, songs, and chants.

In both folk theatre and the folk film, it is the philosophical invocation that initiates the performance. This invocation is the key to the play and the film's structure. At the other end of the performance's horizon, the conclusive note in the folk play and the folk film is also made by a philosophically surcharged song.

Between this beginning and the ending, songs may be used and reused as a kind of chant to veer the audience around to the film's primary mood, to those aspects of the philosophical world view that the drama company or the film-maker wishes to underline. As a vehicle of the overall philosophical mood and various sub-moods, the song in all its varieties becomes the thread that unites the seemingly chaotic structure of the fragmented, episodic, revue-line folk play and folk film.

An interesting irony is that while the song in a film has traditionally been considered by film academics and critics as a distraction and as symbolic of an unwanted breakdown in the flow of the story, we only have to see Indian films without any songs to realize that the larger philosophical dimension is missing from these films. Feature films like *Kanoon, Bhuvan Shome*, and some other New Wave ventures of the early 1970s made a fetish of keeping songs out of the film. They chose instead a straightforward sociological framework to operate in, without quite revealing the ability to weave in metaphysical and philosophical nuances.

It is the tendency of the Indian folk film to stress, in some manner or other, larger questions about man's existence in the universe; to emphasize the philosophical axiom of articulating the condition of human life. This is what leads the Indian film to employ the device of poetry through what we call film songs.

In the conventional Indian film the package of songs chosen for such purposes seems to be a random anthology, chosen possibly without much logic or even without a commendable creative perspective. In other words, the anthology of poems (i.e., songs) in a film may be as chaotic, fragmentary, and episodic in the essential unity as the narrative structure of the film's sequential framework.

In short, we therefore have two similarly chaotic anthologies— one of the poetic word, the second of the visual sequence. Yet the history of audience responses and the staying power of this form of communication would suggest that despite appearances, these two seemingly disparate anthologies coalesce into an effective

entertainment mode which, at its best, is also a powerful instrument for the communication of 'messages' and 'insights'.

The role of poetry in the Indian film, to my mind, is the role of
the innocuous thread that garlands together the scattered episodes
of conventional drama. It provides the anchor and the unifying
thread to a tradition of storytelling in which the action tends to
repeatedly stray away from the main thematic line. No matter how
far it strays, the device of the song enables the film (and the
audience) to return to the core of the philosophical world view
espoused by the film.

Of course, much of what happens between the beginning and
the end of the conventional Indian film is of a flippant, casual, and
ephemeral nature. For those mood sequences, there are supposedly
flippant and ephemeral songs to match. However, the history of
Indian cinema tells us that for successive generations of film
audiences, the best of songs—the best even of the songs written
for ephemeral film sequences—quite outlast the films themselves.
The poetry survives the ravages of time, long after themes, plots,
and film stars become obsolete and are written off.

*Paper presented by the author at the seminar on Literature and Cinema organized
by Sahitya Akademi, 24–26 February 1995, New Delhi.*

* * *

The Southern Locale for Hindi Films

The success of Sholay *saw several Hindi film-makers use the same outdoor
locales off the Bangalore–Mysore road in the state of Karnataka. This locale
remains popular to this day. This essay was written during the shooting of
Esmayel Shroff's film* Suryaa *(1988) starring Raaj Kumar and Amrish Puri.*

The Bangalore–Mysore countryside is not merely the landscape for
writer R.K. Narayan's stories of Malgudi, it also happens to be the

most favoured terrain for the makers of action-oriented, masala-packed, commercial big-budget Hindi films.

Filmy dacoits in these masala films go round threatening people with colourful Bhojpuri invectives, wearing on their heads the *pugrees* of the Chambal ravines, revelling in the idiom and apho-risms, the slang and folklore of the Hindi belt. They actually have celluloid hideouts carved out from the stark, imposing rocks and hillocks of the rugged terrain between Bangalore and Mysore.

About 50 km down the road from Bangalore is the Malgudiesque township of Ramnagar. It is now more famous for the dirt track that the Sippy Films unit had laid behind the hills where Gabbar Singh had his mountain hideout—a hideout that loomed as the distant backdrop of Sippy Nagar, base camp for Ramesh Sippy and the *Sholay* unit.

Early this January, while director Esmayel Shroff was busy shooting his new film *Suryaa* in and around Mysore, Manmohan Desai's unit was working with Amitabh Bachchan on the other side of Bangalore on *Toofan*.

One takes in the continuous roll of boulder-like hills. At least one of them is shaped like the pyramid cone that painter J. Swaminathan's canvases have been full of for the last decade. One focuses upon the odd mix of red dirt and red laterite stone jutting out of the perennial waves of green foliage, and one finds it easy to understand why big-budget Hindi film-makers prefer to shoot their action movies here rather than in exotic Rajasthan or against the static landscape of UP.

The Bangalore-Mysore countryside comes closest to the terrain of the Hollywood Western, a cinematic countryside that John Ford, Fred Zinnemann, George Stevens, and their peers have immortalized for movie freaks over the decades. It is easier, therefore, for Indian directors and stunt masters (or fight directors, as they are sometimes billed) to compose their horse rides, shoot-outs, train hold-ups, and duels to death in an Indian landscape that comes close visually, to the frames of their inspiration—the Hollywood Western.

Also, as actor Kulbhushan Kharbanda once pointed out to this writer some years ago, it is easier for Indian film units to operate in south India than in the north. The crowds in the south are more disciplined and less rowdy than those in UP, Rajasthan, or Bihar.

This certainly appeared to be true, while Esmayel Shroff shot *Suryaa*—with Vinod Khanna, Raaj Kumar, Amrish Puri, Shakti Kapoor, and sundry others—behind Chamundi Hill. Only a few locals from the nearby village hung around the enclosed temple set where Vinod Khanna was battling it out against a gang of lathi wielders. Some of them had sneaked their way into the temple's compound. But when the staff asked them to move out, they did so without protest. Nor, for that matter, was there a melee outside the gates of Premier Studio in the city, a second location for the *Suryaa* unit.

The quiet, work-oriented milieu of a small town location is something that big film stars enjoy as a vacation from the hectic, pell-mell schedule of daily life in Bombay city. Locked in their plush five-star suites, often bringing their wives and kids along, life suddenly becomes a little relaxed, somewhat tension-free and even a bit novel. The big shot in the unit who seemed totally busy on the *Suryaa* location in Mysore seemed to be director Esmayel Shroff. Barely does the director finish with the work of one set of stars than the roll-call is on for the other lot who have been lounging about in their rooms.

The new lot almost always makes its entry with the complaint that they are not shooting enough through the day. But these are complaints that seem to be made purely for the sake of getting a little *bhav* (importance); because nobody is grumbling seriously. They are merely airing their opinions on how the director should go about his work. As long as a star does not play truant, the director is satisfied.

It is on location that film journalists get a chance to peek behind the inscrutable front that film stars generally present. Raaj Kumar likes to write out his lines in Urdu, I observed one evening, when the actor sat learning his lines for the next scene. Raaj Kumar also appeared to be a man with a clear-cut daily routine. While one chatted with him around 6 pm one evening, he insisted that one have a drink though he would have a cup of tea because, he said, 'I only drink after 8.30'. I didn't want a drink either, I said. But that was not possible. A good drink, made by his attendant, is apparently imperative when Raaj Kumar is taking time out to talk to you.

Then there is the memory of an Amrish Puri smile that stands out, days after the *Suryaa* location spell was over. Amrish plays a despotic landlord in the movie. Operating from a lavish drawing room—the palace hotel's conference room—Amrish is confronted by Vinod Khanna, the hero of the oppressed peasants. The scene commences. Amrish and Vinod abuse each other, slowly drawing up in what appears to be a man-to-man confrontation. Anger seethes in the air around them. Amrish Puri's eyes take on a cruel wicked look. The director calls Cut! Asks for a retake. Amrish and Vinod stand rooted to their spots. A thin smile slowly spread over Amrish's tight-lipped face. The viciousness in the eyes fades out. The smile is the gesture with which the actor defuses the make-believe duel of words.

It seems ironic that Amrish and Vinod should spend all the time between shots chatting each other up, when they do little but hurl abuses at each other during the scene. There is a thin line between fiction and reality and a good actor never allows it to be erased.

Amrish is later to expound on the theme of *Suryaa*. It is a movie that delineates how the zamindari system was abolished by the Republic of India. Shakti Kapoor says on another occasion: '*Mere dimaag ki ghanti baj rahi hai*—Esmayel, your film is going to be a hit.'

These words are sweet music to the harried director's ears. He had been trying to sell writer Moinuddin's script since 1980. None of his old producers wanted to touch it then. Now, circa 1987–8, a story about the Indian peasant's revolt against the zamindars and about the government legislation that abolished zamindari is quite acceptable to the tycoons of the film city.

Hindustan Times, *26 January 1992.*

* * *

The Architecture of Illusion

The art director is the least appreciated contributor to the success of a Bollywood film. It is he who creates the right look and atmosphere to lend the film credibility in the eyes of the viewer. Anil's ideas about the pivotal role of the art director holds good even in this age of digital special effects.

The history of cinema is full of untold stories of the small men without whose work that transient journey of celluloid images, from studio backlots to the immortality of the silver screen, would never have been completed.

We remember K. Asif, legendary film-maker, for *Mughal-e-Azam* and that incredible Sheesh Mahal Studio set on which the '*Pyar kiya to darna kya*' sequence was shot. But scarcely anybody remembers the name of the art director who had recreated the Sheesh Mahal inside a Bombay studio. Nor does anybody remember the art director who built an entire village off the Bangalore–Mysore road for Ramesh Sippy's *Sholay*. Or the man who constructed the poignant redlight neighbourhood of Guru Dutt's *Pyaasa*, where Waheeda Rahman waltzed to the sad lilt of Sahir Ludhianvi's poetic fantasy.

Even the best of us will not be able to recall offhand the names of the art directors who constructed that mammoth Roman arena for *Quo Vadis*, the chariot race in *Ben Hur*, the main street of Fred Zinnemann's *High Noon* or, in more recent times, the shimmering contours of the spaceships in Steven Speilberg's blockbuster *Close Encounters of the Third Kind*, and *E.T.*

In the movies, the art directors live in greater anonymity than even the computer whizkids, now famous for the computronic magnificence visible in hi-tech movies from *Star Wars* to *Terminator 2* and *Jurassic Park*.

Understanding the work of an art director is the ultimate tribute to the world of illusion that cinema celebrates. I remember walking into the R.K. Studio floor where Raj Kapoor was shooting *Prem Rog*, to be told by his friend and scriptwriter V.P. Sathe that it was the same studio floor where they had shot Nadira's *'Murh murh ke na dekh* number in *Shree 420*. It was one of Raj Kapoor's favourite floors, long and expansive. It was also the site where many architectural dreams had been dismantled.

Something similar is taking place these days at Bombay. For over four months, a large workforce of carpenters and masons have worked into the late hours of the night, erecting an unusual 'castle' in the outer compound of Film City in Bombay's Goregaon suburb. It is for the most ambitious costume drama being made in recent times—a movie called *Rajkumar*, starring Anil Kapoor, Madhuri Dixit, Danny Denzongpa, Naseeruddin Shah, and Reena Roy.

On 21 April 1994, the unit headed by Tutu Sharma and director Pankaj Parashar began shooting at this breathtaking set of architectural magnificence designed by art director Nitish Roy, who has won three national Film Awards for his work in Mrinal Sen's *Kharij*, Shyam Benegal's *Mandi*, and Gulzar's *Lekin*.

The unit will shoot for a month or so on this set, reported to have cost somewhere in the region of Rs 80 lakh. Then the ramparts, the towers, the balconies, the bell tower, the palatial facades, and the colossal snake-like fountain in the centre of the castle grounds shall be dismantled and gone.

According to producer Tutu Sharma, the exotic set will not feature for more than fifteen or twenty minutes in his film. Once the shooting is over, the 7000 wooden planks, the steel girders that prop up the Westminister-style towers, the Greco-Russian pillars with Egyptian-style hieroglyphs etched around their curves, the grandiloquent turrets made of plaster of paris, the false Venetian panes shall all disappear into dust.

On 23 April, Tutu Sharma unveiled the unique castle of *Rajkumar* to the world at large. A BBC unit went on to include this set in writer Clive James' episode on Bombay for a series titled *Postcards*.

For the first shot of this film, both Anil Kapoor and Madhuri Dixit ran up and down the stairs that led up to a lofty platform where the huge castle bell stood in its pristine whiteness at a height of over 100 feet. The fight director insisted on several takes. If either of them had missed even one step, it would have meant plunging down from that great height. The actors were unmindful of that dizzying height as they kept going up and down doing innumberable retakes. Perhaps actors have nerves of steel.

It seems a tragedy that such architectural splendour should be heading for a quick, inglorious death towards the end of May. Neither Pankaj Parashar nor Nitish Roy want this castle to have any kind of life outside their film. Pankaj Parashar has already refused a couple of offers from film producers from Madras who have offered him as much as Rs 10 lakh each to shoot a song sequence on this set.

Tutu Sharma explained:

I refused because I am not going to let my set be shown by anybody else. We want this to be the highlight of *Raajkumar*. God willing, we want people to remember our film as something to refer to in the history of Indian cinema, that such a set was built for the film *Raajkumar*. Even if we make a video-film on it, we will keep it for ourselves.

However, he has also received an offer that is rather tempting. After *Rajkumar* is released, Tutu Sharma and Nitish Roy plan to accept the proposal of remaking the castle set on a smaller scale on the premises of a Bombay mill that has been lying closed for some years now. There, it will not only be a constant reminder of the ambitious illusions that film people can indulge in but also serve as a leisure and entertainment centre that is a more permanent tribute to the creative skills of Nitish Roy and his team of workers.

Having worked for a number of period films and historical TV serials including Shyam Benegal's *Bharat ek Khoj*, Dr Chander Prakash's *Chanakya*, Govind Nihalani's *Tamas*, and Gulzar's *Lekin*, an alumnus of the Government College of Art, Calcutta, Nitish

Roy decided to adopt a freestyle approach to the design that director Pankaj Parashar and Tutu Sharma wanted.

They wanted a modern look. After they told me the storyline I thought that given my knowledge of Indian periods, why not 'mismatch' the two and invent our own style. That is what I have done. Though many things on the set will remind you of British castles, I have included other elements too. For instance, the swans atop the columns are very Russian. The Egyptian-like hieroglyphs on the pillars, the hydra-headed snake-fountain are all a mismatch. I call it a mismatch because it is like today's music. I mean listen to Baba Sehgal's singing. He will introduce elements from the Punjab into his rap numbers. That is the line I followed.

Having planned the castle set for over a year, before they started on the construction, the producer, the film director, and art director found that as the construction proceeded, new ideas kept cropping up.

Despite the mounting cost of construction, the trio was driven by the ambition to create a unique pictorial look in Indian cinema. They wanted their castle set to be as good as any done in Hollywood, including the 'castle' used for *Robin Hood: Prince of Thieves* which some people believe provided the first inspiration to the film's team.

Of course, the story of *Rajkumar* is very different from that of *Robin Hood*. Writer Vinay Shukla, a Film Insitute director himself, who also has several commercial hits to his credit as a scriptwriter, explained that this was the story of two warring princely families, in the tradition of Rajasthani folklore. 'It is a story of honour and *izzat*, of an evil *wazir* [played by Naseeruddin Shah]' and of a prince and princess who want peace between the feuding royal families. There is a bit of village magic too in the film,' said he.

For Anil Kapoor and scriptwriter Vinay Shukla, there are essential dramatic moments in the script which will provide a very contemporary note on the silver screen. These scenes, they believe, will establish the credibility of this splendorous costume drama.

Said Anil Kapoor who plays the film's title role,

Though *Raajkumar* is a costume drama, it is going to be believable. The people and the scenes are real. The story operates on a serious level. The *Raajkumar* maybe a character out of a costume drama but the characterization is real. There is nothing unbelievable in the story of the film, believe me.

Hindustan Times, *7 May 1994.*

* * *

The Compelling World of Hindi Films

Hindi films have always reflected the prevailing mood of the society. In that sense they have truly been 'entertainment for the masses'. Even in this age of satellite television Hindi cinema continues to play a certain socio-political role, showing the world as it is by the light of its convictions and conventions.

No one really knows when one first became addicted to the Hindi film or why one began to love it. Even those who grow up and forsake the addiction are occasionally tempted into the boudoirs of its fantasies.

One can hate the trash of the films and ridicule everything in them. But that too is a role the Hindi film has come to play. To its devotees it provides recurring moments of love, joy, and happiness; to others a splendid opportunity to vent their spleen against 'balderdash'. But one only has to see a few to discover in them the means of personal and psychological liberation from the inanity and restrictions of everyday life.

The Hindi film magnifies daily suffering into an epic of Good against Evil. It transforms the petty, limited affairs and anecdotes of one's life into a romantic, emphatically significant series of adventures. It instils in us the hope that our life too is meaningful; that the commonplace is not devoid of the heroic dimension.

To the battered body of human beings inhabiting the modern Indian state, always struggling against bosses, poor pay packets and circumstances in general, the Hindi film provides a holiday from life.

The other side of the coin is that it makes accessible to the common Indian's imagination the rarefied world of the affluent and privileged. It takes the pauper through the walls of five-star hotels and gives him a dip in the swimming pool. It takes him inside the bungalows of the rich. It stokes his imagination with pictures of how much money can be spent by one man, how much power can be accumulated by one individual, and how apparently alien people, in their problems and their anger, their sensitivities and humilities, their aspirations, foibles, wit and dignities, are the same as any of us; ridiculous though we might appear in the mirrors of our wives or parents, colleagues or masters.

Yet, ironically enough, cinema is not really the poor man's entertainment in India, though it often bears such a label. The fact is that the 9000-odd permanent, semi-permanent, and touring theatres that dot the country, scarcely penetrate village India. It was estimated by Pune exhibitor and film historian B.V. Dharap in his catalogue, *Indian Films 1973*, that at least '4517 towns and villages with a population exceeding 5000 await this amenity (of local cinema theatres)'.

At present there are but 2500 towns in the country which have theatres of their own. The really poor Indian, the vast majority of whom live in villages, is distantly located from movies. Despite this, the magnetic power of cinema is so strong that each successive wave of rural immigrants into the urban centres helps increase the number that throng the cinema's box-office window. And 65 per cent of cinema halls in the 2500 townships, towns, and cities screen Hindi films.

The popular Hindi film is the dominant, seminal influence on entertainment movies in the regional languages, though it too often borrows stories and themes from the popular regional talkies. The

Hindi film's writ runs primarily in the realm of filmic treatment—both in terms of the stars and the environment it displays. Its dominance stems from the fact that it was the first to champion modernity in daily life. The social mores of the rich, 'the England-returned' characters, might be painted as evil practices, but they are also the vehicles of hedonism in cinema theatres—hedonism that introduced new sensations and new ideas to an audience restricted by too many social taboos and too much poverty of opportunity to otherwise enjoy itself.

As new lifestyles penetrated into the Indian's world during the last three decades, the Hindi film introduced them to its audiences through the villains and the vamps. Smoking, drinking, eating out in five-star hotels, night-club entertainment, swimming pools, fast cars and limousines, air travel and helicopters, slit skirts and revealing blouses, hash and ganja smoking, tape recorders and swivel chairs—practically every new item in a man's personal charter of wants has been first tagged on in the movies to negative characters. It is almost as if the poor Indian's first reaction to the gadgets of modern technology is cynical.

After 1947, the Hindi film became the cultural vanguard, surprisingly though not unreasonably, of a movement against the virtues of ascetism and abstinence, sacrifice and resignation. The poor hero, who charmed the rich man's convent-educated or England-returned daughter, may not have been a true manifestation of social reality, but he was a genuine expression of the common man's aspirations for a better life. Years ago, Sukarno, the first president of free Indonesia, told an American journalist that he welcomed the screening of Hollywood films in his country because they would show his people what life had to offer. That would motivate them to work harder, he said.

The Indian establishment too at one stage envisaged a progressive and reformatory role for Indian cinema. V. Shantaram's *Do Aankhen Barah Haath* (1957) provides a good illustration of the willing subservience of cinema to the national cause. The film was a vehicle for the message of non-violence, as twelve ugly dacoits laid down arms and immersed themselves in social welfare projects. However, what the Establishment had not anticipated was that Hindi cinema would become an 'uncontrollable' medium of communication in the hands of the masses of free India. Two years before *Do Aankhen Barah Haath* came to the theatre, Raj Kapoor's *Shree 420* (1955) had 'exposed' the working of the elite. It showed stock-exchange speculators fiddling with the economy while pavement dwellers burnt in the fire of starvation.

Shree 420, which has a strong resemblance in plot and treatment to Rene Clair's 1932 silent movie masterpiece *Liberty Is Ours*, took Indian film intellectuals by surprise. Other films that dealt with Indian poverty, such as K.A. Abbas's *Dharti ke Lal* (1946), Zia Sarhadi's *Humlog* (1951), and Bimal Roy's *Do Bigha Zamin* (1953), had come a cropper at the box office. Their audience was confined to middle class, university-educated filmgoers. The poor themselves stayed away from the truths that they knew only too bitterly in their own lives.

In sharp contrast to these three films, *Shree 420* became one of Hindi cinema's all-time money spinners because, in Raj Kapoor's world, poverty was coupled with defiance and sensuality. It was a love story of the poor (Raj Kapoor and Nargis) whose music, enshrined in such eternal scores as '*Ramaiya vasta vaiya*' and '*Ichak dana bichak dana*', held its own against the cabaret numbers of the rich men's club. The lower middle class school-teacher played by Nargis rivalled the orgiastic lifestyle of the affluent that Nadira adorned, with the '*Murh-murh ke na Dekh*' number. Raj Kapoor's tramp rose from the pavements and conquered the world of the rich, only to renounce it once again—aghast at its amorality, its dehumanization, and its narrow, money-obsessed perspective of life. The charm and tenderness in the love story of the tramp and the teacher seemed full of life's sensuous pleasures which even money, especially money, could not buy. *Shree 420* blended the traditional Buddhist ideal of renunciation with sensuality.

At the same time, cinema broke through the fossilized world view fostered by the Indian joint family. It insisted on showing us the face of evil, of corruption, and of debauchery. It showed us what the joint family wanted us to close our eyes to—even if these evils were happening within the family itself. Gambling, for instance, or drinking, or going to visit nautch girls in the *kotha* was behaviour in sharp contrast to the ideals associated with the joint family system. Cinema insisted that life could not be divided into two separate compartments—one to be embraced, the other to be totally shunned; one to be discussed and talked about, the other to be totally ignored; one of idealism and the other to be experienced only in guilt.

Above all, the Hindi film struck at the very roots of that pernicious social practice which kept men and women, boys and girls in rigidly segregated isolation. In its own inelegant way, the Hindi film taught a million young Indians how to accept their natural attraction for the other sex. It taught them how to establish some kind of communication with their opposite numbers, despite the great taboos that goverened social intercourse till the early 1960s— particularly in towns and cities other than the four metropolises of Bombay, Delhi, Calcutta, and Madras.

In the early 1960s, as undergraduates in a bustling industrial city in UP, we would laugh and tease each other every time a heroine's father said in the film, '*Main apni ladki ki shaadi us sharabi, kababi aur randibaaz se nahin hone doonga!*' (I will not let my daughter marry that drunk, meat-eating womanizer). The filmy father's exaggerated invective could not hide from us the reality. Even in the early 1960s, provincial towns were overpopulated with a middle class that banned beer and meat, which looked upon the most casual exchange between a boy and girl—even if they were studying in co-ed schools or colleges—as tangible proof of secret orgies between the two!

To the children of free India, including those who came out of the protected shelter of childhood after Independence, the popular

Hindi film has been a surer guide into both adulthood and the twentieth century than parents. Our parents, even those who had studied abroad and been social rebels in their youth, were not uninhibited enough to instruct us in the ways of the world. In their middle age, they were enamoured once again of the platitudes and ideals of an ancient cultural heritage. They might have used short cuts in their own careers, but they did not have the honesty to tell their offspring that this was the only road to success. Nor could they talk to us about premarital sex, divorce, abortion, or masturbation. It was instead the Hindi film that touched on, or suggested, these issues, albeit superficially, through the 1950s and 1960s. It was the popular Hindi film, with its emphasis on the love story, that reared an entire generation of young Indians and taught them to accept the social life of co-educational schools and colleges, picnics and birthday parties, dating and jam sessions.

Shammi Kapoor may well have been the terror of middle class mothers. But his brazenness in *Dil Deke Dekho* immediately fired the imagination of millions of undergraduates who quickly discarded the *Devdas* concept of the passionate lover suffering at a distance, satisfied by a mere look in the morning when his dreamgirl reached college in her rickshaw. Asha Parekh in her jeans and Shammi Kapoor gambolling around with girls in his jeep fired the imaginations of teenage boys and girls, giving them reason to cut through the swathe of their parents' prejudices. If Shammi Kapoor could snatch Asha Parekh's dupatta in broad daylight and if she could tease the life out of him, couldn't the undergraduates muster the courage to speak to each other inside the portals of their colleges?

The realist school critics of the *Bumbaiya phillum* would at this point shriek that Shammi Kapoor was an eve teaser and a road-side Romeo. And it is true that those with minds warped enough in the first place to turn into petty criminals and crooks, would find in the antics of the phillum hero a stimulant to their own latent perversions.

But for the general mass of young people in 1959 and 1960, Shammi Kapoor's articles were not templates for imitation but the expression of a mood. The peppy songs, the iconoclastic mannerisms of both Shammi Kapoor and Asha Parekh created the heady illusion of living out a love story in an Indian city. Just as in 1973, Dimple Kapadia, Rishi Kapoor, and the music of *Bobby* created another kind of mood for young lovers.

Did *Bobby* initiate a rash of elopements in the country? No, not at all! Did *Bobby* tempt every college girl to go around in hot pants and tucked-up shirts? Unfortunately, no! Film-makers realize now that as an instrument of social change the popular film plays a largely enabling role—helping to articulate individual impulses to turn them into social trends.

The examples of Yash Chopra's *Kabhi Kabhie* and B.R. Chopra's *Pati, Patni aur Woh* stand out in this context. Opening in Bombay theatres, *Kabhi Kabhie* began on a lukewarm note but once the film was relased in the north it became almost a sociological phenomenon. Bombay's cosmopolitan permissiveness prevented people from responding enthusiastically to the film's basic theme (an acceptance by a married couple of each other's premarital, romantic involvements). But in the more inhibited, orthodox, and segregated social milieu of Delhi and the rest of the Hindi belt, *Kabhi Kabhie* seemed the catalysing agent for discussions that never took place in apparently modern families.

Kabhi Kabhie evoked intense identification from women of conservative families in the north because even in New Delhi there are families that do not permit teenage daughters to talk to boys, let alone witness adult members discussing their love life with one another. In the same way, *Pati Patni aur Woh* provided an acceptable idiom to wives and husbands to talk about extramarital escapades— a subject that conservative couples would not even allude to in normal conversation.

The popular success of *Dil Deke Dekho* and the films it inspired—*Junglee, Professor, Dil Tera Diwana, Kashmir ki Kali,* and

An Evening in Paris—established once for all the need for the Hindi film to cater to the socio-sexual demands of people supposed to remain blind and ignorant about the human body. When Sharmila Tagore wore a bikini in Shakti Samanta's *An Evening in Paris* all the old inhibitions of the film audience were broken. Films became the standard bearers of fashion and modernity. Moreover, they were schools for some kind of a sex education of youngsters who did not live within the confines of the joint family.

The rapid industrial development of the country after Independence started an epidemic of nuclear families, particularly among the middle class. But popular cinema alone catered to the new psychological and cultural needs. The radio was obsessed, thanks to B.V. Keskar's strictures as the Union Minister for Information and Broadcasting, with classical Indian music. It was an inclination towards high culture that was also to be found in the more respectable magazines then being published—*The Illustrated Weekly*, *Saptahik Hindustan*, and *Dharmyug*.

I was 19 years old, with three painful histories of unrequited love behind me, when I bumped into Rajshree in *Geet Gaya Pattharon Ne*. Shantaram had evolved a bold design to introduce his beautiful, voluptuous daughter. Playing the role of a classical danseuse, Rajshree went around in a number of scenes with her shoulders bare, her albaster-white waist caressing the breeze (flowing out from sighing male filmgoers) and her mouth open in a perpetual pout. Shantaram's design used the camouflage of ancient Indian sculpture to cover up for the creation of a sex goddess.

It was Rajshree and some years later Mumtaz, in movies like Raj Khosla's *Do Raaste* and Manmohan Desai's *Sachha Jhootha*, who made me realize that for young men whose fathers were not members of the big, colonial clubs, the only place where they had the chance to see a pretty girl for a reasonable stretch of time, was in the movies.

Perhaps all that has changed now, in the Amitabh Bachchan era. Perhaps that is why the cabaret dance seems to have disappeared from the Hindi film in the 1980s. Or is it that the heroines have taken over from the Helens, Bindus, and Padma Khannas? This last seems more likely; and I wonder how many college boys go to the movies only to see Zeenat Aman in her, bare dresses, Rekha twisting her hips, and Ranjeeta smiling in a big close-up on the screen.

Sex has of course not been the only magnetism of the Hindi film; but it has certainly been an essential ingredient for a long time. Indeed, it is surprising that like the Hindi film, life outside it too does not seem to change very much. In 1938, Master Vinayak directed *Brahmachari*. Vinayak himself was in the lead role—a roly-poly predecessor of our own Sanjeev Kumar. Dressed in shabby, khaki shorts, Vinayak fell in love with Meenakshi, who went around in skirts.

In 1938, girls from respectable families were forbidden to see *Brahmachari*, because Meenakshi showed a lot of leg in the movie. Meenakshi's modern, anglicized father of course was in a class by himself. He insisted that he would marry his daughter only to a young man who believed in afforestation and family planning and was against the practice of dowry. That was in 1938—and the issues are still alive today.

One reason why the basic framework of the Hindi film has not changed over the years is that, for the vast majority of Indians, life does not yet show any signs of basic change. The changes in our lives and, therefore, in our films are restricted to details. The *mujra* gives way to the cabaret, the bohemian rebels played by Dilip Kumar, Raj Kapoor, and Dev Anand give way to the unemployed student, a stereotype that Rajesh Khanna played with great aplomb in his heyday in the late 1960s. The break-up of the joint family in AVM's *Bhai Bhai* (1956) is re-structured into a new joint family film in *Trishul* (1978). Sunil Dutt plays a psychotic dacoit in Mehboob's Khan's *Mother India* (1957) who speaks the eastern UP dialect, the Purabiya's language. In 1961 Dilip Kumar speaks Purabi in *Ganga Jamuna*; and in 1973 Gabbar Singh alias Amjad Khan is a psychotic dacoit speaking Purabi in *Sholay*.

Nor, for that matter, is there anything new about the action film. Homi Wadia directed Nadia's ballet-like fight sequences in *Hunterwali* twenty-five years ago. Dev Anand was fighting *goondas* with a car handle in *Taxi Driver* (1954) and knocking stuntmen by the dozen in *CID* (1956). Like Sean Connery was to do later in James Bond films, Dev Anand would pick himself up from the rubble, settle his scarf or his necktie and walk away from the scene as if it were but a trifle. A violent prelude to the film's cathartic end was as compulsory then as now.

It took me fifteen years as a Hindi film addict (including four years as a professional film critic) to realize the significance of the obligatory fight scene towards the end of the film. Dharmendra was socking Ajit and his cronies, when things began to gell inside my mind. Every punch that Dharmendra landed began to assonate in my mind with all the rotten things that had gone to make it a depressing week for me.

I felt wonderful after I came out of the theatre in Delhi's old city quarter and I finally understood why the masses wanted the hero to sock the villain on the silver screen. Each punch that the hero swings carries behind it the force of a million admirers who cannot, unfortunately, punch the villains in their own lives.

However, the Hindi film is more than a subliminal discharge of feelings pent up within an audience that is weighed down by the social system. The reason why the Hindi film stole a march on regional cinema immediately after Independence was that it was the first to realize that the old cultural heritage had become a wash out—that the Indian wanted a new lifestyle that was totally different from the one he had inherited from his parents. And yet one not totally different.

Over the years, the Hindi film has evolved its own formula. A formula that is probably unique in the world and which has been adopted wholeheartedly by the popular film in the regional languages. There is a very broad, very generalized morality prevailing on the periphery of the action. This morality pays its homage to conservative social values. It deifies the mother, the values that hold families and communities together, and is often studded with direct religious overtones. Dacoits, smugglers, police inspectors, all worship gods and goddesses in the movies. This overall conservative framework of values is also stressed at the very end of the film. Its main purpose is to reassure the mass audience that the status quo shall be maintained; that they are not being confronted with the possibility and the trauma of a total upheaval in society which is a fairly frightening thing for the average Indian who cannot think beyond survival. It is a psychological obstacle that has drowned successive attempts at an Indian revolution.

Within this broad, general framework, however, the Hindi film injects the very antithesis of that framework's conservative morality. Everything new on the surface of society is picked up and broadcast through the cinema's communicational force for the consumption of the average man. In this area the Hindi film is an unabashed protagonist of modern living, though with a typically Indian middle class hypocrisy, many of the stellar attractions are tagged on to the villains and vamps. In recent years filmgoers have seen through the strategy and are willing to shower as much affection on Amjad Khan's killers and Bindu's whores as they are on regular heroes and heroines. They have learnt to accept Amitabh Bachchan as a smuggler and Rekha as a courtesan. The old black-and-white divisions between good and evil are finally over. The Hindi film can claim a bit of credit for making free India's successive generations a shade more knowledgeable about the way the world functions.

In its pursuit of novelty, the Hindi film has become one of the most sensitive medium to the opinions, attitudes, and perspectives of the common man. Whereas daily newspapers, radio, and TV assume didactic postures seeking to guide the common people with elitist brilliance, the Hindi film knows only the compulsion of establishing a rapport with a large section of the common people.

In 1964, long before it was fashionable in the national press to expose the personal lives of political leaders, producer S. Mukherjee cast Dilip Kumar in *Leader*, a movie in which politics mingled with corruption and love affairs. In 1968, Mehmood unveiled the face of the ugly politician in a bizarre caricature in *Sadhu Aur Shaitaan*—nearly a decade before the press started writing about that creature.

It was this sensitivity to the people's real thoughts that placed the popular Hindi film at the vanguard of modern India's cultural evolution. During the last few years, however, the movies seem to have lost sight of the true nature of this vital connection. They have started taking their own formulas too seriously. Their makers have begun to believe that movies are entertainment alone.

As an addict who grew up on both the Bumbaiya phillum and T.S. Eliot, I can only complain that that is not true, and never has been.

Published in Contour. *This magazine has since ceased publication.*

* * *

Rags to Riches Stories Made Real

Film-making is both an art and a craft that needs to be systematically learnt in an institution. Though written about the famed Film and Television Institute of India, Pune, this piece is about the learning process as a must for students of cinema.

Every young boy who thinks he is brighter and better looking than his schoolmates, has also at some time or the other, thought of a future for himself in cinema. Many young people, indeed, do make a desperate, hoping-against-hope attempt to crash into films. Some of them even run away from home only to hang around the film studios in Bombay (or Madras) waiting to be discovered by the brilliant producer or director who has only to take one look at their face to discover his new star. It is so easy for the young, and the young at heart, to forget the reality of the thousands of 'extras' and 'junior artistes' who starve in Bombay working as waiters and counter clerks for meagre salaries, sustained only by the hope that one day Dame Fortune will bless them with success and they shall be made.

These dreams are sustained by the age-old myths of the cinema. Dharmendra and Manoj Kumar were discovered on the pavements outside Bombay's half-glamorous, half-shabby studios. B.R. Ishara rose from a canteen boy in a Bombay studio to become a noted producer-director. J. Om Prakash worked at a humdrum office job in Delhi before he worked his way to the top as a producer-director. In Madras, Seema made a sensational jump from an 'extra' to transform into a heroine with *Her Nights*.

Cinema provides one of the few genuine areas where rags-to-riches stories actually take place; and there are no rules that cannot be defied, no traditions that cannot be broken. For years, Amitabh Bachhan was considered a very plain-looking man, a man who was too tall to be a popular film hero. Then Bachhan clicked and everything about him became fashionable in cinema. Bachhan's latest rival on the filmy firmament, Shatrughan Sinha, once confessed that he used to think that with his looks he would never attract a girl. Today, beautiful women find him both charming and sexy. Shabana Azmi's admirers, to take another example, would pull out a dagger if somebody said she does not look pretty because she has buck teeth.

No wonder every dynamic young man and girl who feels that there is something special about his/her personality is quite convinced that he/she deserves to be a film star. Most of them are prevented from making an attempt only because of lack of opportunity. But there are others who may come from rich families and who can invest sizeable fortunes in the experiment; they are even willing to partially finance the film producers who will give them a break.

Despite this craze, society will always debate whether cinema can be, or should be, considered a career into which young people should go consciously and in a planned way. Indeed, most youngsters who want to become film actors or actresses always have to struggle with their families to get permission to make their attempt. This is even true of the Film Institute at Pune, officially known as the Film and Television Institute of India (FTII), established in the late 1960s by the Union Ministry of Information and Broadcasting.

The various institutions that have emerged during the last decade or so to impart training in cinematic crafts have been instrumental in giving film a tremendous respectability as a career. Even though the FTII, Pune, has discontinued its acting course, it remains the major film school in the country. It supplements its activities and courses in the other fields by collaborating with the National School of Drama at New Delhi for an acting course.

The other important film courses in the country are at the Institute of Film Technology, Adyar, Madras; Filmalaya School of Acting run at Mumbai; and the film course at the National Institute of Design, Ahmedabad. There are then the two institutions in Mumbai, one run by veteran thespian Gajanan Jagirdar, and the other, by Roshan Taneja who was formerly Head of the Acting Department at the Film Institute, Pune. Her former students include Shatrughan Sinha, Jaya Bhaduri, Shabana Azmi, Asrani, Danny, and Subhash Ghai.

The FTII offers an integrated two-year course for the first two years. In the third year students are selected for different specialized courses in Direction, Scriptwriting, Cinematography, Sound Recording, and Film Editing. The Institute of Film Technology at Adyar, which has been established by the Tamil Nadu government, follows a pattern akin to the Film Institute, Pune.

To a considerable extent, these two institutes receive government subsidies. However, the tuition fees and hostel expenses work out to the same level that students in engineering and medical institutions would normally have to meet. Private schools, naturally, tend to be more expensive.

However, unlike an engineering institute or a medical college, a film institute holds out no assurance to its graduates of getting a job or, to use a more appropriate term, a livelihood. Furthermore, unlike the unemployed Indian medico or engineer, the young graduate of an Indian film school cannot even resort to the final choice of emigrating to America or Europe. He would probably be worse off there because films are cultural products and one understands one's own culture best. Not that film technicians and artistes have not gone abroad and found work, but the going has always been tough, even for Saeed Mirza, Kabir Bedi, and Persis Khambatta.

Therefore, admission into a film institute is only the beginning of a major struggle. First, since the cost of using equipment and film is exorbitant, the film institutes offer a very small number of seats each year. Written examinations are followed by in-depth interviews. At the Film Institute, Pune, the general approach in the selection process is fairly strict. Candidates are tested for their interest in the cinematic art, their awareness of theory, their artistic ambitions, the general level of their knowledge and information, and have to undergo special tests to evaluate their basic talent.

The classes involve a long and arduous training process in which the students are initiated into a world of which they discover, much to their surprise, they had little knowledge. Of course, those who have had prior experience of photography or painting, both of which are among the desirable qualifications along with written work and acting or direction in theatre, have a basic understanding of composition. For that is what, strictly speaking, film-making is all about. Each shot is composed of visual frames which have to be designed, much as a painting or a photograph. Human figures, machines, and objects are but so many images in front of a particular backdrop and have to be visually composed so as to hold together. Moreover, each shot must relate, visually and thematically, to the shots that will precede it and follow it in the film. Otherwise the film would become totally unreal when the viewer sees it. Discontinuity in props and visual design is one of the major flaws in the average commercial Indian film. As so many readers of film magazines complain every month to the editors, dresses, to take one example, often change from shot to shot in the same scene.

The process of understanding the scope and potential of the various pieces of equipment that go into making a film is supplemented by two other basic training courses. One is on the practical use of this equipment. The second gives the students a very thorough and extensive introduction to the theory of film; rather, to the various theories about cinema that have been propounded and occasionally applied. This part of the course is hard work, like postgraduate studies in other subjects. Luckily for the students, the lessons in theory are complemented by the screening of film classics, which are examples of high-quality cinema and which demonstrate the practical application of the main theories. The Film Institute, Pune, offers a particularly wide range of classics to its students, because it shares the campus with the National Film Archives of India, which has a magnificent collection of international and Indian classics now.

The film schools, therefore, prepare the students as much as possible before they face the real challenges of the profession when they leave. In their final year at the FTII, Pune, for example, the students get a chance to work on a diploma film—so called because the Institute offers diploma courses and not degree courses.

For a diploma film, a scriptwriter will collaborate with a director to write a screenplay. This might be based on an idea given by the director or on a short story selected by him. Very often now, after the integrated course for the first two years at the FTII, the director is given thorough training in writing scripts himself. He can, therefore, attempt to write his own script too, if he gets permission from the concerned authorities at the Institute. Once the script is ready, the director begins to organize his unit. He tries to select his own cameraman and sound recordist. In most cases, several of these technicians will be deputed to one unit, not only to provide the various cameramen and sound recordists with as much experience as possible but also to facilitate the director and enable him to shoot with two or more cameras for one particular sequence. As far as the acting crew goes, the official preference is for students of the final year at the National School of Drama, who spend one term at the FTII, and get chosen to play various roles in diploma films. However, outsiders can be also called in by a director if he has characters meant to be either middle-aged, or old, or children. Other exceptions are also made.

The great advantage of studying at a film institute is, first, that the students get a very thorough acquaintance with the history and range of cinema; second, they have the initial experience to adjust quickly to a real film-making situation. For technicians, cameramen, film editors, and sound recordists, the film school's course is qualification enough for regular jobs in the film industry. For actors, directors, and scriptwriters, however, the situation is more complex.

These three jobs of acting, directing, and scriptwriting are the really creative jobs in film-making. Much of the technicians' work depends for its effectiveness on how these three people tackle their jobs. A bad script cannot be photographed dramatically enough, to take one example. Therefore, once the actors, directors, and scriptwriters leave the sheltered enclosures of their film school, the real struggles of their careers begin. And new artistes, directors, and scriptwriters are probably the worst investment bets that a film producer can think of. For these students, therefore, the end of studies marks the beginning of their 'rounds' to the offices of producers. They seek and chase appointments with the men who alone can give them a break in the film industry. Alternatively, directors and scriptwriters can took forward to a loan from the Film Finance Corporation, so that they might launch a film of their own which could also star new artistes.

There are actually two alternatives. First, the directors, script-writers, cameramen, film editors, and sound recordists can try to get jobs as assistants to established people in their respective fields. This indeed is what most students from the film schools do in India. This period is like a period of apprenticeship for them. They work under established directors and technicians as assistants. In other words, the directors and the scriptwriters also convert themselves into technicians and try to work their way up after serving an apprenticeship.

The second alternative is to branch out and seek a career outside the feature film set-up. The major possibilities here are as follows— documentary film-making, either as a staff member of the Films Division of India or as an independent producer working for the various Doordarshan Kendras, or working in the advertising films set-up. In these three fields the film technician can be assured of reasonably good pay and job security. But in the Films Division and in Doordarshan, he has to work under strict restrictions. Very often these become quite frustrating to young creative people. Advertising offers a more glamorous world. But it is also a more difficult world to get into, and demands really high-quality work.

However, in recent years there has been tremendous growth in the demand for short films and documentaries. This offers a con-siderable incentive to those technicians who work in specialized film fields. First, there is a growing market for TV news reports and documentaries form the foreign TV networks. In most cases the visiting TV producer will use technicians already known to his network—people who have worked for other producers of the same network. This is a fairly remunerative job. Moreover, the Indian documentary film-maker can also hope to sell an interesting docu-mentary film, with unique sequences, to a foreign TV network. Naturally, the process is long, painstaking, and difficult. But it is not otherwise in any field. In sports, for example, a sportsman will not get anywhere if he does not dedicate himself to the loneliness and exhaustion of consistent practice. For all its glamour and its excitement, cinema is a cruel slave-driver. It allows people to come up only after they can withstand its worst tests. As a career, therefore, it is suitable only for those who have thick skins and unusual perseverance of spirit—apart from the necessary talent. But then the fruits of success in cinema, both in terms of money and in terms of fame and social status, are unique too.

Since film-making is a team effort, the human element is extremely important. The ability to get along with people, to strike positive chords with them, and make them feel easy and comfortable with you, are very necessary qualities in anybody who works in cinema, no matter how great his skill or talent is. For a film unit is like a small world complete in itself. At its head is the producer and financier, then the captain of the ship, the director, followed by the artistes, the technicians, the scriptwriters, and others. The support unit comprises people who do the odd jobs but who are extremely important for the efficient working of the film's technicians and artistes. These are the lightmen, the assistants to the assistants, the *chaprasies* of the unit. All of them work long hours together, often late into the night. In a successful film unit, a sense of equality and of camaderie floats in the air on its sets. Even the biggest producers will see to it that all the members are happy with their working conditions. For instance, the lunch that the unit eats on location shootings is always the same for everybody—from the biggest star to the smallest errandboy. Though of course a star may get to eat twice as much as others!

Apart from the ability to get along with people, the second important quality that one must have as a human being, if one sets out on the course of making a career in films, is the ability to recognize an opportunity and exploit it. Unless one has a shrewd business sense in managing one's talent, one can make a mess out of the best of breaks.

Look at the state in which Rehana Sultan's career is today. She graduated in the very first batch from the FTII, in 1963. After going round the offices of producers, she finally signed two films—Rajinder Singh Bedi's *Dastak* and B.R. Ishara's *Chetna*. Both these movies turned out to be hits at the box office. Rehana immediately became a star—a new kind of actress whom the public loved for her talent. Unfortunately, the first heady current of success drowned her, as it later turned out. She fell into filmdom's oldest trap. The first mistake she made was to forget that she had become a craze not because she was beautiful and stunning to look at, but because she was a very talented actress. After her initial success, Rehana started concentrating more on her make-up than on her craft. The second major mistake Rehana made was that she became overconfident about her talent. She announced that she would not work with big male stars unless the story gave the heroine an important role. Unfortunately her movies with lesser-known actors flopped at the box office. Gradually Rehana was pushed out of the limelight. Today she is almost forgotten and nobody talks about her phenomenal talent. The film industry has instead opened its doors to successors like Jaya Bhaduri, Shabana Azmi, Zarina Wahab, Ranjeeta, and Rameshweri—all of whom are from the FTII.

Apart from the film schools, another major road to a career in film is theatre. This is particularly true for actors and actresses. A number of talented artistes from theatre have always found their way into cinema. Today we have Dr Shreeram Lagoo, Amol Palekar, Naseeruddin Shah, Kulbhushan Kharbanda, T.P. Jain, and Om Shivpuri, to mention a few of those who have moved from stage plays into the cinema.

Then there are beautiful, dazzling girls like (the late) Smita Patil and Poonam Dhillon who have come to films without any kind of acting experience. Smita Patil was a TV announcer when director Shyam Benegal offered her a role in his children's film *Charandas Chor*. Later, Benegal cast her in *Nishant*. Thereafter, Smita was offered more film roles than she cared to accept.

Poonam Dhillon, on the other hand, was merely a teenager and a rather innocent beauty queen when producer-director Yash Chopra discovered her. A small role in *Trishul* was followed by the leading role in *Noorie*. In this film, incidentally, the hero was Farroukh Sheikh, who comes from the Indian People's Theatre Association, Bombay, and has been acting on stage for many years now. Once *Noorie* began to do well, Poonam Dhillon was flooded with offers. From a simple girl studying at Chandigarh, she became a magic goddess of the silver screen. No institute, no training, no film theory classes.

The same holds true for heroes. If one has luck and certain qualities like star presence, charisma, and perseverance, one can make a glorious career for oneself in cinema without ever acting on stage or ever having gone to a film school. But then one should never really forget that for every person who is successful in the films, there are at least a hundred who have flopped and who have neither the interest nor the talent to do anything else successfully. Can odds like these justify our calling the cinema a career and not a roulette game?

Hindustan Times, *28 August 1993.*

Themes and Variations
of Indian Cinema

The Death of Children's Cinema

Children's cinema has not proved to be a commercially viable proposition in the Indian film industry. This has remained so despite certain films for children having done well at the box office. It is the attitude of the financiers and distributors that is to blame, and to some extent, the lack of initiative on the part of the film-makers themselves.

The children's film movement has more or less died at birth in the movie-making business of this country. To a very large extent this has hapened because Indian film-makers are fixated on feature films.

No children's film movement, or documentary film movement, or a general state of excitement for the other streams of the cinema is visible on the Indian scene—not wildlife movies, or cartoons, or sports films, or experimental shorts. All the substreams exist precariously. Their protagonists often change rapidly. The theoretical frameworks are always somewhat vague. And, perhaps most significant of all, the marketing circuits for these substreams are never quite clear of the shadow of the banyan tree of the feature film that dominates the cinemascape in our country.

The children's film movement in the country is but one more victim of the Indian film-maker's obsession with adult cinema. Even the directors who choose to make films for children during the initial years of their careers seldom return to the genre once they have stepped out into the wider horizons of the feature film.

In retrospect, the 1970s highlighted this enigma with a particular sharpness. One of the noticeable offshoots of the Indian New Wave of the 1970s was the coming together of some of the most dynamic new film directors to make a series of children's films with the support of the Children's Film Society of India (CFSI).

Many of these directors were people with an impressive degree of experience in closely related fields like theatre and documentary films. Soon after their advent into cinema, many were to help open up new windows and a definitive change of sensibility, leading finally to a resurgence of artistic qualities in Indian cinema as a whole.

The personal decision of many of these directors to make films for children in the preliminary phase of their film careers was primarily responsible for a revitalization of the children's film movement. Till then, it was a creature that seemed to have spent too much time in hibernation.

Many film buffs will not perhaps remember that the first feature film directed by Shyam Benegal, who went on to become one of the mainstays of the Indian New Wave, was a full-length film made for children. *Charandas Chor* (Charan Das the Thief) was based upon a popular Chhattisgarhi folk play about an audacious village thief, which had been revived in the late 1960s by stage director Habib Tanvir and a troupe of folk artistes from Madhya Pradesh. Tanvir had reassembled the troupe at Delhi after their folk-theatre company had been languishing for many years. *Charandas Chor*, incidentally, was also the first feature film that Smita Patil acted in. The famous—now unfortunately no more—Indian actress of the New Wave, who went on to win two national awards for acting and inspired a series of retrospectives in India and abroad, actually made her feature film debut in Benegal's children's film *Charandas Chor!*

B.V. Karanth, the exceptionally talented stage director whose contributions to theatre in both Karnataka and Delhi had already won him wide acclaim, has independently directed only two feature films in his long, now seventeen-year-old, association with film-making. He won the national award for best film of the year with

Chomana Dudi in 1976, but before that he had already directed a children's film for the CFSI, *Chor Chor Chhup Chhup ja*, which achieved considerable popularity when the CFSI marketed it commercially.

Kantilal Rathod, who had been a successful ad-film man at Bombay, tied up his debut into offbeat Hindi film (*Parinay*) with a children's film produced for the CFSI. Sai Paranjpe, who was to be later associated with the children's film movement for quite some time thereafter, also made a full-budget feature film for children in the early 1970s. It marked her incursion from TV work into wholetime film-making. And then there was *Ichchapuran*, the children's film that Mrinal Sen directed, based on one of the many entrancing stories that Rabindranath Tagore wrote about the mischievous and topsy-turvy child's world.

By the mid-1970s, it almost looked as if a children's film movement was going to become a pleasant spin-off of the emerging forces of the New Wave. Even the inimitable Satyajit Ray returned to work for children with a series of films with child heroes through the 1970s and 1980s.

But where has that movement and its excitement gone? It is languishing—primarily because these talented directors, for one reason or another, have moved to wider horizons, possibly greener pastures and greater acclaim than children's cinema could offer them.

Regrettably, there were no new or younger directors waiting to step in once the 'seniors' moved out. Nobody was impatient to seize the opportunity that suddenly became available. Even more regrettably, of the luminaries of new Indian cinema only Satyajit Ray was to return constantly to children's films.

It was not a particularly glorious phase for the CFSI itself. The administrators looking after its affairs failed to build on the initiative they had rather successfully taken in the early 1970s. The nascent movement receded to the quieter, less noticed areas of the cinema world.

Two salient factors had much to do with this loss of initiative and both were, as so often happens in cinema, interrelated. The new children's films of the 1970s generated considerable interest among children, parents, and critics but not enough to help establish a viable, independent, marketing circuit for children's films in the country. Irrespective of the figures in the account books of the CFSI, to the outside observer it soon became clear that the children's film movement could survive only through steady government support.

The box-office fate of the children's film *Kitab*, made within the regular, mainstream production sector at Bombay by the noted writer-director Gulzar, was one of the most unfortunate things to happen to the nascent movement. Had Gulzar's film brought in the producer's investment, it could well have become a trendsetter among the movie moguls and big film financiers in Bombay, as one more road to profit through cinema. Released in the mainstream theatrical network, *Kitab* was a very poor cousin to Gulzar's sensitive emotional dramas which represented one of the high points in Indian cinema through the 1970s and early 1980s. Immediately, the money-bags of the film industry shied off from children's films. Even the impressive grosses of *Chhota Chetan* (made originally in Malayalam and then dubbed in Hindi) in the mid-1980s could not tempt the moneybags back.

The absence of small, low rent theatres in cities and towns, the problems of arranging regular theatrical releases, the apathy of school authorities to children's films, the scarcity of good scripts and dedicated directors—all these combined to make a list of difficulties which the movement has constantly had to contend with.

The problems stem from the fact that we do not really have a distinct category of children's entertainment and leisure activities within the modern entertainment format.

Though *Chandamama* and a few other children's magazines enjoyed widespread popularity during the 1950s and early 1960s, there is a general dearth of children's books and magazines in

India. This has robbed children's films of the advantage of drawing upon basic raw material and a basic audience from the world of children's literature.

With the decline in popularity of traditional folk entertainment for children, such as puppet-shows, snake charmers, bear and monkey shows, a void seemed to envelope the children of cities and towns. Television made a half-hearted attempt to fill the vacuum, but without much success.

Therefore, almost without their realizing it, a tremendous socio-cultural responsibility devolved upon Indian film-makers who were venturing into the world of children's films in the early 1970s. They had to create a cinema that would effectively replace traditional entertainers such as puppeteers, snake charmers, and *madaris*.

It was a challenge that the new film-makers could not quite meet. In many instances, the spin-offs of the Indian New Wave produced films on and about children that impressed adults more than children. In a sense, the film-makers were quite clueless about themes, plots, and treatments the young audiences cared for or wanted from their film-makers. The absence of a popular children's literature forced scriptwriters and directors to take shots in the dark. Not surprisingly the endeavour has not succeeded in creating a new sub-circuit in the world of Indian cinema. Children have continued to accompany parents to films that adults prefer to see. The more intelligent of the mainstream film producers and directors were shrewd enough to incorporate in their productions of adult cinema, elements specially designed to please children in the audience. Slapstick, parody, free-for-all action, horseplay, and an element of the fantastic were to become essential ingredients of most blockbuster feature films. One of the most successful propagators of the new trend, director-producer Manmohan Desai, candidly claimed in an interview that his biggest audience was children.

This Gordian knot can be cut only if a tribe, no matter how small, of Indian film directors sets out with a definitive commitment to making films primarily for children. It is only if the film-makers so wish and are fired by the vision, that the movement can be restarted, to etch out a new tradition of entertainment and education for our children.

Hindustan Times, *15 April 1990*.

* * *

Political Themes in Indian Cinema

The removal of poverty—garibi hatao—*holds a greater attraction for the Indian mind than resolving communal tensions between Hindus and Muslims. The film* Garam Hawa *did not do too well at the box office because of this collective preference in the minds of Indians.*

Not since the days when the British authorities banned novels and plays has a single work of art become so involved with national politics as the film *Garam Hawa* has. Most of those who worked in *Garam Hawa* have inherited the legacy of the Indian People's Theatre Association (IPTA). And the Left has traditionally been the major force in the movement of art towards a direct political effect. *Garam Hawa*—both in its making and in its impact—cannot thus be seen in isolation from the artistic and political antecedents of the immediate past.

The heyday of the Naxalite movement saw the arts—particularly drama and song—being forged into a strategic component of the ideological war. Though West Bengal was the main centre of such artistic activity, the influence from there on urban art centres in the rest of the country was immediate. The radical events brought artists face to face with a most significant subject material—the Indian condition, particularly in terms of poverty. As this became the centre of artistic, intellectual, political, and general debate and concern within the framework of the establishment, it transcended electoral alignments and became as respectable a subject as any other for artists.

Yet concern with the Indian situation cannot be confined to air-conditioned theatres. The limitations of the social impact of a play like Vijay Tendulkar's *Ghasiram Kotwal* (outside the regional cultural orthodoxy of Maharashtra itself) may, at one level, be compared with the exaltation of revolutionary chants and gestures in the fantasies of the Bombay film. In both cases, familiar lore from the past may be marginally reactivated (such as Marathi obscurantism about Nana Phadnavis). But it is not possible for the work to activate social currents that are subterranean at the moment, despite their apparent presence in the general flow of the social consciousness. Going beyond such works of art or show business, *Garam Hawa* has now shown the possibility that a work of art can squarely confront society.

I think this is an important development in post-Independence India. For, till 1967, the urban artist was caught in a process that alienated him a little more each year from the 'people'. In that apolitical environment, popular entertainment (in cinema and theatre) took a leap towards escapism, gloss, and sheer fantasy. There is no doubt that this flight into escapism also reflected the general obsession with the opulent toys and façades of the industrial society. Also, popular entertainment could provide some room for the airing of political comment. But the overall feeling reiterated by popular entertainment was that it was impossible to 'change' things, that life would move at its own pace and that resignation and acceptance were the individual's best means of survival.

Since 1967 all that has changed. The birth of the 'new cinema' has, luckily, coincided with this change. The coming of age of the first generation of post-Independence India is also an important factor in the emergence of this new perspective.

The 'new cinema' had a propitious beginning—a beginning that linked the past and the future. The director of *Bhuvan Shome* was the first film-maker of today's 'new cinema' to get a loan from the Film Finance Corporation (FFC) through a personal decision of Himmat Singh, the then Chairman of the Corporation. Mrinal Sen was a man who had grown in the IPTA tradition, but who found his maturity and his time only in the mid-1960s.

In *Bhuvan Shome*, Mrinal Sen handled a subject close to his political and social concerns. Yet he did so in a manner that did not directly use a political terminology. On the surface, the film remained the story of the bureaucrat and the village girl. Under it, it showed the confrontation between an ossifying urbanite and the vitality of village India or, rather, with the depths of our collective potential. It was a confrontation that had a political message for society at large.

The complexities of expression embedded in the format of *Bhuvan Shome* make it more naturally a symbol of the diverse voices that the new cinema has brought to the fore. Young film-makers leaned to this or that side of *Bhuvan Shome* for their individual articulation of form and style. Yet Mrinal Sen's first Hindi film can be taken as a midway point in new cinema.

Over the years Mrinal Sen has pursued his method of using cinema both for purposes of art and of life today. This has provided some sort of continuity to film-making, culminating in *Garam Hawa*. Directed by M.S. Sathyu and based on two stories by Ismat Chugtai, it is a film that seems to mark the beginning of the awareness that contemporary Indian art has a major responsibility in mapping the future of our collective life.

Before one goes on to that, it might not be amiss to mention here that this emergence of a cinema with a direct political bearing also had a curious side effect. Mrinal Sen's second venture in this period—*Interview*—coincided with a major shift in Satyajit Ray's filmography marked by *Pratidwandi*. As Kironmoy Raha pointed out in a review of the film in *Frontier*, *Pratidwandi* was the first film in which Ray directly and urgently dealt with the totality of a contemporary social situation. Ray's later film, *Asani Sanket*, which deals with the Bengal famine of 1943, may also be seen as part of the shift in his career—a shift brought about by, among other things, by the emergence of Mrinal Sen and a socially committed cinema.

Two films of the new cinema—apart from Mrinal Sen's trilogy of *Interview*, *Calcutta 71*, and *Padatik*—are important in the run up to *Garam Hawa*. These are *Samskara* (in Kannada) and *Swayamvaram* (in Malayalam). A brilliantly concise cinematization of Ananthamoorthy's novel, *Samskara* made a major breakthrough in the understanding of religious dogma. What, after all is the Brahaminical concept of 'purity' if the Shudra does little that the Brahmin does not, in terms of the brass tacks of human existence? Through the use of the primordial force of sex, *Samskara* challenges the rigidity in caste segregation. And, to top it off, it concludes that nobody can really be sure about the purity of his or her lineage. This confrontation between tradition and some basic and undeniable common sense—so that the tradition may be redefined to solve the crisis of contemporary society—attacked the roots of political life in our country. The seemingly apolitical theme of *Samskara* thereby becomes a part of the new cinema—a cinema that is always conscious of the Indian body politic and its infrastructure, even when it is not ostensibly oriented to political concerns.

Adoor Gopalakrishnan's *Swayamvaram* is perhaps the most comprehensive film about the post-Independence Indian's social life. By a juxtaposition of the inner and outer lives of individuals, *Swayamvaram* created with both accuracy and imagination the fall of the young into the ancient abyss—an unsung death, or life-in-death. In a particular sequence, Gopalakrishnan articulated his image and observation of this abyss.

The young man, played by Madhu (who starts life as a writer and ends it as a clerk in a squalid timber factory), comes out of the factory and is confronted by another young man. The latter had once worked in the same factory but was sacked and is now unemployed. His job has been given to Madhu. What, Gopalakrishnan asks us, can be the sense of security a young man feels when he perceives that the source of his livelihood has deprived another young man like him? Further, stepping awkwardly past the unemployed man, Madhu walks down the lane to the main road. Here—suggested through sound but not visually shown—he runs into a procession of Kerala government NGOs, agitating for their dearness allowance. The vital link between personal and social life that this whole sequence shows has not, anywhere else, been expressed so specifically as in *Swayamvaram*. Mrinal Sen too has often touched upon this link, but always in generalized terms.

Side by side with these 'public' aspects of the film's central character, Gopalakrishnan sets a curious parallel pattern. Knocking around at life's doors outside his home, and being knocked around in turn, Madhu is shown totally at ease in a strange and intriguing relationship with his wife, played by Sharda. Inside the house, the man is passive—generally lolling about—while the woman is the active member, bustling and doing things constantly. It is a juxtaposition of public and private aspects that provides director Gopalakrishnan with some of the basic premises he needed for his comprehensive account of the young Indian's life today. *Swayamvaram* was easily accepted by society. It did not disturb the sense of status quo as *Garam Hawa* threatens to.

Is it because by the time *Swayamvaram* came about—or for that matter *Interview* and *Pratidwandi*—the problem of the young Indian and of the immediate future of India had already been revealed to society at large by events that are now part of Indian history? The uprising at Naxalbari and its impact on the entire social fabric led to intense public consciousness of the ills of the socio-economic system, specifically in the form of the portrayals of the young as doomed. By the time these films came, we had collectively accepted the social problems the films dealt with, even if we could not solve them right away.

With *Garam Hawa*, it is the opposite. The communal tensions between Hindus and Muslims that the film deals with spell a problem that has not yet stormed the collective mind. A resolution of this conflict has no popularity as a social wish, completely unlike the wish for garibi hatao. For this very reason, as director M.S. Sathyu has said time and again in newspaper interviews, *Garam Hawa* was made with special care. It was meant to communicate and impact with the largest audience of cinema without compromising its essential message. Here is a major social problem, this message says, that still destroys so many Indian homes (twenty-six years after Partition) and we treat it like a problem that cannot be resolved and that does not, therefore, merit public debate and concern.

In this, *Garam Hawa* specifies one major direction along which the urban Indian artist shall have to work if he is to prove the social validity of his work; if art can influence life to make the changes that it needs.

Hindustan Times, *11 February 1990*.

* * *

The Usurper Theme in Hindi Cinema

This essay, written thirty years ago, is both playful and full of mischief. It argues that Shyam Benegal's Ankur *and Mrinal Sen's* Ek Adhuri Kahani *pushed the king pin of Hindi 'phillums',* Manmohan Desai, *into making* Dharamveer. Dharamveer *is about social justice, and how a politician fails to do his duty towards the people and his office.*

Mrinal Sen and Shyam Benegal may chuckle at this but there is a definite possibility that they played a role in ushering in the extravaganza's swing toward history. Bombay's film-makers generally work in a claustrophobic atmosphere. New ideas are scarcer here than space in the metropolis. It is far from imaginable that some intellectual looked around and saw in *Ek Adhuri Kahani* and *Ankur* the seeds of an alternative cinema—one that shows social tension, conflict, and the exploitation and dehumanization of man and woman. Or that anyone considered these as perfect scenario for incorporating fights and exotica. So with Mammohan Desai's *Dharamveer* the big studios went further back into history, before the British Raj that Mrinal and Shyam saw as a house of mirrors reflecting contemporary India.

It may sound absurd to some that *Ek Adhuri Kahani* or *Ankur* could have the least resemblance to *Dharamveer*, or *Azaad*, or *Amar-Shakti*, or that these films could anticipate these box-office extravaganzas. But if you look at it from the perspective that all these films talk about poverty and the poor (yes, the big three do!), perhaps it may not sound ridiculous. It may explain, instead, how popular forms relate to the experiments of art.

When *Dharamveer* was ultimately given the censor's certificate in March 1977, it was clear that V.C. Shukla's ministry (the Ministry of Information and Broadcasting) had been constrained to delay the film's release mainly because of one particular line of dialogue in it where Dharmendra talks about justice as defined for the poor and as modified for the rich and that those who swear by principles to keep the weak in their place would damn these principles if they turned on them.

It is generally, and contemptuously, assumed that the 'uncultured' masses of the Indian film audience will accept a film even if all they really like about it is just one detail. In *Dharamveer* the dialogue that V.C. Shukla's ministry seemed to fear in 1976 and early 1977 stood out like a menacing detail. It was the core of the armed struggle waged by Dharam and Veer's band.

In Pramod Chakravorty's *Azaad*, the essential feature of Dharmendra's character is that, like Zorro, he's not going to let the unjust go unpunished. In A.K. Nadiadwala's *Amar-Shakti* both the princes from the dethroned family—Shashi Kapoor and Shatrughan Sinha—talk again and again of the poor.

It was while watching *Amar-Shakti* that it struck this writer that 'poverty' and the 'poor' were not, in those days, two words the media was particularly fond of. They suddenly seemed to have gone out of fashion and even politicians, who constitute along with films the two dominant communications media on a national scale, do not make much use of them at present.

The compulsions of the commercially produced and marketed Indian film are obvious. But there are occasions when its need to feel the pulse of the people eggs on producers to a blunt and straightforward espousal of the people's demands. This is understandable. For the poor themselves the most important feature in films has always been the narrative and its championing of the poor. In sharp contrast, for the middle class, the Indian film's importance lies in entertainment or, less frequently, the reflection of psychological dilemmas. A situation that is really contrary to the intelligentsia's analyses of the Indian film and its audience.

Intriguingly enough, the simple, unsubtle banner of poverty that these 'escapist' extravaganzas wave now and then is not all. If it was, these overflamboyant films would have been even more crude and unsubtle. On the contrary, a strange, at first nearly incomprehensible, complexity is introduced through the usurper theme. In *Dharamveer*, *Azaad*, and *Amar-Shakti*, to take but three examples, we see a king conspired against, dethroned, and imprisoned—not by an enemy but by deceiving lieutenants. The usurper, being played by a screen villain, is easily defined. But the deposed monarch is in all cases sketchily characterized. He is a vaguely defined 'good' king, a generous ruler misguided by his own administrative machinery, personifying an ideal ruler appealing to our atavistic fantasy. In the inner recesses of the mind's chaos, this fantasy hopes for an end to all dilemmas.

But strangely enough, the usurper theme seems to be easily acceptable to the 78 lakh-odd Indians who frequent the movie halls every day. It thereby introduces into the social fabric a theme that seems totally irrelevant to Indian politicians, political commentators, and scholars.

To go back now from Manmohan Desai, Pramod Chakravorty, and Nadiadwala to Mrinal Sen and Benegal, we can wonder if, in the colloquial idiom of the collective psyche, the harsh factory owner in *Ek Adhuri Kahani* and the confused young feudal master in *Ankur* are not really usurpers. And can we not apply the same sociological-cum-political yardstick and wonder if our rulers have all these years not been usurpers—never performing the roles they know they are supposed to perform?

In our society, where the image is the beginning and end of absolute reality, would the political scientist not agree with the fantasy film and feel that the real validation of public office is something permanent and supreme? Neither constitutional right—through being voted into power—nor the overwhelming powers of office provide a greater justification to the public official than his moral force as the leader of the people in the real, concrete sense. Would there else have been such support for J.P.'s movement in 1974 against a constitutionally elected government or such irritation and despair at the Janata government?

In Indian politics, and Indian society as a whole, there has been and shall remain a consistent pressure on the rulers to adequately perform the functions of their office as defined by popular need. And, as 1977 proved, neither power nor might shall for too long sustain the ruler usurping and encroaching on the functions of his office. The theme of kingship as a contract between the leader and his followers is hardly dead in the labyrinths of the democratic process in India.

Let our rulers think again about the usurper theme that comes through so obliquely in the escapism of cinema. Who remembers the administrative or martial brilliance of Aurangzeb? Dara Shikoh, Shivaji, and his brutal encroachment in religion erase all else about that Mughal's image in the folk mind. And were not the British in India usurpers too?

This Fortnight, *9 November 1978. This magazine has since ceased publication.*

* * *

Popular Cinema Learns from Art Cinema

The early 1980s saw young, unknown film-makers making some memorable films such as Aakrosh and Albert Pinto Ko Gussa Kyon Ata Hai. These films did well at the box office despite initial distribution problems. Certain sophisticated narrative elements were borrowed by commercial cinema to its own benefit. However, popular cinema's gain did not in any way benefit serious cinema.

The world of Indian cinema is a raucous bazaar presided over by the deity of the box office even though the studios churn out dream fantasies about lone vigilantes and romantic idylls. Yet, tucked away in an obscure, partially camouflaged alley at the far end of the marketplace is a row of zealots gabbling about the true god of cinema, each working away quietly at his/her own thing.

Indian New Wave cinema today is not in the most enviable of conditions. An air of déjà vu seems to have enveloped it. Yet, despite symptoms to the contrary, it is still alive and breathing.

Ever since the New Wave was launched in the late 1960s by a clutch of young film-makers from the Film and Television Institute of India, the ideology of the movement continues to impinge upon the consciousness of mainstream Indian cinema. The movement emphasized that film-making did not comprise stereotypes put together on an assembly line for mass consumption, but was a manifestation of the collective impulses of creativity and a search for an Indian ethos that reached towards universalism through its very Indianness.

When the ideologues of the New Wave, led by Mrinal Sen, Mani Kaul, Shyam Benegal, and Govind Nihalani, declared that Indian cinema in the 1960s had become too bland, the movie moguls and technical doyens of the fantasy studios thought that these heretics were just talking airily. Yet, despite the limited, audience to which New Wave films catered, the sheer pugnacity of the movement and the unstoppable flow of new recruits that it attracted along finally began to make the new thinking and approach comprehensible to the dons of cinema's bazaar. In fact, the same period, popular entertainment in cinema gradually tranformed into a more creative medium of cinematic technique. It diffused some of its hot air to turn to more realistic themes.

The influence of the New Wave, and its creative credo, has been very visible during the last couple of years in mainstream Indian cinema. While the New Wave itself has not quite achieved its ambition of reaching out to wider audiences, its spur has made a more sophisticated product out of popular film entertainment. While mainstream Indian cinema earlier had a tendency to be too verbal, it has switched course and is today dominantly visual in its approach. The camera has come alive, even in assembly-line entertainment. The quality of acting is dramatically transformed and even the crassest of stereotypes is now given some semblance of social relevance and reality. These influences of the New Wave have, ironically but not unexpectedly, helped the cinema of box-office formulas to revive and rejuvenate itself and become more contemporary in tone and less melodramatic in its emphases.

Satyajit Ray has been the flag bearer of the artistic tradition in Indian cinema since 1955, when despite considerable odds he put together *Pather Panchali*, the first of his many masterpieces. The 1950s were a kind of golden age as far as cinema sensibility was concerned. The emergence of Satyajit Ray was to coincide with the arrival of another major talent in Ritwik Ghatak, who also worked from Calcutta. Both of them were to go on to become the inspiration and even father figures of the New Wave of the late 1960s. On the west coast, despite the commercialism in Bombay's film world, two extremely complex and significant directors—Bimal Roy and Guru Dutt—kept alive the spirit of aesthetics in India's Hollywood, inspiring some of their peers to occasionally venture into realms nobler than that ruled by the box office and its siren calls. The 1950s were also the decade in which popular Indian films were to establish an international market for themselves. Raj Kapoor's *Awara* headed this list, taking the Asian Republics of the Soviet Union by storm, dominating the silver screen in places as far away as Turkey, Sudan, and Kenya. Built around a format that assimilated Western techniques and sensibilities within a base derived from the Indian folk theatre tradition, the popular Indian film became, in many parts of the Third World, the new idiom in entertainment. And it was to be the inspiration for the growth of native cinemas in many countries of the Third World.

Indian films found it easy to establish this affinity of minds in Africa and Asia because, behind the razzmatazz of glamorized entertainment, they reflected social processes common to the post-colonial era in Asia and Africa, where ancient cultural traditions were beginning to coexist with the mores and norms of an industrial society. The transition to the modern age, the revaluation of the past, and the tensions of the moral conflicts between the traditional and the modern were, indeed, at the core of the quality entertainers produced in the dream factories of Bombay. These corresponded in spirit and impulse to the mood of Africa and Asia as a whole. In turn, Bombay's film-makers were quick to adopt motifs from other Asian and African cultures. This was particularly manifest in the gay abandon with which Indian film scores incorporated and moulded the music of Central Asia, the Middle East, and Africa, establishing through music larger arenas for themselves.

A close examination of Indian film history shows that our cinema has always been inspired, to a very significant extent, by the socio-economic situation of the people. Many film historians believe *Savkari Pash* (1925) to be India's first art-film. This silent-film focused a sharp lens on the abject condition of Indian peasants and recreated their tragedy with a stylized eloquence that wins the pundits' approval to this day. Such was the impact of *Savkari Pash* on the Indian people that many believe that the film paved the way for the subsequent agricultural reforms carried out in the country to free the Indian peasant from the burden of lifelong indebtedness to money-lenders. V. Shantaram, one of the young actors to get a major break in *Savkari Pash*, went on to make a series of unconventional films that were critical of rampant social maladies such as the dowry system (*Dahej*) and communal antagonism (*Padosi*).

It might also surprise the layman to know that the first feminist film to be made in India was as far back as 1936, shortly after the coming of the talkies. The movie, *Amar Jyoti*, featured a gang of women pirates, à la Modesty Blaise, who enslaved men to avenge all the atrocities that they had committed against women down the ages. Other films like *Dr Madhurika* and *Barrister's Wife* (both made in 1935) focused on the challenges, dilemmas, and problems that Indian women faced in the transition from a traditional society into modern times. At the same time, the box-office turnstiles revolved to the cadence of *Telephone Girl* and *Typist Girl* (both silent films made in 1926), starring Indian cinema's first major star, Sulochana.

The early years of cinema in India seem quite astounding. Within a few years of its birth in the West, films captured the imagination of young Indian intellectuals. The first short films made here were in 1897, many of which recorded aspects of India's freedom movement. And once feature films were born— Dadasaheb's Phalke's *Raja Harishchandra* (1913) and the earlier Indo-European collaboration, R.G. Torney's *Pundalik* (1912)—they seemed to share a strong nationalistic aspiration, in tune with the freedom movement against colonialism. Consciously and deliberately, the new technology was used as a bifocal mirror to recreate the national cultural heritage for a people who now wanted to reach out to new horizons.

From the early days, therefore, serious young film-makers were to play an important role in shaping the currents and tides of the celluloid ocean. Whenever possible, contemporary litterateurs too were persuaded to work in the medium. Famous Indian writers like Premchand and Manto were to have substantial stints in the movie business, though not always to their satisfaction. Directors and actors from theatre, like Motilal, Shombhu, and Tripti Mitra, migrated in a constant stream to the new medium. Poets, novelists, and even journalists like K.A. Abbas, Shailendra, Sahir Ludhianvi, and Kaifi Azmi, were to enrich the world of movie-making. The illustrious dancer Uday Shankar ventured to make a ballet film in 1948 called, *Kalpana*. He prompted the new generation of classical musicians—contemporary maestros like sitarists Vilayat Khan and Ravi Shankar—to test their imaginative range by composing the musical scores of feature films.

Cinema is, as technology's child, a wonderful playground for the technique-conscious craftsman. At its best Indian cinema has always had a strong social content. The pioneering vision of the early generations was reinforced towards the end of the 1940s by the large-scale induction of dramaturgists, directors, actors, and musicians from the Indian People's Theatre Association (IPTA), the cultural troupe founded by Indian Marxists in the early 1940s. These luminaries found in the world of cinema happy resolutions to many of their own intellectual dilemmas. Here was a medium that belonged to the common masses, into whose slick, glamorized format the Indian Leftist's social concerns also seemed to find a comfortable niche. Through the 1940s and the 1950s quality cinema achieved a symbiosis between traditional cultural motifs and modern social analysis. It reflected the vision of Jawaharlal Nehru, India's first prime minister, for a new emergent India that would be both modern and traditional, incorporating the best of the two worlds.

It was probably this new infusion of intellectual depth in the early 1960s that prevented mainstream cinema as a whole from slipping into crass commercial grooves. By this time the chasm between the dream factories of Bombay and the aesthetics embodied in the filmography of Satyajit Ray and Ritwik Ghatak seemed to have become unbridgeable. It was a period in which creativity was edged out of movie-making and concoctions borrowed from a variety of other cinemas dominated the scene.

It was in rebellion against this abysmal lack of aesthetic value that the New Wave arose from the cloisters of the newly formed film school, the Film and Television Institute of India (FTII), set up as an autonomous body by the Government of India. The presence of the great Ritwik Ghatak and director Mrinal Sen on the Institute's teaching staff was to motivate a new generation of directors at the film school. Led by articulate ideologues like Mani Kaul, Adoor Gopalakrisnan, and Kumar Shahani, they waged a war of attrition against the bland stereotypes of the film industry. Supported by the Film Finance Corporation (later to merge with a new umbrella organization, the National Film Development Corporation) the New Wave campaigned for a more creative cinema; it emphasized the building up of close bonds with international films. And, for the discerning filmgoer, the new possibilities of the medium suddenly became apparent. Through the 1970s and the 1980s—despite pendulum swings between individual successes and general artistic failure—the New Wave succeeded in changing the perspective of film buffs and, even more significantly, of film-makers. Cameramen, editors, and sound recordists graduating from the FTII were quickly absorbed by established film companies. The new cinema movement burst forth in various pars of the country in a spontaneous outpouring of creativity. But most of all in south India, where FTII alumni Adoor Gopalakrishnan, Balu Mahendra, and John Abraham succeeded in creating a new climate for a new kind of film. People working in allied fields, like short films and advertising, widened their horizons to make feature films on their own; college teachers like the award-winning director Buddhadeb Dasgupta threw up safe jobs to plunge into the risky business of making low-budget films.

It was not long before the impact of this widespread movement began to be felt in mainstream cinema too. And during the mid-1980s, a new crop of young directors, who had one eye on commerce but the other on the film's artistic potential, found opportunities opening up for them in film studios. Gradually, therefore, mainstream movies began to assimilate the virtues of a more creative film movement. The process is still in a state of flux. The moneybags too have had a few lessons to teach the young rebels. But the upshot of this confrontation is that creativity has come to stay as an a priori feature in film-making. Certainly, therefore, the decade to come will see many surprises in Indian film.

Published in Link. *This magazine has since ceased publication.*

* * *

Can Parallel Cinema Survive?

The parallel or art cinema that came about in the 1970s was supposed to be a sophisticated answer to the crudeness of commercial Indian cinema and was supposed to create choices for the more discriminating viewer. That did not happen. Most of the films made in Hindi, at any rate, were too dull and pedantic to find a paying audience—even a small one.

Any assessment of the prospects of parallel cinema in India must take into account the traditional division between urban and folk culture. It must also consider whether Western influences on academic approaches to studying and making films are really part of the cultural assimilation that Indian society is supposed to be undergoing today. Or are they but a cultural affectation of the ruling elite of a society that is actually inert and feigns dynamism?

Most people who talk about parallel cinema see it as a means of bolstering dynamic movements in Indian society. And yet, while the parallel cinema exists in that films like Adoor Gopalakrishnan's *Swayamvaram*, *Ranur Pratham Bhag*, and *Samskara* have been made in recent times, it is also true that parallel cinema does not exist without state help. Even the demand for art theatres has been made to the Government of India, which would of course like parallel cinema to be parallel in the sense that AIR, the Films Division, the Publications Division, and TV now are.

One would have thought that Indian film-makers on the offbeat track would have shown the sort of ingenuity in handling material problems that they are only too eager to claim on the aesthetic level. One would have wanted film-makers to seek a parallel cinema in 16 mm and Super 8 also and not simply in 35 mm. One would have expected them to avoid the banal publicity campaigns that have riddled the film industry with narcissism, arrogance, and overconfidence. And one would have expected at least one genuine film experimentalist (as different from derivation experts) experimenting in terms of audience attention.

More than anything else, one would have expected parallel cinema to throw up artists who were not megalomaniacs; who were objective; who were searching for truth and not for personal glory; who are so confident about their efforts that they do not demand instant applause; and who represent the post-Independence generations that have rescued their idealism from the mire.

This did not happen. The possibility of film-makers creating another financial circuit, on a lower scale than the big-time racket, with films creating operators of smaller theatres, was a possibility that has been aborted. This is so largely because the new film-makers chose to relate in simplistic positive or negative ways to the big-time circuit. Either they wanted to be accepted by the existing distribution and exhibition set-up or they stood totally against it (and expected the government to arrange distributors and exhibitors for their films).

Whenever that happened, it amounted to parallel cinema denying itself a chance to set up shop on is own. It was a choice made out of fear that this cinema was too distant from a large enough audience to allow it to stand on its own legs. But then why could feature films of parallel cinema not be made on 16 mm? This could also have accommodated the innumerable film societies and film clubs on whose membership parallel cinema sought to build itself. Why must feature films be made to a length of at least ninety minutes running time and with an eye to international film festivals? Why should it be said that parallel cinema cannot exist without government aid and intervention? Why should the government have restrained private entrepreneurs from setting up art theatres in the private sector?

Yet, as it always happens with us, the situation is not entirely hopeless. Sufficient highbrow interest in the cinema had been created by the film societies before the government established the Film Institute of India (now FTII, the Film and Television Institute of India). The FTII itself fits in with the old socialist thinking that the state must look after the core sector of national economy. It defines the furthest point away of the state's contribution to Indian cinema but it also sets itself limits! I don't think that state financing of film is likely to be as fruitful as the setting up of basic institutions. One only hopes that government will also make some investment in research on technical development in the manufacture of raw film, the innovation of cinematographic and processing apparatus, and into film technology as a whole. But perhaps inventive filmmakers will make technical innovations, inventions, and discoveries whenever they turn inventive.

Despite the fact that a recent rule requires applicants to the FTII to be graduates, the FTII draws upon a sufficiently diverse section among the middle and upper classes. It gives a thorough enough training to create a potential film-maker out of everyone who has gone through the Institute. In ten to fifteen years time, FTII graduates, because of sheer numbers, will be forced to seek alternate means other than status quo possibilities as new Indian film-makers. In the first instance, an unduly high reliance on wangling a Film Finance Corporation (FFC) loan will give way to greater entrepreneurship than there now is among FTII graduates. It will also lead to far greater competition in the documentary film world, in ad shorts, and in audiovisual development programmes. And, considering some general Indian responses, such enterprise and competition is bound to improve the quality of films and film technology.

But that is a long way off. As of now, parallel cinema exists only through the FFC and through the effort of a small section of people in the film industry. (Asit Sen ranks very high in my list here, though people generally refer to Gulzar and—mistakenly— to Hrishikesh Mukerjee in this context. There are also Basu Chatterjee, B. Bhattacharya, and, if you like, Rajinder Singh Bedi, Ishara, etc.)

In this transitional phase—of parallel cinema existing and not existing as it were—there are some important ramifications to consider. We have had several efforts in which young film-makers have reworked for filming the literary structures of older generations. Barring the rare examples like *Swayamvaram*, *Samskara*, and *Garam Hawa*, most of the literary material used by the new film-makers has been of the kind that gets dated within the decade. Nirmal Verma's story for Kumar Shahani's *Maya Darpan* is one of the strongest examples of such short spans of survival. What we haven't really seen is new writing for cinema, what in Hollywood's golden era was called an 'original', that is written specifically for film and not for stage or literary purposes. If a new Indian cinema is to emerge as a symbol of social dynamism and as a motivation for it, much will depend on new writing done specifically for film—even more perhaps than on the choice of literary pieces reworked for the screen by film-makers. While the constant coming out of young directors and potential directors (and cinematographers, editors, etc.) from the FTII is bound to lead to a few genuine sensibilities in Indian cinema, it is film writers I am worried about. Most of the present-day leaders of parallel cinema have not been able to select and, what is more important, handle the basic literary material, however worthy. (Even a writer film-maker like Girish Karnad can be caught flatfooted, as in *Vamsa Vrishka* and, to a lesser extent, in *Kaadu*). Nor, for that matter, have we heard much about the Film FTII students who did their courses in scriptwriting.

The second most important thing about parallel cinema is its permanent number, particularly directors. Take Mani Kaul, for instance. His latest offering, *Duvidha*, is simplistic and defensively explanatory in a manner reminiscent of Shakti Samanta's slow, slow 'social dramas', and of Hrishikesh Mukerjee's 'social drama' phase that lasted till the advent of the 1970s.

Over the years, how many directors will prefer to stay on in the alternate parallel cinema circuit and not inch themselves into big-time movie making? Similarly, will parallel cinema create its own stars? To what extent, and for how many years, will they look the other way when the carrot of big-time cinema is dangled in front of them?

What is perhaps the most important question is whether parallel cinema itself is going to last. Is it possible that in the next ten to fifteen years the commercial circuit becomes so shrewd, that parallel cinema's avant-gardism becomes so much less arrogant about Indian film audiences, that parallel cinema returns to the folds of big-time operators? After all, good 'different' films (the progenitors of all the textbooks that in turn fathered parallel cinema) have always been made no matter how ugly the bosses tried to be.

Is the parallel cinema demand a class demand made by the upper class Indian (defined by his university education or by his espousal of the lifestyle of the university-educated Indian)? Over the decades the citizen of the modern Indian state (the 'upper-class Indian') has come to a simple conclusion. He has come to believe that his environment—from school to university to a white collar job, carrying a stress on the scientific and rational approach and with a constant awareness of the world at large—is the natural utopia that all Indians must be provided with.

It is a difficult conclusion to quarrel with. And yet the Indian who lives in the shadow (but never on the surface) of the modern

Indian state is constantly resisting metamorphosis. Not in the simplistic sense that he doesn't want a brick house with water, sewage, electricity, sofas, with transistors, and motorcars. But culturally, he is resisting the doing away of dowry and the caste system and old fashioned business methods and attitudes (including profiteering and hoarding). And the main reason why the Indian living in the shadow of the modern Indian state is doing so is because the modern Indian state does not really appear to offer an alternative to what he already has. The work processes, the methods, the apparatuses, and social values of the modern Indian state don't give even its citizens a total confidence in it. This is why we have so many contradictions and so much confusion.

Where does all this tie up with art? With the way Satyajit Ray makes films or John Abraham intends to make films? With M.F. Husain or Rajesh Mehra? With Utpal Dutt or Mahesh Elkunchkar? With Vatsayan Agyeya or Giridhar Rathi?

Let us go back to the so-called neo-renaissaince of modern Indian history, to Rabindranath Tagore, Sarojini Naidu, and Prem Chand; to Madan Mohan Malviya, Gandhi, and Jawaharlal Nehru.

Ever since the reformist movement began in the nineteenth century, Indian society has been enclosed in a parallelogram—the bigger sides made up of the constant rejection of several important elements of the prevailing structure and of the perpetual addition of new possibilities, coming mainly from other societies, to serve as replacements for what has been rejected. The smaller sides of the parallellograms are made up of (1) the absence of a wholesome system of either works or thought to take Indian society past a chaotic transitional phase; and (2) the constant floating of false messages of hope—from Sat Sai Baba to Mani Kaul who was described by the Chairman of the FFC to be a greater film-maker in the making than Satyajit Ray.

The trouble with modern Indian art has been that it has been contained as it were by the last-mentioned side of the Indian parallelogram—constructing and floating false messages of hope, out of an unimpressive stock of modern Indian art and out of a historical abyss. Which is why modern Indian painting, literature, theatre, and now films, are but games of intellectual escapism most of the time. They change nothing in the Indian parallelogram only helping the parallelogram to live longer by justifying things in the eyes of those who drive the Indian parallelogram. Thus killing any chance for better vision and for a better approach to coming down from the driver's cabin up above. The Indian parallelogram survives because of the great divide between the court and the subject people—the court in a way now extending to all those who have the privilege of social mobility in the modern Indian state.

It may be that the Indian economist, entrepreneur, engineer, technologist, and technocrat face both physical (inclusive of legislative) and psychological hurdles in their attempt to bring the environment of the ruling elite closer to everyman. But surely artists could face only psychological problems to such an effort. After all, while artists have always cried about their poverty and their lack of influence on everyday affairs, within the domain of art they have asserted their identity as artists in the face of overwhelming physical handicaps. And they finally do get to influence everyday working methods, sometimes long after they are themselves dead.

Today, to a certain extent, Indian cinema provides a platform outside the political establishment for public debate. But more as a safety valve for mass attitudes than as a forum. Will the protagonists of parallel cinema use cinema as the most immediate medium to grapple with both our material condition and the topsy-turvy sea of ideas, thought processes, and attitudes as one of the means of bringing about some dynamism instead of the psychological inertia ossifying us?

Diwana, *January 1975. This magazine has since ceased publication.*

* * *

Some Ground Realities of Art Film-making

Two decades ago, Indian art film-makers were a committed lot, pursuing film-making against tremendous odds. This piece is a plea for being patient with the efforts of young directors who take risks, often against tremendous financial odds.

Over the last decade, the Indian art film has assumed an identity and an importance that runs parallel to Bombay's filmdom. Drawn from the various film societies of the country, this assertion of its individuality by the art or serious film has been an arduous task. Undoubtedly, the biggest boost to its status that serious film-making in India received was the acclaim that Satyajit Ray's Apu trilogy achieved at international film festivals abroad. At Bombay, nonetheless, there had always been a handful of directors seeking to amalgamate the pressures of the box office with imaginative efforts and the standards pertaining to intellectual satisfaction. The requirements of the film-making process, however, tie the art form to a sizeable audience, within or without the film societies.

Satyajit Ray continues to be the doyen of the art film world in India, though his status is now hotly contested by the fans of other Indian directors. Ray has dominated the field long enough and, in the natural order of things, his relationship with the art form is now much more controversial on the debit side than it was, say, five years ago. Writing in a Satyajit Ray number of *Montage*, a magazine on films published by a Bombay film society, Mrinal Sen pin-pointed Ray's inability to lead aspiring film directors who saw in his first films the hope for the serious film in the country. Sen argued that the situation had thrust leadership upon Ray. But, he said, Ray successively appeased the film establishment by his increasing use of matinee idols. This was inherent in the very logic of the situation which he himself had heralded, Sen said. It adversely affected the efforts of others who wished to make films that financiers would not unhesitatingly back and that audiences might not easily swallow.

The most adversely affected were the films of Ritwik Ghatak. The persistent search for metaphoric associations and the intensity of feeling in Ghatak's films are in opposition to the restrained documentation significant to Ray. Explicitly, while Ray's films held popular appeal, his influence on new and emerging film-makers is considerably less than that of Ghatak who has not had proportionate success at the box office. A reason may be, speaking in general terms, that Ghatak has sought to express himself as ingeniously as possible through the components of his medium. He has sought a complexity in form simultaneously with the storytelling. Contrary to Ray, his method is not to choose the genre as a framework which he proceeds to fill in. In their fluidity of style, Ghatak's films concretize the aesthetic premise that the 'story', as understood conventionally, is the name for the form of a particular style of writing about people and things. Both his preoccupation with the ability of the medium and the violence of his feelings form, in this writer's opinion, a major contribution to Indian artists. Our artists are caught in the strange situation of having to produce art and also contribute to the non-existent tradition of the oeuvre. Neither the form nor the content, if the two must be spoken of separately, can be omitted from the probings of the imagination.

This has been the result of certain things that happened in the Indian social and art worlds in the last two hundred years, particularly in painting and theatre. The grafting of British aesthetics as it then existed in British academies upon subterranean, if not defunct, Indian traditions created an untoward attitude towards these arts. No amount of popular and state patronage has been able to bring about the necessary sense of freedom from petty inhibitions without which the imagination cannot create. The impact on writing became near-disastrous, mainly because of literature's seminal position among art forms. Many of the violent deviations in favour of foreign trends that can be witnessed in twentieth-century Indian writing are the result of this blind, fear-driven adoption.

Though this has also broken down many of the barriers and reduced some of the crampedness of classicism, the achievements remain in isolation and have not affected the mainstream of artistic values and practices in our society. The degeneration in Bombay to the film financier's tune has, on the one hand, distorted the possibilities that the new medium of the film could otherwise have realized. Nowhere has this distortion shown itself more disturbingly than in the effect it has had on national radio and the TV programmes. On the other hand, the art film has grown in complete opposition to the Bombay film and, as such, is inclined to be elitist. While the intellectual arrogance might sustain the new film-makers, there is no less a danger that it might deny them the opportunity to exert their image of cinema over a larger audience.

There is no gain saying that the art film, like all other art activities that are not integrated with daily life in the manner of folk art, shall never have the mass-appeal of diluted and popular concoctions. However, as the European experiences proves, the art film must not only have its own audience, it must also influence the making of popular films so that these latter can imbibe, if belatedly, the discoveries of the avant-garde. Only then can there by an avant-garde.

Most of our newer directors have not yet overcome the charms and the distractions of the abundant technical improvisations made abroad. The evolution of a multifaceted international language in cinema has drawn our film-makers too dramatically. The assumption is that by knowing in depth, through an eclectic application, the complex language of cinema as it has been created by others, one inherits the artistic complexity and the relevance of the language too. For cinema is as yet the most ephemeral and most journalistic of the art forms, apart from the musical and the operatic concert, though these can now be preserved by recordings.

Perhaps the very speed at which the frames are seen is responsible for this, along with other, more material factors.

Though it is obvious that these new directors are aware of the conceptual originality necessary to cinema's formal and institutionized journalism, it is equally obvious that they have not succeeded in arriving at it. They have instead relegated it to secondary importance. This is not better elucidated than by the merits and limitations of the documentary films made by Sukhdev. In most cases, Sukhdev either links sequences along new directions only to conclude on very old ground—as with *India 1967* and *And Miles To Go*. Or, as in his more standard Films Division documentary, he detaches himself from the experimental self. The former point is also true of Chari, Sastry, and Wadhwani. To reduce Pati's *Explorer* to its essential non-visual concept leads to the journalistic cliché that traditional or rural India, and modern or urban India are too contradictory and that the consequential tension is almost untenable. In cinema and in theatre, to stress the audio-visual too exclusively over the non-audio-visual aspects is to prefer the frilliest aspects of the 'art for art's sake' movement.

The orientation of our new directors is too severely occidental. And because of it they have failed to reflect, in any of the new films, the relevance that the films of Akira Kurosawa have to our own contemporary situation. An emphasis on the morbidity of life and the helplessness of the individual against circumstances may be an accurate reflection of our psychological morass. But what is the way out? Artistic imagination must grapple with this. As opposed to the European director, Kurosawa discovers the human strength that will overcome the situation—morally, if not physically. Not boredom but poverty and our inertia should be the points with which artistic juxtaposition is sought. For this the imagination must throw up new possibilities and directions.

The psychological nature of most of the new films at least focuses on the issue. For our socio-economic difficulties are as much due to psychological inabilities as to economic penury and the stranglehold of tradition. The economics can be handled by intelligence complemented by a moral sense of priorities. Tradition continues through myths and images. The modern Indian artist—and the prominent role that the film-maker must play cannot be overstated—must offer myths and images that can be alternatives to traditional ones and that can induce both the sense and the actuality of intellectual and material movement.

One also feels that the weight of education in the film institutes is so heavy that few of the new feature films—neither the short nor the commercial films—consider humour as a human outlet. It was left to Mrinal Sen's *Bhuvan Shome* to draw a lesson from the Czechkoslovakian style to suggest the homicidal nature of the edifices of bureaucracy, the humour of their crumbling down, and the solemnity of the individual being resurrected. The absence of a complex idiom and the technical looseness for which Sen's film has been criticized do not hold against the anthropomorphic saga of social processes and of history that it becomes. As Basu Chatterjee's *Sara Akash* emphasized by negation, it will not do to express states of mind and situations through more complicated syntax. It is necessary to discover how the human being can perform, more quickly and more rationally, whatever life demands of him, with whatever choices it gives him. An inert society is ignorant about how it should perform for the ambitions that it holds. One does not wish to counter the canon that the artist is concerned with the most indirect and, therefore, the most comprehensive manner in which human beings perform and live. One only wishes to criticize our new film-makers for not being able to suggest, more comprehensively, the directions that are open to men in our society and to all men in similar situations.

On a lesser though not unimportant scale, creditable work has been done by the new films in showing us our environment in detail and by making us see that an awareness of its paradigmatic complexity reduces our scientific and aesthetic ignorance. Moving out of the studio, these films apprehend the environment in the strictly artistic sense. Art being a veritable mine of information, the new film has initiated a study of the physical shape of the country. In the immediate future, this will do much to erode some fictions that were, unfortunately, formulated in our academies. Perhaps the newer film-makers can consider the suggestions that the Bombay film has offered and has crudely and inadvertently designed. A detailed study of the geography the new films have initiated can be juxtaposed with the invention of geographical regions that do not exist outside the film but are implicit in it.

The documentation has, of course, to be supplemented by imagination and those Indian writers who are recruited by the art film, will have to constrain their own sensational inclinations to the discoveries and the inventions abroad, and face the problem squarely. The fact that we are a pantheistic society where psychology has only a limited field to function in, makes it all the more important that those who work with the plastic arts discover patterns in which images succeed each other, not to support or to refute a monotheistic philosophy but to create a concrete representation of psychic processes as they affect the pantheistic mind. In this regard, the influences of Antionini, Fellini, Ingmar Bergman, and Jean-Luc Godard cannot exceed technique or we shall be saddled with new myths that are relevant to the societies to which these directors belong but that are fictions and yet, by the structure of their myths, come to seem undeniable truths about us. As most of these films are among the first that are being made by their respective directors, one hopes that the essentials will clear up in time. One hopes that the technical excesses will be balanced by the requirements of the human being manifesting human existence and by showing ecology as art.

We have also to see what will become of the distaste of Bombay's hodge podge. The Bombay film is a larger though drearier version of the Nautanki. The aural and visual aspects of cinema compel a consideration of both song and dance. The Hindi film has been distorted to create a peculiar oeuvre in Bombay. But as the new films shall have to deal with many of the same people in the audience as for the Bombay film, they could well redeem songs and dances in their structure. Perhaps in times to come, such redemption will force the Bombay film to reorganize its own song-and-dance numbers so that these no longer remain standalone eccentricities regardless of the rest of the film. A more intelligent usage will prompt greater variety in the lyrics and the music and reduce the repetition and the plagiarism from Western 'rock' and from Arabic music. Another aspect that the Bombay film has often exploited and which the new directors can pick up as their own, if they can refashion it sufficiently in their manner, is the ability to shock the audience with phenomena that are related to the fantasies of the audience but that are seldom manifest in its life outside the cinema theatre. A persevering compilation of such phenomena—in a way the compilation has already begun—would satisfy the ideological aspirations of the new directors as well as their audience. The creative process must be analytically selective and selectively analytical, both with the doings of the Bombay film and the accomplishments of cinema abroad.

Meanwhile, one ought to consider the new films without setting too much stock by them. There is no doubt that these, and the conveyance of these films to the people at large, require sustained effort and investment. The new directors must not succumb to the workings of either an intellectual or a material rat race. Most of them are beginners, many just out of the Film Institute at Poona. The awards that they may or may not win at film festivals ought not to become the dominant measure of their merits or demerits. Obviously, film criticism in the country will be overhauled and reoriented in the process.

Link, *published around 1972. This magazine has since ceased publication.*

* * *

Should Art Films be Subsidized?

Art cinema certainly deserves state funding, but the clumsy efforts of the Film Finance Corporation during the 1970s did not produce the desired results. The main reason for this was that the aesthetic and intellectual needs of the audience of art films were not addressed by the concerned parties.

While the Government of India and state Akademies do offer subsidies and grants in the other arts, it is only in cinema that the state has set up institutionalized means for assisting new, often young, artists to have the means to undertake their own projects.

The argument for this commonly given by the government, by young film-makers, and by many journalists and intellectuals is that institutionalized finance is necessary for film-makers. It is, thereby, implied that such assistance is not so urgently necessary for the writing of a book or for painting to hold an exhibition. While this seems only too true at first glance, the actual situation is somewhat different. The writing of a book may not involve large expenses but the publication and distribution of a book do. Similarly with painting. Given the present costs of hiring art galleries and the exorbitant percentages taken by gallery owners as commission, the argument that new films need institutionalized finance more urgently than new literature or new painting is fallacious. It exposes chinks in the government's cultural policy. This is felt most in the stalemate affecting the new movement in Indian cinema. This is a tragedy. First, because the development of a stable offbeat cinema could have served as a sounding board for new film styles and for the grooming of new talent in all aspects of film-making. Secondly, because a substantial section of the Indian film audience hoped to find in offbeat films the satisfaction of those intellectual, social, and aesthetic needs that lie outside the scope of popular films, in India and everywhere else.

A common argument advanced by government officials and the supporters of the so-called Indian 'New Wave' cinema is that despite the prospective and long-term advantages to popular cinema from the offbeat cinema, the moguls of the film-industry have tried their best to choke the life out of the new cinema. Even if this argument is wholly true, it is not a comprehensive statement on the prevailing situation.

In the first instance, the war between the established film-maker and the prospective, new film-makers is part of an ancient and unchanging pattern. In Indian cinema too, as in the other arts, the opposition to the new has to be accepted as a fact of life. Anything contrary to this has never been witnessed anywhere in the world at any time in the history of the arts. The old shall always oppose the new. Each generation of artists rises in intellectual and aesthetic opposition to its immediate predecessor. It would be naïve to suggest that old film-makers should help new film-makers destroy the very values and attitudes that have sustained them. Every new artist must establish himself through his work and through the impact of his work on the people.

This basic unavoidable challenge to new artists was distorted by the government's approach, causing harm to the new film-makers. Supported by a section of the press, it placed so much trust in their work as to make it appear that only certain kinds of films were films, the rest trash.

This logically untenable and impractical opinion was justified by a vague argument—that people's taste cannot be trusted because it has been defiled and vulgarized by long years of conditioning. It is a view that runs counter to any belief in humanity and in any human society's ability to bring about change in itself. It is a belief that insists that social and cultural change can only be thrust upon people and that it does not ever result from an interaction between the few who wish to thrust change upon the rest of society.

The emergence of such a dogmatic policy has had two significant consequences, both fatal to the quick growth and maturity of Indian cinema. They are also responsible for the fact that while there is a public need for an art film movement in the country, an art film movement still does not exist.

These two significant and inter-related consequences are as follows. On the one hand, new film-makers who are making films with public money have developed a tendency to avoid self-analysis and criticism of their own work. Thanks to the government's unlimited support, these new film-makers have countered public rejection of their films with a hysterical exaggeration of their aesthetic and intellectual value. The basic facts of growth that must be faced by new artists, and the process of learning by trial and error, have been conveniently transformed into delusions for the new, state-supported, film-makers.

Not only were these new film-makers able to exaggerate the artistic value of their films, thanks to blind and total support from the Government of India, they were able to get away with the fact that there is little that is new in their style. Most of it is borrowed from European film-makers and a proportionate section is little more than a modification of Satyajit Ray's style, assembled from the influences upon him of Jean Renoir, Rossellini, Vittorio De Sica, and other European film-makers.

It is surprising that none of the new film-makers and their supporters have realized that a 'new Indian cinema' dominated by European influences would not be wholly suitable for Indian needs today. After all, the same circles do accept the premise that traditional Indian philosophy and culture are distinct from European philosophy and culture and therefore have something to offer it— a belief that Prime Minister Nehru extended into the domain of international politics.

It is also surprising that the Government of India did not see that the new film-makers would mix up Indian culture and European technology into a terrible mess, unless they realized that the interaction between the two was but a process of regeneration for Indian culture. The government did not see that the mess might satiate the desires of certain sections of urban elites but would have the most disastrous and retrogressive effect on the course of Indian development.

The new, state-assisted film-makers have not lived up to the hopes placed on them. This is the second fatal consequence. They have not given the public the sort of films that large sections of it have been wanting for nearly a decade now. They could not do this primarily because they alienated themselves from the very people for whom they were supposed to be making the films. They were so obsessed with ideas of their own importance that they sought to impose their amateur cinema and philosophical whimsies on the people.

These new film-makers behaved as if artists were made in heaven and discovered by governments. They forgot that a genuine movement in film could come about only through a strong relationship with the people. They, unfortunately, began with the premise that they had nothing to learn from the people. They donned on the masks of prophets. For their own reasons, the Government of India and its concerned institutions helped in this make-believe of the new prophets. No wonder the people rejected these films that did not take them—their lives, needs, and aspirations—into account.

Once it became clear to the new film-makers that, despite their prophetic stance, their work was as much of a gamble vis-à-vis the people as that of big-budget film-makers, they fell into an even more vicious trap of their own making. Throwing to the winds their need to develop a closer relationship with the audience, they concentrated on developing personal ties with officials of the Government of India. Personal pressures, relationships, and high-level politicking in official circles began to take up as much of the time of the new film-makers as film-making. No wonder all chances of establishing an art-film movement took a backseat. The new film-makers now no longer care for the birth of such a public movement, as long as the government, or somebody else, is willing to serve their personal ends. It is, of course, necessary to analyse why the Government of India and its aid institutions gives such wholehearted support without any critical assessment of results achieved.

At a seminar on the Role of the Short Film, organized several months back at New Delhi by the Films Division of India, I.K. Gujral, the Union Minister of Information and Broadcasting, said that Indian cinema had suffered because of the social prejudice against it. He hoped that Parliament and the union government would no longer consider the film as a temple of sin. Yet this is precisely what the Government of India considers popular Indian cinema—the cinema of the Indian people—to be. This implies that the films the government likes are films and the films that the people like are but temples of sin. To mistrust the people so intensely is a cardinal sin for any government to commit, whether in implementing a cultural policy or an economic policy with cultural ramifications.

One block that develops in the arts, when the government interferes in the field, is that mistakes cannot be acknowledged. A bad film made with governmental assistance will not be shelved even after bitter lessons from the experience. Instead, the government bends backwards to prove that it was no mistake. Nothing can illustrate this better than the recent case of Kumar Shahani's *Maya Darpan*. A box-office flop, it was pronounced by a large section of critical opinion to be an unoriginal film, greatly influenced by Robert Bresson's *Une Femme Douce*. However, in 1974—one year after it was awarded the Best Hindi film for 1972—it is being sent to innumerable international festivals as India's official entry.

The explanation given was that we make very few films that can be sent to international festivals at all. This is untrue because there are several films that can be sent, with a little editing, but which the government will not consider at all, because they are made in a world with which the Government of India does not associate international festivals. Kumar Shahani, and other direction course graduates from the Film and Television Institute of

India (FTII), boast of their association with Ritwik Ghatak. But Ghatak's working assistant, Asit Sen, finds his powerful films not even being considered to represent India. The Government of India's prejudice against the cinema patronized by the people is incomprehensible except for two possible reasons.

The first of these seems to be a hangover from the British Raj days. The British considered amateur drama productions in Westernized schools along the basic precepts of European theatre better and more serious theatre than the folk theatre of the Indian natives, with the accoutrements peculiar to the native *mehfil*. A similar cultural superiority complex is to be found in the approach of the government, the new film-makers, and their supporters to people's cinema. They see themselves as the natural heirs to the mission of civilizing the natives, undertaken by the British. All the nonsensical criticism that a film becomes a good film if it has no songs, dances, and other popular Indian elements—if it has been made in the grammar of the film—is criticism that the Indian intelligentsia makes only to identify itself with European and other Western audiences. European audiences do not like these elements in our films because they do not form part of their cultural environment.

This approach to Indian cinema is not without precedent. The approach of the upper-classes and the West to Indian folk theatre was similar till Bertolt Brecht came along. Brecht proved that while these elements do not make for art by urban and classical standards, they can provide a genuinely creative artist with vast potential for original drama. Since Brecht's theories have become accepted and legitimate, the Indian intelligentsia has simply transferred its outdated arguments to cinema. It forgets that while popular Indian films are not works of art in themselves, they can provide a genuinely creative film-maker with the elements necessary for making a film that communicates powerfully with the general Indian film audience and also measures up to Western aesthetics.

Something very close to such a creative graft has been achieved by several Japanese film-makers whose films have all the elements of popular Japanese films on the one hand and, on the other, are also meaningful to western audiences.

It is very Indian, indeed, for our directors not to learn something from the successful experience of an Asian people but to pursue their notions as to how Godard or Bresson can be outdone in their individual styles! Needless to say, the Government of India blindly backs the new film-makers because it seems to share with these film-makers some sort of inferiority complex as far as European culture is concerned. Since it is a well-recognized fact at international level that cultural elements play an important part in building a country's international image, it is understandable that the Government of India should wish for a development of those Indian films which could, like the films made by Satyajit Ray, help boost India's international image.

However, this should not lead to the view that the new films desired by the government are in total opposition to popular Indian cinema. Such a view can be, as it has so far been, detrimental to both popular Indian cinema and the Indian art film. For a work of art is not in opposition to popular culture but is a dialectical counterpoint to it. Indeed, they are each other's measure and provide to each other the source material necessary for the independent growth and maturity of both.

It is commonly known in Indian film circles that the art film provides an array of styles and ideas to popular cinema and functions as the avant-garde. What is not commonly accepted, but is nevertheless true, is that the serious urban artist has a twofold relationship with popular culture. Like Brecht in theatre and T.S. Eliot in poetry (through nursery rhymes, Roman Catholic hymns, beer hall songs, and Cockney speech rhythms), the serious urban artist may pick up elements from popular culture and transform them into new means and forms to perceive reality and express the human condition. In the second place, the serious urban artist is related to popular culture and the popular artist because both, in their own different styles and world views, are commenting on contemporary life.

It is not, therefore, surprising that time should disprove the validity of the argument that classicist art is in total opposition to popular cultural artefacts. In cinema itself we have the examples of K.L. Saigal, John Ford, and Alfred Hitchcock, all of whom worked in the realm of popular culture and who were, in time to come, transformed into deities of classicist art.

In India itself, we see the new art films concerned with sex, physical and mental violence, and economic injustice—themes that are concurrently handled by popular films in their own fashion. However, nobody in the Government of India or its aid institutions or among the new film-makers (with the exception of M.S. Sathyu and Girish Karnad) or the journalistic supporters of the new cinema, has given even an inkling that they realize this basic fact.

Instead, we find that while most of the new film-makers are happy to make films in the European tradition, the Ministry of Information and Broadcasting's New Film Policy is taken wholly from the new film policy formulated and implemented in Britain in the recent past. Thereby a circle of plagiarism from the much-condemned popular cinema to the art film scene to the government itself, is complete!

Given the situation we have today, with the Film Finance Corporation (FFC) as the government's aid-giving institution, and art theatres in the offing under the National Film Corporation, perhaps the momentum for an art film movement can be initiated if there is some drastic reorientation on at least three basic levels.

First, the people directly associated with the Film Finance Corporation and with the various advisory committees concerning cinema need to be chosen on strictly non-political grounds. There are a large number of well-known and established Indian writers, artists, and intellectuals associated with cinema, such as Sri Sri, the Telugu poet, Samar Sen, the Bengali intellectual and journalist, Utpal Dutt, the actor-director, and Shamsher Bahadur Jang, the Hindi poet. They are never consulted or used by the government simply because they oppose the ruling party on political grounds.

The need for the government to use such talent as theirs seems all the more necessary today because those writers, artists, and intellectuals who politically support the ruling party have failed to deliver. They have not been able to give the guidelines for a film policy whereby the Indian art film movement really becomes a movement and does not get further alienated from audiences that would like the art film to coexist with popular films. Also, it would be advisable for the FFC to persuade itself that since it must sell at the box office, it must have on each script advisory panel at least one established film distributor. The business acumen of the distributor and his assessment of a film's communicability can be used to advantage by the film-maker without compromise.

The second drastic change needed by the FFC has to do with scripts. After the script advisory panel has recommended a script, the FFC should ask the prospective film-maker to rework the script. He should rework it in such a way that it explains the meaning of each scene in terms of its relevance to aesthetics and also in terms of what each scene shall mean to the Indian people if and when they see it in the proposed film. Film-makers asking for loans should also be asked to explain how their film would affect the people and the development of society. Of course this would mean more labour for the film-makers seeking an FFC loan. But it would help them see their own ideas more clearly and also solve some of the possible problems in the film in advance. At the same time, this will give the FFC a clearer idea about the sort of films they will be financing—a clarity that is extremely necessary if the mistakes of the recent past are to be are to be avoided and learnt from.

Third, the FFC should ask all those who seek a loan for their first feature film, to first make a short feature film, preferably with their own finances, and submit it along with the script for which they seek the loan. The FFC may decide that only after a new film-maker has proved himself repeatedly should he be considered mature enough for a loan for a full-length feature film.

Finances permitting, there is no reason why the second or third short feature film of a new film-maker should not be financed by the FFC. Television centres too could provide such finances.

Since there is a substantial international market in short feature films, there is no reason why a short feature film circuit cannot be introduced in India. For one thing, short films can provide enough exhibition material for the proposed art theatres. In addition, in recent years the short feature film has become an accepted medium in international cinema. There are innumerable international short film festivals and a good Indian shortfilm can help India win international prestige.

Screen, *published around 1974.*

* * *

Renaissance in South Indian Films

This essay was written fifteen years ago in response to many films being made in south India that went on to win at the national level awards. This trend is even more interesting because Tamil and Telugu cinema have strong commercial affiliations. Only Malayalam cinema, and to a certain extent Kannada cinema, retain space for art house films.

For almost twenty years now, film directors, artistes, technicians, and musicians from south India have been bagging a majority of the national film awards given each year. The year 1993 was no exception. Films made in Tamil Nadu and Kerala last year won a grand total of eleven national awards; in addition, another four national awards were secured by south Indian film-makers working in other languages.

The most surprising and commendable aspect of the film renaissance in the south is the artistic emergence of Tamil cinema. Malayalam and Kannada films have long enjoyed a standing for artistic ventures, whereas it is only in recent years that Tamil films too have begun to be noticed for the superb quality that marks them.

The two individuals who are at the centre of this renaissance in Tamil cinema are actor-film producer Kamal Haasan and director Mani Ratnam. Over the past many years, Kamal Haasan has been involved in an impressive list of films which have been most unusual and unconventional in approach. Made by different directors, such Kamal Haasan starrers as *Apoorva Raagangal*, *Moondraam Pirai*, *Nayakan*, *Appu Raja*, *Pushpaka Vimanam*, and *Thewar Magan* have brought Kamal Haasan recognition and acclaim as a great actor from filmgoers all over India. It is in fact generally accepted that there are certain roles—such as those in *Appu Raja* and *Pushpaka Vimanam*—which no other Indian actor could have done justice to. As an actor who is closely involved in the conceptualization of the film script and in his directorial approach, Kamal Haasan has grown as one of the pillars of the movement in south India for high-quality films.

The 40th National Film Festival 1993 saw Kamal Haasan in a new role—as the producer of *Thewar Magan* which won the award for best Tamil film. *Thewar Magan* has been a stupendous box-office hit, grossing over Rs 60 million in 1992–3. It is also one of the most brilliantly picturized and mounted films ever made in India, technically extremely slick.

The story of a Thewar feudal family in which two brothers fall out, leading to a feud between two familial branches, the film has been directed by Bharathan and produced by Kamal Haasan in a style that is unmatched in Indian cinematographic history. The performances are marvellous and it is difficult to choose between Sivaji Ganesan (who plays Kamal's father with unexpected restraint), Kamal Haasan, Gowthami, and Revathy Menon. Of the four, Revathy went on to win the national award for best supporting actress and Sivaji Ganesan was honoured by the special jury award.

Made with all the ingredients of a good, conventional commercial film—romance, family drama, the individual's struggle for dignity against evil forces, and first-rate action sequences— *Thewar Magan* glows with technical brilliance. Every frame in the film is a telling composition. It is a film that rivals any of the best ever made.

The other individual whose name has become synonymous with top class cinema from south India is director Mani Ratnam. He is now widely accepted as the most original director in mainstream (or popular) cinema. Mani Ratnam's emergence as a director of the first calibre has also helped persuade many film experts in the country that the dividing line between commercial cinema and the so-called art film need not rigidly separate them into two different compartments. His best films have always been part of the set-up of commercial cinema but have also demonstrated an extremely high technical quality.

In a sense, Mani Ratnam has also influenced certain trends in shot taking and song picturization in mainstream Hindi cinema. *Nayakan* (1987), which starred Kamal Haasan, was re-made in Hindi by Feroze Khan as *Dayavan*, and Mani Ratnam's *Anjali* (1990) was dubbed last year in Hindi.

Mani Ratnam first grabbed the national limelight when *Nayakan* won the national award for the best film with popular appeal and wholesome entertainment. He was to win this particular award for two other films, *Gitanjali* (1989) and *Anjali*. This year, his new film *Roja* won three national awards—for best film on national integration, best musical score (by A.R. Rahman, whose real name is Rahuman), and best lyrics (Vairamuthu's song 'Chinna chinna Aasai'). Moreover, *Roja* captivated Indian film-goers because it is the first Indian thriller on the contemporary theme of terrorism.

Roja is the most exciting film to have been made in India in 1992–3. First, it tackles a completely new subject in Indian cinema, that of an average person's confrontation with terrorism. Second, as scriptwriter-director, Mani Ratnam effectively brings home the diversity of Indian life. We have a village girl from the heart of Tamil Nadu marrying a Madras-based, thoroughly urbanized, and liberal-minded scientist. Their honeymoon has scarcely begun when the young husband (Arvindswaimy), a cryptologist, is sent by his office on a mission to Kashmir. There he is kidnapped by terrorists. His wife Madhubala, who insisted on coming along, is a Tamil-speaking girl at her wit's end in a northern state where she cannot communicate with anybody.

With this basic material, Mani Ratnam makes a truly Indian thriller, adorned with many human (and humorous) nuances. Moreover, his style of film-making is so rich emotionally, his picturization of songs and dramatic sequences so expressive of feeling, that one can easily say of *Roja* that it is a film that crosses the barriers of language. Even filmgoers who do not understand Tamil will find themselves gripped by this film.

The pride of place in this year's national awards went of course, to the Sanskrit film *Bhagavad Geetha*, produced by Andhra Pradesh's famous businessman, T. Subbarami Reddy, and directed by that grand old man of celluloid from Karnataka, G.V. Iyer. Iyer had earlier won the national best feature film award for his first Sanskrit film, *Adi Shankaracharya*, about eight years ago.

Bhagavad Geetha is an extremely artistic attempt to translate the philosophy of the great Indian epic into film. It starts off by setting the historical atmosphere of the Mahabharat, with the battle about to begin on the fields of Kurukshetra. As Lord Krishna seeks to clarify Arjun's doubts and fears, the film is transformed into a symbolic explanation of the origin of the world and of the basic instincts that govern human emotions.

Naturally, this interpretation of the epic deals with the gist of its philosophy, and Iyer, according to experts, does not make any mistakes in its rendering. It is also to be expected that such a philosophical film is not going to be easily understood by the average filmgoer. But there is no doubt in this critic's mind that for those who know the Gita, or are interested in being educated about it, this film is one of the best interpretations of the great epic.

Once again, as in so many south Indian films of recent vintage, the technical qualities of Iyer's film are superb, especially the camerawork and musical score. What was unexpected is the stellar performance by the Bombay-based actress Neena Gupta. A graduate of the National School of Drama, New Delhi, Neena had hitherto been cast on screen in the mould of a sensuous and voluptuous woman. But in *Bhagavad Geetha*, she reveals herself to be an extremely sensitive and subtle actress. This is one of the many discoveries that film buffs will make in the film.

The three Malayalam films to feature in this year's national film awards were *Swaroopam* (best Malayalam film), *Sadayam* (best screenplay award, for M.T. Vasudevan Nair), and *Sargam* (which won the award for best popular film providing wholesome entertainment). Directed by Hariharan, *Sargam* is another example from the south to prove that classical Indian music can be interwoven with a popular film story without jarring the senses. Set in a family of classical musicians, *Sargam* depicts with great sensitivity the emotional turmoil faced by three teenagers—Hari, a talented singer, Kuttan, his friend with a violent temperament, showing no sign of following his friend's musician father, and the young girl Thankamani, who is actually in love with Hari but is married to Kuttan. Set against the backdrop of the ethereal world of classical music, *Sargam* was one of the biggest box-office hits of 1992.

Director K.R. Mohan's *Swaroopam* belongs to that respected class of Malayalam films that experiment with very unconventional themes and are extremely sombre in their cinematic style, a school of cinema long represented by the work of Adoor Gopalakrishnan and Aravindan. *Swaroopam* deals with the unusual theme of a poor farmer becoming increasingly involved with spiritual matters. Sekharan (played by Sreenivasan) becomes obsessed with the homage he must pay to his illustrious ancestors and he begins to cut himself off from the daily troubles and tribulations of a peasant's life. Just as he seems to be attaining sainthood, he locks himself up in a temple he has built and dies.

The celebrated Malayalam writer and journalist, M.T. Vasudevan Nair, has won several national awards for writing the best screenplay of the year, as well as awards for many of the films he has directed. His screenplay for *Sadayam* marks a break from his earlier work in cinema, in that he chooses a modern and contemporary theme for this film. *Sadayam* comments on the degeneration of Indian society as seen through the eyes of an artist who, in order to save two young girls from prostitution, kills them. This is obviously a film that makes a strong comment on Indian society today. It is not so much the story of a man who looks back on life as he awaits his execution in prison as a comment on the hopelessness of living a clean, ethical life. It is this dimension of the film, and the screenplay, that sets off many echoes that will haunt the minds of filmgoers.

The Telegu film *Ankuram* marks a distinct break from the routine high-budget Telegu films. Few realistic films are made in Telegu, although it enjoys a standing as one of the most prosperous of popular cinemas in India at present. Winner of the best Telegu film of the year award, director C. Umamaheshwara's *Ankuram* is a moving and emotionally charged story that takes up a minor incident at a railway station and goes on to explore the political crisis in Andhra Pradesh, as epitomized by the Naxalite struggle in a part of the state.

Returning from a train journey, the young woman Sindhura (played by Telegu actress Revathy) is given a baby to hold by a fellow passenger, Satyam, at the railway station. Thereafter, Satyam disappears and Sindhura has to take the baby home, to the great discomfort of her husband and mother-in-law, who accuses her of having an illegitimate child. Sindhura's search for Satyam is in vain. He has been wrongly imprisoned by the police as a suspected Naxalite and dies in custody. Sindhura's search for him soon gets transformed into a journey in which she discovers the corruption of the local police system and the helplessness of the common people. *Ankuram* is not a great artistic film, but it is a superb piece of realism, making a strong social comment on life itself. As such, it marks a definitive departure in Telegu cinema.

Another simple but captivating film from the south this year is Girish Karnad's *Cheluvi*, which won the national award for best feature film on environment. Made in Karnataka with Kannada artistes, *Cheluvi* is, however, in Hindi, which makes for an interesting experiment along the same lines as Shanker Nag's popular TV series, *Malgudi Days*.

Cheluvi has the format of a fairy tale, in which a poor young girl is given a boon by the gods—she can turn into a tree bearing incredibly fragrant flowers. The girl and her sister use this magical boon to sell the tree's flowers and help their family survive. The beauty of the flowers persuades the son of a rich man to marry the young girl. Unfortunately, her secret soon becomes known to her adolescent and spoilt sister-in-law, who forces the girl to turn into the magical tree and then breaks her branches while playing with her friends.

This enchanting tale becomes director Girish Karnad's means of conveying the message of environmental protection, a topic which is gaining increasing importance in India. Director Visu's *Neenga Nalla Irukanum* (Tamil), won the award for best film on social issues. The other award-winning films from south India together present a picture of an extremely rich and diverse cinema.

It has long been recognized that southern films have very powerful and original themes and scripts, but what this year's collection proves is that technically too they are head and shoulder above the films made in other parts of the country, including Bombay.

India International Magazine: A Monthly Review of Events, *July 1993*.

Perspectives on
Indian Cinema

How Socially Conscious is Hindi Cinema?

The moralistic nature of Hindi cinema makes it weave a moral punch or 'sabak' into its storyline. From the time of silent movies to the present, cinema has reflected the social realities of the day. Cinema draws sustenance from both the prevailing social norms as well as political environment.

The motion pictures were first imported and exhibited to India on July 7, 1896. The earliest short films to be photographed in India were by unknown foreign cameramen in 1897. An Indian ventured to make his own short film in 1899. India's first narrative feature came in 1912. And the Indian talkie film arrived in 1931.

Firoze Rangoonwalla, *Seventy Five Years of Indian Cinema*

The record books tell us that the first short films photographed by Indian pioneers included such titles as *Coconut Fair*, *The Wrestlers*, *Splendid New Views of Bombay*, and *Tabcot Procession*.

Harishchandra S. Bhatvadekar (popularly known as 'Save Dada') and F.B. Thanawalla set up the first Indian documentary units, and their early projects—as the titles indicate—manifest the entertainment-orientation and the spectacle-like inclination which is traditionally associated with Indian cinema. However, one of these documentaries is also said to include footage of one Mohandas Karamchand Gandhi! In later years, Gandhiji's tragic assassination was to inspire several songs in the talkie *Majboor*. A company called The Documentary Films at Madras made a full-length feature in 1948 titled *Mahatma Gandhi* and Patel India compiled the documentary *Gandhiji*, which drew on newsreel coverage of the freedom movement. One of the earliest films to be banned by the British India government was the Madras National Theatres production titled *Congress Girl*.

These, too, are part of the history and the heritage of Indian cinema. Their significance does often seem to get lost in the melange of adolescent frivolity and stereotyped vendettas that crowd the Indian silver screen, but for the film-makers themselves the tradition of incorporating social commentaries within a raucous explosion of seemingly unintellectual entertainment is not totally absent. The placing of a photograph of Mahatma Gandhi or Pandit Jawaharlal Nehru, in the backdrop behind a particular character, in a wholly 'commercial' film may seem to the intellectual critic to be a clichéd exploitation of the collective sentiment of the Indian people. But for the film-maker himself it serves the purpose of using a popular iconography which reinforces his attempt to underline the moral dimension of the dramatic conflict delineated in that particular sequence. Such debates about the style—or, as some would say, the lack of style—of popular film-making belong to the area of the aesthetics and anti-aesthetics of popular cinema. They need not occupy much of our attention in an attempt to trace the close interaction between modern Indian social history and the popular Indian film.

In the silent film era, as far back as 1925, Baburao Painter made the film *Savkari Pash* (with the English title *Indian Shylock*) which was one of the earliest films to feature V. Shantaram in the lead. It can be said to be our first art film. It certainly painted an extremely realistic picture of the Indian poor in the rural vastland, focusing on rural indebtedness, feudal oppression, the poverty of the peasantry, and a myriad problems that Indian economists and social reformists had already been campaigning against.

Around the same time, P.C. Barua, who was to later achieve great fame for his version of *Devdas*, made a film titled *Farmer's Daughter*. Twelve years later Ardeshir Irani was to use the same title for *Kisaan Kanya* (1937).

From its very early years, the Indian feature film developed the admirable ability of focusing on both the urban and rural facets of Indian life. It has been a lively, dynamic tradition which only very recently, in the mid-1990s seems to have tilted excessively in favour of wholly urban themes. The films *Mother India*, *Ganga Jamuna*, *Mughal-e-Azam*, and *Sholay* are considered the four biggest, longest-in-demand, popular classics of the Hindi cinema. Of these four, only *Mughal-e-Azam* is not set in rural India!

A child of modern technology, the cinema industry is a very urban enterprise. However, its market and its audience encompass both urban and rural societies and the truly popular films suggest in their contents a cultural homogeneity between the ostensibly divided world of urban and rural India. Even recent box-office successes like *Hum Aapke Hain Kaun...!*, *Karan Arjun*, and *Maine Pyar Kiya* either include the rural landscape in their narrative or espouse social mores and norms common to urban and rural India.

Yet, because of the undeniable urban sensibility and family background of a sizeable majority of directors, writers, and technicians of the Indian film industry, the popular Indian film's content has always been greatly influenced and inspired by social philosophies dominant in urban intellectual circles. As a result, many social reform movements impelled film-makers to present reformist ideas and concepts for the so-called common man.

The films of V. Shantaram are perhaps the most obvious illustrations of this phenomenon. *Dahej*, *Padosi*, *Do Aankhen Baara Haath*, to mention three of his most popular films, were strongly reformist and didactic in approach. So, too, the classic from Bombay Talkies, *Achhut Kanya* (1936). A little later Ranjit Studios produced a film on the same theme, *Achoot*, which starred the legendary Gohar and dealt with the struggle of the Dalits.

The amalgam of social reform and stylized entertainment proved to be particularly heady in the 1930s and 1940s. A film dealing obliquely with rural immigration, *Street Singer*, immortalized K.L. Saigal. With *Mela*, another film set in rural India, we saw the birth of another legend—Dilip Kumar. Dilip Kumar, in particular, was to consciously espouse the personage of the rural Indian. Right up to the mid-1950s, in B.R. Chopra's *Naya Daur*, Dilip Kumar was not just the most popular (and acclaimed) star of Hindi film. He was also the protagonist of rural India in an increasingly urbanized world order.

Right through the 1960s from the 1930s, cinema's concern with social problems continued to be overtly expressed in a handful of very significant films—Mehboob Khan's *Aurat* and *Mother India*, K.A. Abbas's *Dharti ke Lal*, and a number of Bimal Roy films including *Do Bigha Zamin* and *Sujata*. Along with Raj Kapoor's films that highlighted the conflicts between the rich and the poor, there were Dilip Kumar's *Ganga Jamuna* and Sunil Dutt's *Mujhe Jeene Do* that focused on the socio-economic roots of very Indian social problems.

One stream of social reform came very easily to Indian feature films in the natural course of events, as it were. Since all cinema has at its core the primal relationship between man and woman, a very specific role has been played by female characters in the feature film, reflecting the changing image of women in twentieth-century society. In India, as in many other Asian countries, the twentieth-century saw womanhood gradually breaking out of unwanted, archaic, and burdensome orthodoxies. In many cases, popular leading ladies became the protagonists of the twentieth-century woman, in her varied hues through the decades. The social evils of dowry and child marriage, women's education, the dignity of the working woman—all the social reform movements that dominated the Indian scene in the early half of this century—were to find their rationale echoed and their arguments expounded in a continuous stream of films.

In the silent film era itself, we had Dhiren Ganguly's *Lady Teacher* and films by others that focused on the personality of the working woman—*Marriage Market*, *Telephone Girl*, *Typist Girl*. In 1935, *Dr Madhurika* put forward an analysis of a lady doctor's life. Gohar starred in *Barrister's Wife*, and Kadar's *Sharda* and Shantaram's *Duniya Na Mane* became extremely powerful and popular attacks on the traditional practice of child marriage.

The 1970s are often referred to as the decade that witnessed the emergence of the dominant status of the action film. Yet film sociologists would be committing an intellectual misdemeanour if they were not to notice that the 1970s was also the decade that unveiled new portrayals of contemporary womanhood. In Hindi cinema alone, this was also the decade of Shabana Azmi and Smita Patil, two great actresses whose portrayal of contemporary characters quite changed the tone of Indian films as a whole. Starting off with low-budget, so-called art films like Shyam Benegal's *Ankur* and *Manthan*, Shabana and Smita were soon to become cult figures in the Indian cultural scenario and, in the 1980s, were to greatly influence the concept of women characters in Hindi cinema.

Shabana Azmi and Smita Patil were path breakers whose achievements provided new inspiration to other leading actresses of their time. The queen of showbiz, Hema Malini, broke from tradition and worked in offbeat films like *Khushboo* and *Kinara*. Raakhee established a new niche for women characters in the cinema through films like *27 Down*, a national award winner, and *Tapasya*. Rekha and Sridevi have from time to time revealed themselves as consummate artistes capable of tackling such complex roles as in *Ghar* and *Umrao Jaan* (in Rekha's case) and *Sadma* and *Sauten* (in Sridevi's).

The 1970s also saw the unique case of a film actress working in the commercial cinema set-up, but giving it a dignity that was at once acceptable to social reformers and intellectuals. Such was the rare achievement of actress Jaya Bhaduri Bachchan. With her roles in such films as *Abhimaan*, *Parichay*, *Koshish*, and *Mili*, Jaya Bhaduri Bachchan immediately enlarged the range of characterization and realism that would be popularly accepted. It has been a rare achievement and one that deserves an exclusive analysis of its own.

This group of talented actresses of the 1970s and the 1980s did, as a matter of fact, follow in the footsteps of two other generations of great actresses. First, the generation represented by Geeta Bali, Nargis, Meena Kumari, and Madhubala and then that generation represented by Nutan, Waheeda Rehman, Sharmila Tagore. All these actresses are immortalized in a number of extremely significant and socially relevant films, that form the jewels in their respective crowns. From the years immediately after India attained Independence in 1947, actresses and women characters have, from time to time, embellished the quantum of Indian films with a contribution that is no less than that of men. And it can be argued that these three generations of great talents are representative of three chapters' in the history of Indian womanhood during the last sixty years or so. A reflection, as it were, of the changing face of women in Indian society.

One of the interesting aspects of cinema, Indian cinema in particular, is that it has never espoused the cause of social evils or projected them in a positive light. This, indeed, is the reason why popular cinema has become a cultural symbol for the Indian people, who see films in close interaction with life as they know it outside the cinema hall.

At the same time, whenever society itself has seemed to have lost a sense of direction, cinema has been equally afflicted by the social confusion. At such times, film-makers have confined themselves to the limited concern of producing only entertainment of one kind or another.

Whenever the larger process of social development has been clearly defined in the body politik and has been lucidly articulated Indian cinema has quickly picked up the cue to propagate the ideas and concepts that direct social development in the country. On the other hand, whenever social development has slowed down to a listless pace, popular cinema has tended to move away from realistic themes and escape into the realm of pure entertainment.

However, any list of the most popular films in Indian cinema will show us unequivocally that the most popular films have always been those which combine the ingredients of popular entertainment with aspirations of social amelioration and humanist development. Like the novel, the feature film 'tells a lie in order to tell the truth', as literary critics say. Popular cinema has a hybrid style which has evolved from folk traditions but which now also includes 'pop' elements. An analogy here is that while modern development programmes seek to implant new technologies in 'a historically backward' landscape, the popular Indian film attempts to enrobe the economically backward individual in the trappings of new technology. In that sense, cinema is quick to pick up the symbols and icons of technological developments and economic evolution, and incorporate them as part of the backdrop in which the emotional drama takes place.

Since cinema is itself technology's child, it has always been aware that new technological environments cast their own shadow on human relationships and on human aspirations. To that extent, no matter how much a film may depart from the realistic facets of contemporary life, it can never snap its umbilical bond with social development. Social struggles and social achievements provide the inspiration for many a film. For at its best our cinema is a fair image of what is happening in society at large.

Yojana, *August 1995.*

* * *

Violence in Hindi Films

Indians are not as non-violent as they fondly imagine themselves to be. Notwithstanding the reverence in which Gandhi, Buddha, and Mahavir are held, violence is as much a part of the history of this country as is non-violence.

The resounding success of Sholay (1975) bears this out. In a sense, violence became institutionalized in Hindi films after the release of Sholay.

The three classics of the box office in India are Mehboob Khan's *Mother India*, (1957), K. Asif's *Mughal-e-Azam*, (1960), and Ramesh Sippy's *Sholay*, (1975). The only other movie which film industry pundits are willing to accept as a close fourth in this all-time list is the Nitin Bose directed *Ganga Jamuna* (1961).

Mughal-e-Azam is not the odd one out in the all-time list of the top three, as may seem at first glance. Though it purports to be a love story, *Mughal-e-Azam* is the one that projects in the most overt terms, the conflict between lovers and the state. The shadow of the armies of the Mughal potentate crowds the corners of the narrative. Soldiers in full martial gear decorate the outer durbar as a war of emotion rages tempestuously within the imperial family. And the full might of state power most violently puts an end to the life of the beautiful commoner with whom the young prince became infatuated. *'Jab pyar kiya to dama kya'*—the war cry of the passionate lovers reverberates across the tragic tale, in brazen defiance of the state. War and violence is the common thread that runs through these three box-office classics and closely links the fourth also to them.

However, a salient feature common to both *Mother India* and *Sholay* needs to be kept in mind. *Mother India*, the seminal source of inspiration for a myriad formula films in the 1970s and the 1980s, was located in the easily cognizable turbulence of the Hindi belt of north India, a rural landscape of intense caste divisions, feudal agrarian machinations, and extreme disparities.

Sholay has a more contemporary texture, adapting Akira Kurosawa's *The Seven Samurai* and its Hollywood imitation *The Magnificent Seven* to the Indian world view of the 1970s. However, despite the Bombay style pop culture mannerisms of the film's leading characters, played by Amitabh Bachchan and Dharmendra, and notwithstanding the fact that the film was shot at a specially chosen location in south India off the Bangalore–Mysore road, the film's ambience highlights the semi-feudal countryside of north India's Hindi belt.

First, there is Thakur's family, steeped in the traditions of north India. It is this family, with Sanjeev Kumar's Thakur as the patriarchal head, which provides the *raison d'etre* for the narrative. A significant characteristic of the film which has scarcely evinced any analytical interest over fifteen years is the linguistic persona of Gabbar Singh, played by Amjad Khan, the one character from the movie who passed instantaneously into folklore all over India.

In truth, Gabbar Singh speaks in a diluted dialect derived from the spoken idiom of the villagers of east UP and west Bihar. Against the denim jackets and jeans worn by Amitabh Bachchan and Dharmendra, and in contrast to the Bombay-style slang spoken by them and by Hema Malini, Amjad Khan's Gabbar Singh recreates the oral ramifications of the anarchic countryside of the Hindi belt.

In a sense therefore, both *Mother India* and *Sholay* draw upon the thread of menace from the violent culturescape of UP and Bihar, the two states that have long had the highest annual crime rates in the country. Incidentally, *Ganga Jamuna*, at the fourth spot in the list of all-time favourites, uses the same linguistic idiom and has important dramatis personae in dhoti and kurta.

Mother India was, of course, not the first rural saga of the Robin Hood type dacoit. Stunt and action-oriented films have been one of the constant elements in Indian cinema from the time that it became entrenched as a regular medium of entertainment.

War and violence became intrinsic to the Indian feature film because of the living myths of the Indian people. The Ramayana and Mahabharata are the seminal epics for the larger corpus of folk ballads and folk theatre and, thereby, of Indian cinema. This is reflected in the fact that Dadasaheb Phalke, the pioneer of Indian cinema made his fourth feature film on the burning of Ravana's kingdom (*Lanka Dahan*) in 1917. The next year saw S.N. Patankar's

Exile of Shree Rama, a four-part serial. In 1920, Madan Theatres produced the first film on the Mahabharata and two years later brought out a silent serial film on the Ramayana.

Perhaps the one premise of modern Indian history that is seriously challenged by a study of the history of Indian cinema, and the folk tradition to which it owes its roots, is the much-touted belief that Indians are a non-violent people and that the apostles of non-violence—the Buddha, Mahavir, and Mahatma Gandhi—exemplify the land and its people. But in truth a detailed study of Indian history would show that the land has witnessed incessant warfare and conflict, even before the Muslim invasions began in the medieval era.

At empirical level, violence has been an obvious, but unfortunately ignored characteristic of the actual history of the subcontinent. Because the concept of a pan-Indian nationalism was born only under the aegis of Mahatma Gandhi, we have trended to emphasize the non-violent aspects of the Indian lifestyle, glossing over the bitter truth—the ideal being substituted for the actual.

The folk imagination, however, has taken a more comprehensive view of the totality of the collective impulse and cinema has reflected this non-didactic viewpoint of historical reality through movies like *Prithviraj Chauhan, Sati Padmini* (*Siege of Chittor*), *Shivaji's Escape from Agra, Veer Ahir* (all made in 1924); *Chhatrapati Sambhaji* (1925); *Murder of Narayan Rao Peshwa, Naharsinh Daku* starring the stunt queen Jilloobai (1926); *Karna: The True Battler, Kichak Vadha, Traitor* (subtitled *Maratha War Cry*) (1928); *Fall of Mauryas, Mewad nu Moti, Rajput Swar, Rajputani* starring Gohar, *Rukmini Haran, Siraj-ud-Dowla* (1929); *Jeejabhai—The Fall of Raigad, Ran-Chandi—Goddess of War, Outlaw of Sorath* starring Putli, and two movies co-directed by V. Shantaram and Dhalber, *Khooni Khanjar* and *Rani Saheba* (1930); *Karma Veer, Prithviraj, Teerandaz, Throne of Delhi* (1931); *Bhawani Talwar, Sinh Garjana, Tiger of Rajputana* (1932); and *Drums of War* and *The Lion of Girna* (1933). And these are just among movies of the silent era!

Yet it was not till 1970 that violence was to become the pre-dominant mood in popular Indian cinema; notwithstanding the tremendous impact that Mehboob Khan's *Mother India* (1957) and the Dilip Kumar–Vyjayanthimala starrer *Ganga Jamuna* had on the film-going public.

The advent of the new trend in 1970 was epitomized by the resounding and unexpected popularity of *Johnny Mera Naam*, with Dev Anand, Hema Malini, and Premnath and directed by Vijay Anand; and the palpable excitement that Dharmendra and Vinod Khanna generated in theatres in Raj Khosla's dacoit drama *Mera Gaon Mera Desh*.

Until these two films changed the very climate of the audience's psyche, 'action', as a physical ingredient of the popular formula, was but one of the many spices that helped give a tang to the movie as a whole. Though occasionally, of course, there were movies— like Sunil Dutt's *Mujhe Jeene Do* (1963) and Dilip Kumar's double-role movie *Ram aur Shyam* (1967)—in which popular cinema even got down to focusing some kind of an analytical eye on the well-springs of social violence.

As the 1970s began, mainstream entertainers still seemed far removed—if not moving in the opposite direction—from old-style stunt films like Raja Sandow's *Veer Kunal* (1925), Jilloo's *Midnight Rider* (1926), *Princess Laila* (1927), Sulochana's *Vengeance* (1928), or Nadia's *Hunterwali* (1935). All that was to change within a matter of years. Suddenly, all the other traditional ingredients of the basic formula—the crude sequences of comic relief, the measured dose of voluptuous dances by well-endowed actresses, the idyllic run-round-the-trees by the romantic lead pair, the sentimental bonds of the family—became subsidiary to a clear-cut, black-and-white confrontation between two warring sides. The trend for an increased demonstration of violence in cinema had begun on a much wider scale, but from the mid-1970s and right through the 1980s, it seemed to the casual observer to devolve into a mere trend resorting to the gimmicks and cinematic tricks of ancient mythological movies and Nadia-style stunts. The origins of the trend, in my opinion, are reasonably revealing of the changing sociology of the modern Indian state.

Within mainstream popular cinema, the three pivotal trend setters in the first phase were Vijay Anand's *Johnny Mera Naam*, Raj Khosla's *Mera Gaon Mera Desh*, and a little-known Amitabh Bachchan starrer entitled *Parwana*. These were the movies that opened up new avenues to the box office for the *Deewar*s, the *Sholay*s, the *Amar Akbar Anthony*s, the *Muqaddar ka Sikander*s and the *Jugnu*s to roll in in quick succession.

And beyond the portals of mainstream cinema, offbeat formats in the shape of *Nishant* and *Ardh Satya* were to reinforce the relevance of the angry, gory, bloodthirsty cry against injustice. It is not at all an irony that the offbeat films most successful at the box office through the 1970s and 1980s should also have been the ones that voiced the inherent conflicts within the Indian nation.

But to return to the variations that started from 1970, *Johnny Mera Naam* was the movie that, in a sense, opened up the cinematic possibilities of showing organized crime. The urbane, sophisticated modern-day criminal running a parallel government of his own beyond the reach of the forces of law and order—operating from a luxurious villa set in the mountains just beyond the Indian border, protected by a large private army of his own—all these elements made their advent into Indian cinema. Films incorporating them were our own counterparts of *Dr No* and *Goldfinger*.

Johnny Mera Naam updated the crime film by showing the box-office potential of the urban underworld; projecting a with-it, urbanized criminal. His emergence on the screen ushered in the new face of the archetypal, mythic, personification of virtue, who would destroy the evil dragon. This was the face of the urbanized Indian committed to a just, dharma-based violence. *Johnny Mera Naam* established his mythic credentials on the same scale as the *baaghi* (rebel/dacoit) heroes of rural Hindu India.

Understandably, the actor to represent this trend was none other than Dev Anand, who had consistently portrayed, through the 1950s and 1960s, the personality of the urban Indian. Of the trio of actors who had captured the devotion of the wider film audience, Dev Anand alone had specifically urban characteristics. Dilip Kumar's screen image had a strong rural orientation. Raj Kapoor personified the urban bohemian who secretly yearned for the tranquillity of rural India. Dev Anand, on the other hand, played one urban hero after another. He was a taxi driver, a CID inspector, a pickpocket, a professional gambler, a truck driver driving down from Delhi to Bombay, a conman, even an urban destitute in *Funtoosh*. Unlike Dilip Kumar or Raj Kapoor, it was Dev Anand who influenced youth fashions year after year with his scarves, his shirt collars, the props he used, the way he smoked, and in other minor but crucial details of fashion. It was appropriate, therefore, that he was the man who raised the status of the urban man of action to the same scale as the legendary *dakus* of the Chambal valley.

In 1970, the legends of the Chambal valley too received a fresh lease of life through Raj Khosla's *Mera Gaon Mera Desh*, which was shot entirely on location in a village in Rajasthan. In *Mera Gaon Mera Desh* the slick cinematography of the 1970s coalesced with the ethnic lustre of authentic rural locations—showing the way for a whole new trend of dacoit films which were to have equal appeal for urban, semi-rural and rural audiences.

The era of violence was, therefore, ushered in in the year 1970 through a two-pronged attack. On the one hand, there was a streamlined showcase demonstrating how the routine dacoit story could transcend its rural roots and appeal to the worldly viewers of urban India; on the other hand, Indian film audiences were given their first good look at the then little-known scenario of organized crime, stretching its tentacles beyond national boundaries.

Incidentally, *Johnny Mera Naam* was the second attempt at introducing this new underworld scenario to Indian filmgoers. The first attempt, *Jewel Thief* (also starring Dev Anand and directed by Vijay Anand) had flopped in 1968.

Why did *Johnny Mera Naam* storm the popular imagination in 1970, when the same story had failed in 1968? The answer, to my mind, lies in the sudden upheaval in independent India's polity in 1969, when the Congress Party split and politics broke out of its distinct state and spilt onto the streets. The breakdown of the status quo in the body politic set off similar reactions in the broad social fabric because the process of change had been particularly intense in the two preceding years. In 1967, the monolithic hold of the Congress Party over the nation's affairs had first been broken, with the Congress being edged out of power by improvised alliances in nine states. Secondly, 1967 had also seen the birth of an ideology that justified the use of violence to hasten the process of change and revolution. The Naxalite upsurge had begun in West Bengal but the ideological fire had spread across the country and the basic premises of the Naxalites were quickly assimilated into the political lexicon.

Indian politics was never to be the same after 1969. Nor, as it turned out, was the popular Indian film. The age-old platitude that 'India is the land of non-violence' was buried in the streets and fields of the country. A new impulse was upon us hereon. In 1971, the Indian army took the initiative of lending its arm and arms for the liberation of Bangladesh. A new era in Indian history had been initiated. The new consciousness responded to new motifs and new visual patterns on the screen. In popular cinema, every-thing gave way to the new struggle—a clear-cut war between Good and Evil, between the just and the unjust, the old-style bigshots and the rebellious underdogs. In a sense, cinema of the have-nots now came into its own, perhaps for the first time in the history of the popular Indian film.

Power, rather than emotion and sentiment, became the new lingua franca of popular cinema. In its own—should we say, irrelevant and illogical— manner the popular Hindi film seemed to accept that power at the box office was born out of the barrel of a gun. Bombay's film studios now began to produce their own version of the Maoist aphorism. *Jugnu, Raja Rani, Hera Pheri, Chacha Bhatija, Charas, Saat Sikke*, etc. a mushroom growth rose around the *Deewar–Sholay* syndrome.

Within two years of *Johnny Mera Naam* and *Mera Gaon Mera Desh*, the entire perspective of commercialized film-making began to be transformed. Raj Kapoor complained to this writer in an interview in early 1973 that even he had been forced by his distributors and exhibitors to incorporate fight sequences in *Bobby*. 'Imagine,' said the film-maker querulously, 'a fight sequence in a Raj Kapoor film! It's never happened before! But I had to,' he confessed, because 'people say a film won't run without a fight sequence.'

Even the Indian government shifted the angle of its censorious eye. Through the late 1960s, after the G.D. Khosla Committee report on films had been submitted, the primary debate had been around 'to kiss or not to kiss'. In the 1970s it became 'to kill or not to kill'.

Fortuitous violence would not be tolerated by the film censors, declared the then Minister of Information and Broadcasting, I.K. Gujral at sundry gatherings and press conferences. At a luncheon meeting in Bombay with the Indian Motion Pictures Producers Association, the minister even had a public row with a group of film-makers led by Vijay Anand. Said Vijay Anand, 'Films are only reflecting the violence that is taking place in Indian society'; and he proceeded to reel off a list of horrific instances. That did not, nor was it expected to, persuade the government to quit carping about excessive violence in cinema. In 1975, taking advantage of the extraordinary powers bestowed on officialdom by the declaration of an emergency in the country, a new Minister of Information and Broadcasting, V.C. Shukla, implemented a 'Stopwatch Scheme', under which a film could not have violent sequences beyond a total of six minutes and the duration of individual sequences was restricted to a maximum of three minutes each. All manner of problems began to arise in the clearing of films by the censors. But the film-makers responded with a clever sleight of hand. They would shoot other varieties of excessive and blatant sequences to distract the censors from what they did want to carry through.

The more officialdom denounced screen violence, the more popular it seemed to become with the masses, right through the 1970s. My personal theory on the government's anxiety about the new trend of violence was that it was prompted by the fear that, obliquely and indirectly, the popular film had begun to convey and propagate the essential premise of the Naxalite movement—that in the Indian social order justice could be achieved only by taking the law into one's own hands, that the common public would find its saviour in a lone crusader rather than in the police force or the legal system. It was all heady stuff for the mass audience, but it was also clear-sighted, valid indictment of a system of justice that had begun to fail.

Even Raj Kapoor, the eternal romantic, found fault with the censorship of social violence in films and said, in 1973, that it was absurd that an Indian film-maker could not even show a policeman taking a bribe on the cinema screen. He said he had wanted to make a film on graft and corruption but knew that the censors would not let him show what everybody knew was happening in Indian society.

The one man who most helped the film industry to carry on its battle with the censors was Amitabh Bachchan, the new superstar. His phenomenal popularity as the 'People's Warrior' compelled film directors and scriptwriters to conceive of most ingenious ways in which to drive past the obstructions created by the film censors, till the censors seemed to give up the fight, beleaguered by the rising tide of the action film's popularity.

Amitabh Bachchan's image as the Angry Young Man of cinema was born in the little-known film *Parwana*. An unsuccessful actor for some four or five years till then, in the emotional angst of a rejected lover, one willing to kill his rival, Amitabh Bachchan first discovered the seeds of a distinct and original screen image. This was quickly perfected in films like *Zanjeer* and *Deewar* and became the credo of a new faith for Indian filmgoers all over the country; its popularity resounding across the border in Pakistan, in the Asian republics of the USSR, among NRIs in Europe and the USA, and wherever else Hindi films were shown.

The combination of features intrinsic to the Amitabh Bachchan persona embodied a subtle and contemporary mix of the real and the unreal. Since the popular Hindi film operates (like Kathakali and Indian folk theatre in general) on a larger-than-life, bigger-than-real scale, there is incredible exaggeration to every type of drama in the Hindi film.

The fight sequences, for instance, were only too obviously fantastic in nature and a bit farcical in the physical dimension and intent. To the inherent unreality of the popular Hindi film's *mise-en-scene*, and the studio's artificial ambience, Amitabh Bachchan brought something of the reality of the north Indian psyche. He borrowed elements from the local culture and lifestyle of the Hindi belt—proclaiming himself as the one actor from Uttar Pradesh to become a leading film star in Bombay—and merged the essentially rural code-of-honour cult with the iconoclasm of urban youth.

Though, like Dev Anand, most of the characters Amitabh Bachchan played in the movies came from a noticeably urban background, the persona of his Angry Young Man also incorporated the traditional value system of rural north India. The song sequence '*Khaike paan Banarswala*' in the movie *Don* typified the conscious attempt on his part to suggest a subliminal link with the Hindi belt. But it is a sequence in Yash Chopra's *Deewar* (1975) which best illustrates the fusion of contemporary urban and rural sensibilities that his screen image embodied. The dramatic point of transcendence for Amitabh Bachchan's character in *Deewar*, the movie that first elevated him to superstar status, is a scene in which he takes on the dockyard's bullies into a warehouse. He enters their den, locks the door from inside, puts the key in his pocket and then, in full exaggerated filmy style, proceeds to bash the goons into pulp. The bravura of entering the warehouse alone, and locking its doors before the commencement of a combat unto death, fits in easily with the tradition of the *daku-baaghi*s of north India—*Sultana, Putlibai, Man Singh, Lakhan, Roopa*—which still colour the texture of heroism in the Hindi belt.

Carefully written sequences that cast a jean-clad, denim-jacketed, lone ranger into the kind of combats that echoed the legends of the north Indian *baaghi*, created a fusion of the urban and the rural, something that Indian filmgoers hadn't quite experienced before. A hero was either urban in personality or distinctly rural. The Amitabh Bachchan persona fused the elements of the two together. He added to his sophisticated, public-school background the essential features of the folk-theatre hero; conveying the impression that he was as comfortable in a three-piece suit as in a kurta-pyjama with an *angochha* tied round his head like an ethnic sweatband.

As an actor, Amitabh Bachchan seemed to positively revel in this symbiotic cultural myth. Revealing a depth of talent within the demands of popular cinema's format, he seemed to bring off one surprise after another. And in the wake of his success, the commercialized, one-track producers and directors of Bombay's entertainment industry began to turn towards greater experimentation. The all-macho tough guy Dharmendra was rediscovered as an irreverent comedy man. Mithun Chakraborty was cast as an Indianized James Bond. The versatile Amjad Khan was transformed into a superstar villain. And leading actresses like Hema Malini and Rekha took up the gun in dacoit sagas that seemed to recall the pyrotechnics of Nadia's *Hunterwali*. The elements of violence were woven together into a complete fabric, blanketing all the conventional elements of popular cinema's potpourri.

This transformation in the priority list of the ingredients of the box office formula also led to a major reorientation of the ends towards which filmic violence was directed. Almost as if submitting to an inexorable law, till the 1970s the popular Hindi film used to conclude on a positive, peaceful, idealistic note, something along the lines of 'and they lived happily ever after'.

The happy ending in Indian cinema (the affliction was rampant in Hollywood too) persisted as a generalization till the early 1970s. For, unlike the art film, the masses demand of their movies that they conclude on a note of hope, so that cinema can serve as purgation of the filmgoer's sense of oppression and rejuvenate him to come out and face the world again.

In the conventional sense, 'the happy ending' marks a final declaration of 'peace and harmony' in the world after all the drama and conflict, the emotional upheaval, the confrontation with individual or collective disaster, the calamitous unhappy coincidences and, in the case of the action film, the suspense-ridden tightrope walk for vengeance. All art, if one may repeat so obvious a generalization, aspires to lead man to a higher state of existence. In the popular movie circuit, it offers a cliche of hope, of a golden sunset enveloping the audience's mythic heroes in the embrace of its warmth, of Good triumphing over Evil, of the quintessential peace of human existence on earth despite all the temporal wars and depressions.

In a sense, cinema in particular churns up a veritable storm of fears and doubts before it punctures its own mirages of disaster with the predictable 'happy ending'. A bland, stereotyped, artificial generalization about *shanti* and 'peace' is also, perhaps, incumbent upon cinema. There have been few films in the history of cinema which have succeeded in effectively demonstrating the dramatic nature of peaceful life in graphic detail. In Indian cinema such instances are even rarer. An analytical, detailed narrative about life's bliss or pure joy and happiness is beyond cinema's ken. At best, it can begin with an idyllic existence which is sabotaged by the birth of unexpected, unknown fears, which actually dominate the movie's mood till the abrupt finale of a generalized resolution of the crisis.

Because cinema administers its dose of pleasure only by taking viewers on a roller-coaster ride of danger, it can temper the concept of life's eternal peace with such realistic variations as the death of the main protagonist in the penultimate sequence. This twist to the happy ending became increasingly possible in the Hindi action film because of the 'grey' characterizations that Amitabh Bachchan was to portray right through the 1970s and 1980s, giving a melancholic twist to the final resolution of the filmgoer's catharsis, thus tingeing his sense of hope for tomorrow with the indelible stain of having to pay a price for a victory in an oppressive social milieu.

The equilibrium between violence and shanti in popular cinema responds with great sensitivity to the elements of violence that endanger life outside cinema. The popular movie not only reflects the happenings of the actual world, it also articulates the unspoken and undeclared impulses of the collective psyche of a given society. In that sense, trends in popular cinema reflect the collective unconscious; and for a film critic become a means to gauge how real life is being perceived by the larger film audience.

India, *December 1990.*

* * *

Movie Idols are the Soulmates of the Young

Hindi films have always reflected the preferences of their audience. The changing tastes of college students and the unspoken desires of rural India for material well-being, find wish fulfilment in this cinema. The quest for a narrative strategy to express this dialectic has remained one of the main endeavours of Hindi cinema.

The relationship in India between cinema and the youth and the common man is unique in the history of the arts. It resembles the 'jaagran', public recitation of religious books, though there is very little that is religious about Indian cinema except in the minds of its youthful devotees. It is like Ram Lila and folk dance rolled into one. It is more like an event than an escape into fiction. And this is what makes the relationship between Indian people and cinema unique.

Except for Hollywood films, which have a gargantuan distribution network in nearly all parts of the world, Indian films are the most popular. French, German, Japanese, and Czechoslovakian films may win awards at international festivals, but Indian films are more popular—in Asia, in Africa, and in Latin America. The Indian film industry has already begun wondering how it can expand on the Hollywood pattern, and no wonder.

It would not be incorrect to say that to a very large extent, trends in Indian cinema are dictated by its young audience and by the values of Indian college students in particular. Indeed, the growth of Indian cinema has been linked to the growth of literacy, which perhaps needs a little explanation.

Before Independence, it was the literate and urban-oriented middle class audience that dominated trends in cinema. Today, the trend has been reversed, primarily because the Indian student has been de-classed culturally. Film tastes among college students, workers, and villagers living on the periphery of the cities and towns are intricately related and it would be safe to say that if they are unidentical at times, they are similar just as often.

That the growth of Indian cinema is linked to the growth of literacy in India is because the extension of cinema is dependent on the growth of modern technology, with which the literacy pattern is linked. This need not be so of course and we do have some sort of an effort in this direction at two levels. In the private exhibition sector there is the semi-permanent touring cinema. In the public sector the Directorate of Film Publicity goes deeper into the interior with instructional and educational films. The setting up of the SITE network which can carry the message farther into the rural heart of the country, wherever electricity is available, is one of the benefits of sophisticated electronic technology. Nor should battery-operated TV sets be far off. Electrification is the basic key to the development of Indian cinema. The touring theatre and the Directorate of Film Publicity do, of course, overcome this disadvantage by having mobile projection units.

The touring theatres of south India, which have a bigger exhibition network anyway, are a good example of what can be achieved with enterprise and initiative. Travelling by train in south India, one sees the landscape dotted with innumerable theatres made of thatch and bamboo poles. The cost of cement, steel, and mortar, so commonly associated with the cinema halls of towns and cities, are easily avoided. If the air-conditioned or air-cooled theatres of cities and towns are like mammoth edifices erected in devotion to the entertainment of the technological age, the thatch-roofed theatres of south India are like local arenas for Ram Lila.

To a very large extent, the concept of 'arena' describes the experience of Indian cinema perfectly for it is a live spectacle that Indian audience, desire from their films. And like the bull fight for the Spanish, for the Indian filmgoer the social relevance of the film-maker's statement should be intricately woven—indeed, camouflaged—into the colourful and glamorized sequences of an out-of-this world dream. The urgency of life and death so perceptible in the bull-fight's ring must pulsate in the drama of cinema.

The search for excitement in the dark theatre is a search for the immediate present—to live it and forget all else. This is why the popular film—whether it is a comedy, a tragedy, or a mix of the two—is so undiscursive, so unlike introverted thought and meditation. These are the characteristics of an intellectual activity that involves a to-and-fro journey between the present and the past, the present and the future, and the past and the future.

The Indian filmgoer would rather have all this intellectual movement be invisibly present, lying behind the scene and the surface confined to direct expression. The song, the dance, the dramatic scene—all these must be more of their own self than of a preconceived message. They must be complete in themselves and, in being complete themselves, each of them becomes an event located in its own timespan. As long as one watches it, one is consumed by it. To be captivated by a scene is to participate in an act. The glory and strength of Indian cinema lies in the participation of the filmgoer; in his total involvement.

It is the common aspiration of today's young, and of workers, villagers and the poor, to act and participate. This common aspiration unites them into a cultural affinity and identity of thought, making for a cultural homogeneity, though intellectuals frown upon it.

In a sense, the Indian film has always been an expression of a cultural unity between the rural and the urban peoples of this land. In the old days, when the majority of film audiences consisted of urbanites, film stories, their directorial treatment, acting styles, and the social needs expressed by the films showed an Indian lifestyle, where the man of the town was not alienated from the traditional cultural patterns of the country.

Today, these elements seem to have undergone substantial change and urbanization, because now it is not the townsman who wishes to be closer to the villager, but the other way round. Otherwise, would the lower-class filmgoer identify with the film hero who sings songs in cars, dresses flashily in multicoloured bush-shirts and bell bottoms, drinks Scotch, and carouses around with mini-skirted damsels? Would he otherwise identify with heroes playing characters that are supposed to be doctors, lawyers, business executives, army officers, and professors? Could the cabaret else have become popular at all as an essential ingredient of a film?

It is generally thought that the enticements of cinema for the young are escapist in nature, both in terms of the cultural milieu and material circumstances. This therefore, the thinking goes, prompts idle young people to waste their days inside cinema halls and in gossiping about films and film stars. If that alone were the truth of the matter, why is it that things 'filmy' influence so much the creative sprit of young people?

In college canteens and at bus stops, it is not uncommon to hear young people improving on certain choice scenes or performances from films. One of the most popular items in college variety programmes is the parody of things filmic. Hairstyles change over-night with the ascent of new monarchs on the screen, and that sort of a thing is popularly accepted.

What is not talked about by social commentators of cinema so often is the inspiration the creativity of young Indians receive from films which can be sensed only at the level of their social life, though traces do appear, as mentioned above, in college variety programmes. However, it is largely to be found through direct contact with the young—in slang, for instance. And the two keep evolving. In recent months, for instance, the fine *Purabi* UP accent displayed in the film *Sholay* by young Amjad Khan has become the vogue for any number of improvised dialogues among the young.

This phenomenon of uninstitutionalized or unchannelized creative activity by the young—which is different from getting poems published, paintings exhibited, or plays performed—can also be heard in conversations at such public congregations as cricket test matches, college sports events, and at festival melas.

Another important aspect of cinema's lure for our young is that from the very beginning, cinema has been a catalyst for successive generations of young Indians in their quest for a social identity independent of the rigid framework of the joint family. And in its own oblique way the feature film has also had an educational role to play in the realization by young people of the adult world.

This has particularly endeared cinema to young people, who are curious, if anything. And the genuine film-maker has always taken into account the directions in which social forces are moulding the curiosity of the young. In the natural process of things, the curiosity of the elderly tends to follow the curiosity of the young and that is how the young easily influence trends in films.

A gradual awareness of their influence on cinema and of how they can get their parents and elders to accept their modifications in lifestyles, their social attitudes, and their moral and ethical values has led Indian youth to develop a very intimate and sub-jective fraternity with cinema. It is their thing, even as it has lovers, both male and female. And that explains their obsession with all its paraphernalia and ancillaries.

A corrollary to the liberation of Indian youth by cinema is the fact that a film is the one thing that immediately computes the audience reaction to it. One may dislike a book but one cannot express one's dislike of it as easily as one can of a film, to which one simply does not return or which one stops one's friends from seeing. It is like a swiftly conducted vote.

This is important because liking or disliking a film means not only the appreciation or criticism of the artistes, the direction, the musical score, the narrative, etc. but also of the countless social trends and attitudes that are expressed in films, for each film is like a slice of life of the period and social milieu in which it is set. Popular films, indeed, are a very competent tool for the Indian sociologist to understand which way the undertones of social attitudes, particularly those of the young, are going. And what is an undertone today becomes an overtone tomorrow. No wonder that in India the reaction of people to topical elements in films is even more indicative of the state of society than the reaction of people to—or through—the newspapers.

An interesting study in the history of Indian cinema is the change in attitudes to working in cinema. In recent years, a career in the film industry has become a prized one for the middle and upper classes. If the first decades of Indian cinema were dominated by the children of the poor, the scions of the professional middle class are now flocking to the Film and Television Institute of India. Indian TV centres are, like All India Radio stations, providing equally attractive careers as, say, journalism and teaching for university graduates.

The present state of Indian cinema ranging from *Uski Roti* to G.P. Sippy, B.R. Chopra, and Raj Kapoor represents to a certain extent the great variety of options open to it. Both the art film and the regular film are embroiled today in a situation that underlines change, innovation, and novelty. Like the state of society, the state of cinema is one of flux and of great potential.

The new ground that has been broken since the mid-1960s in the area of operations of the Film Finance Corporation, in the film industry itself, and in the land lying between the two happily reflects important events in Indian cinema. In the first instance, a picture has emerged of a composite post-Independence India. A society has matured somewhat in its vision of the contemporary era and sees itself as an independent period of time in the history of the land.

Second, the mid-1960s have marked the entry of post-Independence generations into active film-making. The diversity of Indian cinema today reflects largely the influence of the diversity of feeling and ambition of the post-Independence generations.

However, despite the feverish nature of film activity we have witnessed in the last decade, the actual achievement has been unhappily less than it initially appeared, or what it ought to have been. After all, the Czechoslovakian 'Wave' and the French 'New Wave' that did so much for the international reputation of the cinema of these two countries, had their first phase that lasted a decade too. Why, then, has the Indian 'Wave' not led to the maturity of Indian cinema? For we see that in the film industry there is great emphasis today on unoriginal narratives. And at the same time, the Indian art film is not able to realize its artistic ambitions because of too many creative 'blocks'. Both our commercialized professionals and our serious artists are not able to bridge the gap between word and deed. Apart from the temperamental 'blocks' of the individual film-makers involved, there is also a crisis of communication, though it takes different forms in the two branches of the cinema.

While the commercialized professionals of the film industry have tremendous talent for captivating the audience, their initial problem is to exercise their own judgment as to what a film should be. Most of our established producers and directors are not as satisfied with the popularity and success of their films as it would seem. For they are successful on the audience's terms but not on their own.

In this context let us take the examples of Raj Kapoor's *Mera Naam Joker*, B.R. Chopra's *Aadmi aur Insaan*, Shakti Samanta's *Amar Prem*, Vijay Anand's *Tere Mere Sapne*, Raj Khosla's *Prem Kahani*, Gemini's *Ek Gaon ki Kahani*, Hrishikesh Mukherjee's *Mili*, *Sabse Bada Sukh*, and *Buddha Mil Gaya*, and the recent films of Asit Sen and B.R. Ishara.

All these films were made by film-makers who, in most cases, have proved their ability to make good and popular films. These films were made as per their own inclinations and desires, as films they wanted to make from their concerns as artists. Yet the people more or less rejected these films. At the same time, they thronged to films made by these producers and directors more as saleable projects and not too much from personal involvement. Vijay Anand followed the thinly popular *Jewel Thief*, with *Johnny Mera Naam* that broke box-office collection records. He came out with *Tere Mere Sapne*, a film his very own, but it knocked him so hard that he still hasn't recovered psychologically.

Similarly, Raj Kapoor made *Mera Naam Joker* as the culminating finale to a grand career as film-maker and actor, but this auto-biographical showmanship sank him into colossal debts. Only the tremendously popular youth film *Bobby* helped him recover his reputation.

It has been a strange time, this, for film-makers. The illustrious Dilip Kumar found himself treading on thin ice with *Daastaan* and *Sagina*. Dev Anand received severe shocks with *Heera Panna* and *Ishk Ishk Ishk* while he hit silver jubilee with his conventional role in *Amir Garib*.

No wonder even the most powerful film producers are conscious today, more than ever before, of the total unpredictability of people's aspirations and desires. This time round it is the film-maker wooing his audience.

In its own way, the crisis of communication is also to be found among the makers of art films. Much has already been written about the obscurity of the modernistic film, both in the Indian and international press. What needs deeper study, however, is why seemingly intelligent, talented, and committed film-makers are not able to express their own talent and concerns more genuinely, without making what may be called the compromise of easy communication. For our young experimentalists have not made much of an impact with the sophisticated and intellectualized film audiences of India on the international scene. Their limitations of course, makes for an independent study in itself.

What may be mentioned here is the strange case of Mrinal Sen's Bengali films. When *Calcutta 71* was released in Calcutta in 1972 (as far as I remember), both the director and cameraman K.K. Mahajan were carried shoulder-high by the crowd when they made a personal appearance. However, in 1974, Mrinal Sen's *Chorus*, an intellectualized extension of the earlier film's theme, and a film that later won the highest film award in the country as the Best National Feature Film, was summarily rejected by the Calcutta filmgoer.

Nor should one forget that of the so-called Indian 'New Wave', a number of films that were popularly accepted, such as *Dastak*, *Anubhav*, *Phir Bhi*, and *Rajinigandha*, had several cinematic flaws. Whereas better-made films that were substantially different in style, such as *Garam Hawa* and *Nishant* did not do as well at the box office. This may be because of some factors involved in the themes the films tackled, for these are not stylistically obscure films.

The limited popularity outside Bengal of the films of Satyajit Ray, the most distinguished Indian film director, should make the serious Indian film-maker restudy both his style and his thematic concerns. For it is not very difficult to see that the audience does not exactly flock to theatres even though the films of Ray, and films like *Garam Hawa* and *Nishant* deal with themes that do concern the Indian people, the lucid and straightforward narrative form utilized by Ray notwithstanding.

Unfortunately, it does not appear from the outside that enough deliberation is being done in this direction. And the makers of the Indian art film and commercially motivated films are both trying to solve their puzzles without quite catching the bull by the horns.

Link, published around 1973. This magazine has since ceased publication.

* * *

Hindi Cinema Denies Space to the Writer

Good writing is the basis of good cinema. Producers and financiers do not seem to quite understand this fact. A film-maker alone cannot adapt cinematic material available to him. This is the task of the writer. The occasional, well-written film script, therefore, continues to be an exception rather than the rule.

All the major New Waves and movements in world cinema, especially in the last five decades, have been stimulated by a collaboration between film directors and writers writing specifically for film. Two of the New Waves that had pervasive influence on Indian film-making went on to commemorate some of their writers as superstars: Zavattini in Italian neo-realist cinema and Carrere in the French New Wave of the 1960s and 1970s.

Nor were Zavattini and Carrere isolated figures in the cinema of their time. Zavattini's tradition of script writing was continued by Vittorio de Sica, Federico Fellini, and others who started as scriptwriters and went on to become great film-makers. In France, the New Wave directors ventured out and even experimented with the writings of novelists who had already made a niche for themselves in contemporary literature, such as Alain Robbe-Grillet and Marguerite Duras.

From Ingmar Bergman to the New Hollywood era of Steven Spielberg and Francis Ford Coppolla, narrative cinema has thrived on this collaboration between the film-maker and the writer. Indian cinema is no exception and the names of literary writers like Vijay Tendulkar and M.T. Vasudevan Nair have been closely associated with some of the best films in India's alternate cinema.

The history of our cinema in the Hindustani language, on which alone I may claim some expertise, also throws up innumerable instances of writer–film-maker collaborations, despite the popular notion that Hindi cinema has no space for the writer. Rajinder Singh Bedi, K.A. Abbas, Krishan Chander, Manto in parts before his migration to Pakistan, Abrar Alvi (Guru Dutt's scriptwriter), Rahi Masoom Raza, and Gulzar are some of the notable examples from a legacy that survives to this day.

Yet the notion persists, not without reason, that Hindi cinema, especially mainstream Hindi cinema, has no space for the writer. A Delhi–UP film distributor told me some years back that the story content of mainstream Hindi films followed a tortuous route. If not lifted from Hollywood/foreign films, the stories for Hindi films often come from Malayalam literature, just as they came in the past from Bengali fiction, of which Sarat Chandra and Bankim Chandra were the most popular sources. In the more recent past, a Malayalam film based on a good story would be remade in Telugu and Tamil, and if it proved successful in all three film circuits, it would be remade in Hindi.

Suresh Jindal, who in his early days produced *Rajnigandha* and Ray's *Shatranj Ke Khilari* said some years ago that he had stopped dreaming of producing a new film because of the lack of good scripts. A behind-the-scenes scriptwriter of more contemporary vintage at Bollywood says that film-makers dump a load of VHS copies of foreign films on the 'story-writer' and even specify the film/films which are 'likely to be extensively used'. This writer also confessed that he was not yet in the same league, as far as money went, as Javed Akhtar or Javed Siddiqui.

The late Arun Kaul (the film society buff who produced Mrinal Sen's *Ek Adhuri Kahani*) told me at the 1991 International Film Festival of India (IFFI) at New Delhi that he had been writing film scripts for Bollywood. However, he had decided to give it up, shift to Delhi, and make TV documentaries because the money paid to the scriptwriter at Bollywood wasn't good enough. He and his co-writer were 'rated' at Rs 6 lakh a script. This worked out to Rs 3 lakh apiece, but over the two-year period that the film was produced!

Indian cinema's more active trend these days is for young film directors to write their own scripts as writer-directors, or for the more artistic film directors to script novels or short stories of their own selection. The latter is a convention most notably established by the late Satyajit Ray. However, the trend of young directors writing their own original scripts is only now becoming widespread practice in Hindi cinema. John Mathew Matthan's *Sarfarosh* (1999), Ashutosh Gowrikar's *Lagaan*, and Madhur Bhandarkar's *Chandni Bar* (both released in 2001) are three important instances.

These three Hindi films have instilled new optimism into young creative writers across the country, aspiring to make an entry into the seemingly inaccessible world of films. Their perception is that doors have been opened which will enable creativity to enter on its own steam into film production. True enough. But as John Matthan Mathew said to this writer recently, successful film-makers soon realize that they can function more efficiently as film-makers if they also have good writers to work with—a writers like Sooni Taraporewala, who has been the backbone for director Mira Nair's string of successes (with the exception of *Monsoon Wedding*, which Sooni did not write).

However, the number of these films is abysmally small. It works out to an average of three or four per year at Mumbai, even if one includes such films as *Gadar*, *Godmother*, *Fiza*, and *Dil Chahta Hai*, out of an annual production of over 125 films. The crisis of 'no writers' thus haunts the cinema at Mumbai, as elsewhere in the land.

The primary reasons for this crisis, in my opinion, are:

1. The paucity of popular novels and fiction in the Indian publishing world.
2. The inability of a large number of novelists and playwrights to accept the essential idiom of the Indian film and the requirements of the product's market.
3. The inability of film producers, financiers, and directors to comprehend the significant though intangible contribution good writing can make to a film, and to give the writer a respectable status in the film-production hierarchy—specially the pecuniary hierarchy.
4. The lack of desire of directors to go out in search of 'filmable' books and stories. Instead, both film and TV serial directors do not see beyond the writers who come to them.
5. Translating great literature into cinema is one of the most arduous undertakings imaginable. It is more difficult than translating great poetry from one language into another. Second, on the film's release its comparison with the book—generally unfavourable—is inevitable.

Nonetheless, cinema always thrives on the possibilities thrown up by contemporary 'popular literature'—novels and fiction and plays that intrinsically cater to a wider audience than 'literary' writing, for example George Bernard Shaw's *Pygmalion*. Not necessarily among his greater plays, but delightful material to adapt for a musical as *My Fair Lady*. Similarly, the stories of Daphne Du Maurier cinematized by Alfred Hitchcock.

The phenomenon of 'New Hollywood' has been possible because directors like Steven Spielberg, Francis Ford Coppolla, Christopher Columbus, et al., could pick up appropriate novels by new writers like Peter Bentley, Mario Puzo, and John Grisham. The thriving world of popular fiction in American publishing provides New Hollywood directors with a ready source of 'filmable' material to pick and choose from. American publishing is the fountain from which New Hollywood springs. Every year new novels as well as new novelists emerge in the American book market and a steady stream of fresh ideas and concepts flows in with them. Popular literature keeps the film industry ticking.

In India, on the other hand, popular literature exists like an endangered species, thanks to the crooked intent of Indian pub-lishers who believe that writers can subsist happily enough seeing their name in print. It is only in regional languages where the pub-lishing world is dynamic and honestly remunerative for the writer, such as in Kerala, that popular literature prospers and blooms. In turn it provides Malyalam cinema with its essential plots and themes. Today, Malayalam literature may well boast of the largest number of fiction writers who manage to survive on their writing alone—more perhaps than in Bengali, Marathi, Tamil, and Gujarati.

On the other hand, in Hindi, Urdu, and English, the book publishing world is so exploitative that many a capable popular novelist, especially in Urdu and Hindi, goes wholly unnoticed both by the film-making crowd as well as the film-going public. Nor, for that matter, do Indian film directors evince any keenness in looking at the back of the cupboards or under the carpet, as it were, to discover for themselves such popular novelists as do happen to exist to this day in Hindi and Urdu. The financial hierarchy and the lowly status of the writer in mainstream Indian cinema makes it seem undignified and embarrassing for a film director to go out in search of a good writer. In turn, good writers protect their minimalized sense of self-respect by refusing to make countless numbers of bus trips to film-production offices.

Indian publishers do not seem to be alive to the potential vein of prosperity that they could mine for themselves—the reading public and cinema. The paperback book market in India is terribly undeveloped. It presents itself in worn-out colours, looking always like a set of discarded clothes that do not deserve a second look. Book marketing is pitiably low and book covers of popular fiction are unattractive.

Indian publishers have not shown any enterprise in establishing a dynamic paperback market for popular fiction that would command an all-India readership—through translation if necessary—in the manner that dubbing has extended markets for film production. By adopting such a stance, they have undermined Indian writing, Indian publishing, and Indian cinema. Writers themselves despair about the neglect and dissipation of the potential of popular Indian literature. No one is concerned about this state of affairs—least of all Indian producers.

Published in Hindustan Times.

* * *

Indian Goof-ups at International Film Festivals

Is the state doing enough to promote new talent in cinema? International film festivals provide a key meeting place where film-makers from across the country can interact. Unfortunately, they are not being provided with a proper forum. In addition, India continues to ignore the post-colonial countries of Asia and Africa, which have been our traditional, overseas market.

The success of an international film festival—and there are many crowding the calendar now—depends primarily on the equations and balances it works out between the senior film-makers and the new, emerging talents.

The older names from the roster of contemporary cinema's hall of fame, give an international film festival its sense of tradition and quality and also reinforce the festival's institutional character. The presence of some of these directors at the festival helps the event to raise itself above the din and bustle of the market section where producers and distributors explore the possibilities of pushing their films into every corner of the world.

An extremely important feature of the innumerable small-sized events that go to make an international film festival into a major event is that it brings the senior film-makers into informal dialogue with the vigour, impatience, revelations of new entrants in the field. Every festival has an army of young film-makers to fill the ranks, and only a few senior film-makers.

Film festivals in India, such as the 8th International Film Festival of India organized at Delhi from 3 January to 17 January 1981, have also placed a very noticeable emphasis on bringing together the older and the younger generations. Yet our festivals have failed to achieve a status that would make them more than 'also rans' on the international film scene.

This failure, and the comparatively fewer successes our festivals have achieved, stem from a basic flaw in our approach to the organization of a festival. Hitherto we have been satisfied with inviting one or two very famous names, a few directors from Third World countries, and several Indian film-makers. Also our organizers at the Directorate of Film Festivals have also seen to it that a number of important film critics, from England primarily and other European countries, attend our festivals and discover for themselves the new talent in film-making that India is constantly throwing up.

It is the presence of the foreign critics that really reflects the success of our efforts. During the past six years—since the 6th International Film Festival of India (IFFI) at New Delhi in 1977, whereafter festivals have been held regularly in the country—the Indian Panorama section has drawn more and more attention from foreign film critics. This has led to the showing of Indian films by younger directors at festivals abroad. This helps in giving these new film-makers the kind of support they need to prove that the art film in India does not begin and end with Satyajit Ray and a handful of peers like Mrinal Sen and Shyam Benegal.

Adoor Gopalakrishnan—the maker of *Swayamvaram* and *Kodiyeltom*—and G. Aravindan—who had made *Uttarayanam*,

Kanchana Seetha, Thamp, Kumatty, and *Esthappan*—are two film-makers from Kerala who have had considerable impact in art film circles abroad, after they were discovered at Indian Panorama programmes here. Incidentally, Aravindan also won an award at the 1980 Mannheim Film Festival with *Kumatty.*

Another notable projection, particularly during 1979 and 1980, has been that of Buddhadeb Dasgupta; the 36-year-old Bengali director (*Dooratwa* and *Neem Annapurna*), has been invited to nearly a dozen important film festivals during the last two years. Dasgupta's projection peaked with his winning a silver medal at the Karlovy Vary festival in 1980.

These discoveries have, naturally, highlighted the success of our efforts. But they also mark the limits of our achievement. Over the past five years there have been a number of important films by newcomers that have not been shown at our festivals. They have been overlooked despite the fact that they were films that would have had a better chance of making an impression on foreign film buffs than some of those included in the Indian Panorama's programmes. Very often the selection of some of the films has unfortunately been dominated by vested interests and by a totally Indian framework of film values. The film-maker from Kerala, P. Abu Backer (who has made *Kabaninadhi Chuvanna, Manimuzhakkam, Chuvanna Vithukal,* and *Sangamam*) is one who could have been more forcefully projected by us among foreign critics.

We have also made the mistake of concentrating on Europe for opening up a market for the art film. This has been at the cost of pushing away younger directors from the traditional overseas markets for the Indian film, which are mainly in the post-colonial countries of Asia and Africa.

It is clear that one possible role that an international film festival in India can play is that of being an important film centre for Third World countries. We have tried to bring this about but without much success. The representation of Asian and African cinemas at our festivals is rather meagre and 'officious'—half the berths being given to films by government officials from those countries.

Krystoff Zanussi, who is now a name to be reckoned with on the international scene, illustrates one of our fortunate moves. He was discovered by us at a time when he had not yet established an international reputation for himself. Over the years, as he kept coming to festivals in India, in tandem with his growing international stature, we also began to derive a sense of reflected glory—deriving a sense of glory, even if reflected, is crucial to a film festival. As the director of such films as *Illumination*, *A Delicate Balance*, and *Spiral*, which are very popular with Indian film buffs, Zanussi has become an accepted member of the art film milieu in India.

If only we had also succeeded in discovering, in similar ways, young film-makers from Algeria, or Senegal, or Iran or Japan! If our film festivals had played a part in the international discovery of such films as *Chronicle of the Years of the Embers* (the Algerian film which won a Grand Prix at Cannes, 1976) or the Tunisian film *Hyenas under the Sun* (shown some years after its international discovery at the 1979 Delhi festival)—we could have taken credit for the fact that films by new film-makers, first shown at an Indian festival, were significant enough to become famous the world over.

The discovery of an important young and new director by a film festival is significant on two definite counts. First, cinema is nothing if not the child of the young. Young film-makers have always dominated fashion and public taste. The introduction of new talent in a festival's programme immediately excites the festival's audience. It gains recognition as a venue that can make important contributions internationally.

We, in India, have not conceived of this role for our film festivals. If and when we have performed this role that festivals all over the world have come to perform, it has only been accidental, as in the case of Zanussi.

At least one other film-maker—Reinhardt Hauff of (former) West Germany—slipped through our hands. Hauff first came to

India in 1973, as a delegate to the West German Film Festival held in India under the cultural exchange programme. He came again to the 1974–5 film festival at Delhi where he entered his film, *The Brutalization of Franz Blum*, in the competition section. It was a film that had tremendous impact on the festival audience but it won no award. Nor, for that matter, did the French film, *Empty Chairs*, which was one of the first films we have seen here dealing with the problem of the single woman and mother.

Though Hauff likes India too much to admit something like this publicly, people in West Germany say that after he returned from the Delhi festival, he felt that it was pointless for a young film-maker to send his films to the competition section of the Delhi festival. Hauff's word carried considerable weight among young film-makers in West Europe—*Brutalization* and *Empty Chairs* became symbols of what could happen, in terms of neglect, to young film-makers at the Delhi festival. Immediately thereafter, at least for the 1977 and 1979 festivals at Delhi, important West European films by new directors were not competing.

Today, of course, with the public success of *Knife in the Head* in Germany and West Europe, Hauff has graduated into the major league of the European art film. But any attachment he will still have for our competitive festival is bound to be limited.

The tragedy has been that the Indian festivals have not been able to realize the importance of young directors competing from abroad or of striking a balance between the older and the younger film-makers. A festival should attract both by offering them a meeting place, an arena where they can indulge in fruitful dialogue with each other; apart from just having a holiday in the exotic East.

What our international film festivals have tried to do is to meet two main ends. First, to get a couple of very important names, so that their presence becomes a feather in the cap of the organizers. Secondly, to cater as much as possible to young *Indian* film-makers, even at the cost of those from abroad. As a result, for the visiting film-maker, we are constantly selling ourselves and looking after our own interests, but not giving anything really stimulating or really international for them to take the trouble of flying down to India with their new films.

Hindustan Times, 29 January 1989.

* * *

Black Money as the Mainstay of Hindi Cinema

The labyrinthine paths to financing which make Hindi films possible have been highlighted here. Earlier, it was possible for small- and medium-level businessmen to invest their money in Hindi films. By doing so, they could convert their black money into legally-held wealth. But things became somewhat difficult when the underworld began to finance films and drastically alter their content. Now a third element is emerging. Corporate houses are also financing films and this has seen the content of Hindi films undergo a cosmetic change.

Despite the onslaught of TV and the increasing popularity of video, there has been no major drop in the number of feature films produced in India during the last two years. The Indian film industry continues to produce the largest number of films in a year, and is still considerably ahead of Hollywood.

This output is amazing and intriguing considering that during the last two years the film business touched the nadir of a recession. Audiences dropped substantially in the theatres, there were few box-office successes, and many big-budget films flopped disastrously.

One important reason for the high production figures of the last two years is that a much greater number of small-budget, offbeat, artistic films are being made, often produced or financed by businessmen unconnected with the film industry. The number of offbeat, low-budget films has increased substantially during the last two or three years, even though the distribution and release of films by award-winning directors—such as Buddhadev Dasgupta (*Andhi Gali*), Saeed Mirza (*Mohan Joshi Hazir Ho*), and Ketan Mehta (*Holi*)—remain major headaches.

A second and more significant reason why there has not been a slump in feature film production in the country is that finance—often from new sources—is still readily available for commercial films; recession or no recession. As filmwallas rightly believe, there will always be people ready to invest money in popular commercial films because the Indian film industry is one of the few avenues open to the medium- and small-scale investor to convert his black money funds into legitimate money. Film financing remains one of the best means to invest black money and reap 'white' money returns.

Since film production in India has evolved a highly specialized method to cover up black-money investments, the commercial film industry continues to attract such undeclared capital generated in other businesses without fear of repercussion. Most of these investors prefer to remain anonymous. They operate through a regular film financier who invests their money in various feature films and offers lucrative returns to his depositors. These investors come from various walks of life. They could be businessmen, professionals such as doctors, engineers, chartered accountants, or smugglers for that matter.

Apart from the opportunity the film industry provides for the investment of black money, businessmen from other walks of life are also tempted to get into films because of the opportunities films provides to befriend, woo, and socialize with the famous screen faces.

The bulk of the black-money operations in the Indian film industry appears to be concentrated in the production sector, though there is also a considerable amount in the theatre and exhibition sector. Ironically enough the process through which black money is converted into legitimate 'white' money, hardly provides any advantage to film stars. As far as the black-money–

white-money circuit is concerned, the stars are saddled with black money as the major percentage of their remuneration.

Film producers, however, after they achieve a certain status in the industry, will not accept finance in black. But they do keep a finger on black-money funds, because their stars, or other people involved in film production, have become used to the luxury of having a personal cache of black money.

The conversion—laundering, as it is termed—of black money into clean money is critical to a film producer's job. A man who does not know how black money can be laundered through the process of making a film can hardly survive in the commercial industry.

Broadly speaking, this process of conversion operates along the following lines. A major percentage of a film's budget is the payments made to the leading star and other members of the cast, the music director, the playback singers, etc. Fifty per cent of these remunerations is made with black money. But when the film is being sold to distributors, the cost of production stated by the producer, along with his fee for launching the film, incorporates the legitimate and undeclared investments made by him. The incorporation of black money in the film's cost of production is through many ingenious methods. The most common is through fake accounts for publicity expenses.

Apart from the overt publicity campaigns launched to sell a film to the audience, a number of other means are also used. For example, many film producers distribute expensive publicity souvenirs. The accounts for these souvenirs and for the regular publicity campaigns are generally shuffled to accommodate the black-money payments made during production.

A film producer while selling the film shows smaller payments to the film's artistes, though it is understood between him and the distributors that the actual payment made to the artistes is in fact much more. The distributor, therefore, is willing to buy the film at a greater margin of profit for the producer than the film's budget would normally warrant. In such cases, the larger margin of profit works to the advantage of the film's producer and its financier.

Though the average producer is not very keen to raise his taxable income, the film financier is mainly looking for a way to convert black-money investments, made on behalf of a number of depositors, into legitimate returns.

While many traditional film financiers have come into the business from real estate and building construction, or from traditional moneylending families, during the last decade professional chartered accountants and income-tax consultants have come in prominently. This is important. For it is through them that a very large clientele of depositors has been making undeclared investments in films.

These financial consultants are also important because they arrange for 'bank entries', which helps the producers and film stars to convert black money into white. The 'entry' system is rather simple to operate, provided one makes the right connection. Any person with a reasonable bank balance can use the 'entry' system to his advantage. For example, if you have Rs 50,000 in the bank, you can offer a loan of this amount to somebody who needs to convert black-money into white. On paper an 'entry' is made through which you give a loan of Rs 50,000. In actual fact, however, for the loan of Rs 50,000 by cheque, you are given the same sum in black money. That is, in fact you do not really loan out the money but offer a bank entry to somebody who needs it. For this favour you may receive a small commission for a specified number of years.

Since film production involves the payment of expenses under a large number of heads and because a very large number of people are involved in film production, it is more or less impossible for tax officials to check and counter-check the actual payments made. It is common knowledge that film producers will often ask lesser artistes and technicians to sign receipts for larger sums than they have actually been paid. This process helps a film producer create his own black-money resources, which he uses to pay the main artistes of his film. These luminaries in turn need black money to live the lavish life that show business requires of its luminaries.

Another method used for creating black-money resources is through hotel bills. On location shooting, the staff of the production team collects all the hotel bills of the personal expenses incurred by the unit's members, even though the bills may have been cleared by those who incurred the expenses. The purpose is to show the amount as expenses incurred during location shooting thereby enabling the producer to convert this amount into black money.

The lead stars, of course, hardly spend any money of their own during a shooting schedule. On the contrary, their personal expenses, including those for trunk calls, excess air baggage, and air fare for their personal retinue are all paid by the producer.

Since most of the expenses incurred while a film is under production are met with black-money payments, and because of the lucrative returns, the film industry will continue to attract finance from outside. And as long as finance is available, there will remain a reason to produce more and more films. Until, that is, a more successful method is discovered to convert black money into white.

Published in Screen.

* * *

Bollywood Goes on Strike

The first and only time Bollywood went on strike was in the 1970s when the Maharashtra government imposed a 177 per cent tax on cinema tickets. The 50 per cent entertainment tax on the sale of every cinema ticket these days is a legacy of those times. The high prices being charged at multiplexes today are a continuation of the high taxes of the 1970s.

The recent film industry strike is perhaps the only instance since, 1947 when all segments of the trade have come together for an indefinite strike. And the only reason why this industry, riddled with internecine commercial strife, politicking, and factionalism, came together briefly is because had the dreaded sales tax proposal been enacted by the Maharashtra legislature, the film industry's survival in Bombay would have been at stake. It would have meant a complete reorientation of the industrial milieu in which films are made in Bombay.

The Maharashtra government had proposed that entertainment tax be increased substantially. The Godbole Committee however recommended that entertainment tax on cinema tickets be reduced from 177 per cent to 97 per cent. It also recommended that the dreaded sales tax which would have applied to both goods and tickets be pruned down. Once these recommendations were accepted and the bill withdrawn, a mood of quiet elation mixed with feelings of relief spread through the film world.

For a start, if the bill had gone through, it would have become essential for film-production units to shift their headquarters out of Maharashtra, since the proposed sales tax envisaged a tax even on the sale of film-distribution rights. That is to say, that if a producer of an A-class, big-budget, multi-star cast extravaganza (like *Karma*) sold the distribution rights of his film for a period of ten years for an amount upwards of Rs 2.5 crore—an amount that decided by him as one that would cover his costs and also incorporate a reasonable profit for his efforts—then the amount of Rs 2.5 crore would also be subject to a sales tax of 4 per cent.

Film producers, and the rest of the industry, felt that the film trade was anyway paying far too many taxes at every stage of production and marketing, and that the current economic depression in the film market emanated from the fact that while films were regularly being produced, there were few distributors willing to invest their money and buy distribution rights of completed films.

Over the last six years or so, when the end of the boom first began, distributors have been complaining that rates have been raised far too steeply by producers and that the distribution sector of the trade (which is the crucial marketing sector since distributors function in the manner of wholesale dealers and agents) cannot afford to retail the product at the manufacturer's price.

While this quarrel between producers and distributors has been going on for some years within the industry, the Maharashtra government's sales tax proposals would have enormously increased the cost of film production and—the sting in the tail—the sales tax on the sale of distribution rights would have been a further compounded levy, adding to the cost that the distributor had to bear. Since the price of film tickets is controlled and licensed by local administrations in most parts of the country, the film distributor would not have been able to pass on the increase to the consumer as other industries tend to do.

Faced with extinction, Bombay's film industry began to work out alternative channels of survival. Undoubtedly, most of the film industry's unit would have shifted their head offices out of Bombay and Maharashtra so that they could escape paying a sales tax on the sale of the completed film's distribution rights. Another significant proposal that was being considered seriously was that a gradual shift of film production from Maharashtra should begin. The industry toyed with ideas of making films in Hyderabad-Secunderabad, Gujarat, and even West Bengal.

Such was the militancy during the heydays of the film industry's strike. Today, evaluating the pros and cons of all that has happened since October, many people in Bombay's film world believe that the most important gain of their strike has been a simple lesson— the government will not bother about the film industry unless it takes a militant stance.

Behind this fighting posture is a history of interactions between the film industry and the government. A history that film people think has always given them the raw end of the bargain. And since the world of Hindi films has been a community of 'politically aware' professionals and businessmen, their responses have not been apolitical. At this point one must specify the special manner in which the film community has been, and is, politically aware.

The first golden epoch of the Hindi film industry, to take the most dominant segment of Indian cinema here, coincided with the social reformist atmosphere in the Indian body politic dominated by the ideas of Gandhi, Nehru, and the freedom struggle as a whole. V. Shantaram and K.A. Abbas are perhaps the most famous living representatives of that era. In the period after 1947, two significant trends occurred. On the one hand, a number of leftist artistes and creative people—many drawn from the Indian People's Theatre Association (IPTA)—went to films in search of a creative means of livelihood. And on the other, there was a contrary and opposite development—moneylenders and financiers moved into the film trade.

Many of these investors came from Sind after the partition of the country, and their presence attracted business people from other parts of the country too. But—and Raj Kapoor's films are perhaps the best amalgam of these two diverse trends—the creative work continued to be largely influenced by people with a social commitment to their society. In that era began the first public interaction between political leaders and film people, epitomized by the presence of some leading film personalities at an All India Congress Committee (AICC) session, following an invitation to them by Jawaharlal Nehru.

Coming back quickly to the present, the film industry which was largely supportive of the Congress, though there were minor sympathies for other causes as well, struck a rough patch in its relations with Indira Gandhi. During the early 1970s, shortly after the 1971 Lok Sabha elections, the Ministry of Information and Broadcasting began cracking down on sex and violence in commercial cinema. Censorship of films became a problem through the 1970s, corruption in the office of the Censor Board began to be openly talked about, and, worse, some producers managed to get the Censor Board's decisions revoked in New Delhi.

This uneasy relationship worsened during the Emergency and when the 1977 Lok Sabha elections came about, Bombay's film world was sharply divided between those who supported the Congress and those who were against it. While stalwarts like Raj Kapoor, Dilip Kimar, Manoj Kumar, and, most of all, Sunil Dutt and Nargis, campaigned for the Congress, the larger section of the film world took a public stand against the Emergency.

With the Janta Party coming into power the financial decline of the Hindi film industry began and an economic pattern emerged in the government's policies which rudely shocked the film trade. While Raj Narain was being photographed at the *mahurats* of various films at Bombay, his erstwhile mentor Charan Singh, the then Finance Minister, imposed an exceptional levy on the number of prints that a producer took out for the release of a new film. While the first twelve prints were levy-free, additional numbers of prints were subject to a 15 per cent surcharge.

Then, after 1980, the film industry received yet another jolt. Though the majority of the film people in Bombay had supported the Congress in the 1980 Lok Sabha elections, within a couple of years the new government imposed a fresh levy on the film business. The levy on film prints was again raised, inspired by the measure Charan Singh had initiated during his tenure at the Finance Ministry. While the surcharge was not raised, for every additional lot of twelve film prints there was an increased levy per print for a big-budget film, requiring a minimum of sixty prints, reached a ceiling of Rs 15,000.

In effect, this doubled the cost of each print for the distributor, onto whom the producer shifted the burden. As a result, film distribution found itself confronted with an odd economic situation— levies and taxes had raised the basic cost of film production along with a price escalation in all commodities and services used in film production; entertainment tax rates kept rising; theatre rentals rose continuously; and the audience began to shrink because of rising ticket prices, the general rise in the daily price index, and the alternative possibilities of watching feature films on TV or video.

Consequently, the film-distribution network outside Bombay simply collapsed. The old distributors shut up shop, preferring to stick to films they had bought previously. Though films continued to be produced in Bombay, there was difficulty in releasing them through the old distribution system. Film producers operating on medium or small budgets therefore found it incumbent to release their films on a commission basis to the distributors for organizing the marketing of the film, instead of selling the distribution rights to a wholesaler (the film distributor) in different parts of the country. But for this new system, half the Hindi films released in 1986 would not have come to the theatres.

Also, it was apparent that the boom of the 1970s was over. There were no guarantees that a big star line-up would ensure a viable box-office return. One after another, in the 1980s, distribution offices found that releasing 'prestigious' ventures was setting them back anywhere between Rs 10 and 20 lakh. The impact of the escalated costs and, therefore, of the shrinking market can best be seen through the plight of producer G.P. Sippy's *Shaan*. G.P. Sippy followed up *Sholay*, the most profitable film of the 1970s, with an even more expensive movie in *Shaan*. Ironically, however, *Shaan* found no distributors willing to buy its distribution rights and Sippy was forced to release the film in several parts of the country at his own risk.

Interestingly, while film distribution came to a virtual standstill, film production carried on blissfully. Since most of the big film producers were able to willy nilly release their films, the smaller fry kept having illusions of economic viability round the next bend. A lot of 'new money' came into film production during the 1980s and enabled film production to proliferate. The Indian film business has a long history of surviving on fresh blood. That is to say, the circle of investors in the movie business keeps changing at a less perceptible level. The economics of this process is simple.

Films, along with hoteliering, are a business where black-money investments can be made while the profits accrue largely in white money. To simplify the picture, let us take the illustration of a dozen persons working in non-film-related businesses or professions. If these gentlemen have black-money incomes in their respective (non-film) fields of activity, they would naturally like to invest their black-money capital, if that were possible.

Let us say that these dozen businessmen come into contact with a film financier who can provide an avenue for investment, and they deposit a total of Rs 36 lakh with him as investment. The film financier will promise them interest (in black money) on their investment and seek to invest their money in a project under his fiscal control. He will approach a producer he can trust and offer to invest Rs 36 lakh in black money and a certain amount in white. Between them, the producer and the film financier may manage a given sum of money in black and in white. This becomes the capital on which the film can be made.

Now since the investment of capital in film-making is required at periodic intervals, the traditional method was to find a distributor on each of the five and a half domestic circuits and the overseas circuit, who'd offer to buy the film, making the major share of his payment in white money.

The distributor himself is the focal point of a new investment circle. In his city or region, he attracts a business group to become his partners in the purchase of distribution rights. Once ready, financially, he pays the producer in instalments, making the last, major payment at the time that the film prints are delivered to him.

Traditionally, this entire process was conducted mainly on the basis of trust. The distributor had no clue, when he bought the film rights, about the kind of movie he was gambling on. He banked on the producer or the financier's past record and on the marketability of the star cast and the rest of the unit, especially the music director and the director, as the basis to finance and market the film. The hiring of theatres was the distributor's responsibility, though the total publicity expenses were to be shared between the producer and the distributors.

The sum total of the producer's contract with the distributor helps launder the black money invested in film production. The film financier and the producer very conveniently insist on making black-money payments (at least upto of 50 per cent) to the film stars and the lesser artistes and, in other percentage proportions to the technicians, members of the film crew, and other production staff.

In the budget of costs presented by the producer to the distributor, black money investment is laundered cleverly—generally through false bills submitted by various small businessmen who supply goods and commodities required for production and publicity. This laundering of accounts is crucial and a person who can understand this can easily produce a film in Bombay if he knows a couple of stars and has money of his own.

The trick is to ensure that the profits on the film are all in white money. That is, they are made white by the sale of tickets at the box office, each ticket being serialized and registered and accounted for by the entertainment tax departments of the district. In other words, while a combined investment of black and white monies is made to produce a film, the profits are absolutely clean money.

Since the motion picture business is one of the few businesses in the Indian economy that can help convert black-money investments into white-money profits, despite the oscillating graph of financial crises that have bedevilled film-makers, businessmen with black-money resources in other sectors of the economy have always felt tempted to make an investment in cinema. And these, to be frank, include politician businessmen too in small measure.

Therefore, though the distribution network of Hindi films had become completely crippled by 1985, since the shrinking market made it unprofitable for businessmen to gamble their money in film distribution, film production carried on smoothly, thanks largely to the 'new money' that kept coming in. For the new investors the most interesting part of the business was that once the deal came through, when the film was released it was for other people to worry about the black money the financiers had invested—the film stars, playback singers, music directors, character artistes, technicians, junior artistes, commodity suppliers, and so on. As a matter of fact, film stars are saddled with black money and it is their headache how they handle it. This is why we have seen over the years that the income-tax department's list of defaulters has more film stars than producers.

The magic world, however, was threatened, as never before, by the proposed sales tax that the Maharashtra government wanted to impose. The financiers and producers baulked at the threat. Film-making, for all its nefarious jugglery of accounts, could no longer survive with increased taxes. Both businessmen and film professionals, who are 'victims' of the black-money economy in cinema, came together because the proposed sales tax was not going to cleanse the industry. It was simply an additional levy on film-making itself. A levy that the trade honestly cannot afford to be saddled with at this juncture in its history.

Moreover, as film people never tire of saying, the total turnover of black money in the film industry (which is said to have an overall turnover of around Rs 800 crore) is so small in comparison to the turnover of most other industries and trades in the Indian economy, that to single out the film industry as harbouring the evil of black money, or as a target for additional revenues, is to completely miss the point.

Fiscally, this comparatively small industry is expected to produce a proportionately large ratio of revenue for the state governments, while the bigger fish are left largely untouched.

Link, 4 January 1987. This magazine has since ceased publication.

* * *

Young Film-makers Strike Gold

The rise of a new cinema made with little money and plenty of enthusiasm came about because of the repeated failure of big budget films at the box office. The signs of a new cinema emerging from the debris of the old one have been examined in some depth.

The impossible seems to be happening at the box-office window of the great Indian film bazaar. Finally, after a series of false starts over three decades, the gun-and-tears cinema has made room for another kind of film which is not a potpourri of the Ram Lila and the Mahabharata, fantasies and aberrations, big stars and clichés.

This could well be the year of the new cinema's box-office debut, of a quiet revolution in popular taste that has begun to open the eyes of film distributors and financiers living in their plush, air-conditioned cocoons. The average Indian filmgoer is bringing about a radical upheaval in the nature of his celluloid entertainment. The new cinema has already taken root in the metropolitan centres and big cities and it is only a matter of time before the influence of the big city begins to seep through to smaller towns and provincial outposts. It is perhaps a natural process of the history of modern India. Two decades ago the terylene bush shirt, the transistor radio, the ballpoint pen reached out into rural India; now they are entrenched. They could well be the forerunners of the new cinema in the countryside. Rural culture is getting imitative of city culture. Now that the cinema of *Aakrosh* and *Albert Pinto ko Gussa Kyon Aata Hai* has finally established itself in the big cities, it is perhaps only a question of time before it seeps onto and into the whole canvas..

This is not to say that the formula film is ageing or is suffering from poor health. On the contrary, the amazing box-office draw of Manoj Kumar's *Kranti* should make the lovers of the new cinema more cautious in their optimism about the pace of change. Indeed, there are people like Shabana Azmi, Shashi Kapoor, and Gulzar, who have a foot in both the art film and the commercial film camps, who feel that the trend is not changing at all. For Shabana the success of the new films is no more than an irritant for the commercial filmwallas—'They can just flick it off; moneywise, these films are not in the same bracket.'

However, there is more to it than money. The new films—made on small, reasonable budgets, without big star casts and by directors for whom a film is not simply a money-making proposition—involve us in issues about the future of both Indian cinema and Indian society. They raise questions about the kind of films that are going to be popular in the days ahead.

Shaan, for instance, may eventually manage to recover its colossal investment (said to be around Rs 5 crore) but surely it is not going to win the kind of plaudits that Govind Nihalani's *Aakrosh* has won from common filmgoers in the big-city audience. *Kranti* may well churn out a profit of Rs 10 crore. But it is unlikely that Manoj Kumar's blockbuster will trigger off the kind of cultural explosion that Saeed Mirza's *Albert Pinto ko Gussa Kyon Aata Hai* has in Bombay, where advertisement hoardings and newspaper columns are taking off on the catchy title of Mirza's film. In early February, the popular afternoon daily *Mid-Day* was inspired to advertise one of its forthcoming columns with the caption *Shobha Khilachand ko Gussa Kyon Aata Hai*. The same week, B.K. Karanjia, editor of *Screen*, the popular film weekly, wrote a front-page editorial titled *Filmi Logon ko Gussa Kyon Aata Hai*. Within a couple of weeks after its release at Bombay and Calcutta, in mid-January, the title of Saeed Mirza's film had attained remarkable distinction. It has entered the language, become an integral part of the slangy, colloquial cultural idiom that had hitherto been influenced only by the big-budget spectacles of the commercial industry, films like *Sholay*, *Bobby*, and *Amar Akbar Anthony*.

And to think that Saeed Mirza, as recently as in the middle of 1980, could not sell the film to a distributor in Bombay! *Albert Pinto* was completed by July 1980, and producer-director Saeed Mirza began showing it to distributors at 'trial' shows from August. He held as many as forty 'trials' up to December and could only manage to sell the film to two and a quarter circuits—east India (comprising West Bengal, Bihar, Assam, Orissa, and the north-east), Delhi-UP, and one of the three sub-circuits in south India. For the Bombay circuit, Mirza had negotiated the sale of the distribution rights but the distributor backed out when it came to signing the agreement contract. He said that he wanted to pay Rs 10,000 less than the amount they had agreed on earlier.

If Bombay businessmen were still sceptical about the revolution in public taste, there were other people who were not. Film producer and distributor Dhiresh Chakravarty, who has produced Mrinal Sen's award-winning *Aakaler Sandhaney*, has not only bought the distribution rights for the east India circuit, he will also be producing Saeed's new film, tentatively titled *Five Star Hotel*, which they will shoot in 1981. For the Delhi-UP circuit, traditionally regarded as one least favourable to films without the usual formulas and *masala*, the sale of *Albert Pinto* happened 'in very strange circumstances,' according to Mirza. The distributor saw a few reels while the film was being dubbed—that is when the soundtrack was being married to the visual track—and decided immediately that he would buy the film for Delhi-UP. This enabled Mirza to think of distributing the film on his own in the Bombay circuit. Having taken a loan from the National Film Development Corporation (NFDC) to produce *Albert Pinto*, Saeed took the risk of asking for an additional loan of Rs 75,000 to distribute the film. The NFDC had already given loans of similar amounts to producer Suresh Jindal for the distribution of Satyajit Ray's *Shatranj Ke Khiladi* and producer-director Muzaffar Ali for *Gaman*. Because by 1976 the government corporation was finally persuaded to acknowledge that it must enter film distribution, too, if the films it backed were to find their way to the theatres.

With additional NFDC support, Saeed Mirza and *Albert Pinto* finally made their bow at two Bombay theatres on the same opening day that distributor Dhiresh Chakravarty released the film in Calcutta. *Albert Pinto's* start was fairly modest in Bombay. In a metropolis where big-budget films are released in fifteen to twenty theatres spread across the main city and suburbs, *Albert Pinto* found only two theatres, Gemini at Bandra and Liberty in the Grant Road area.

Gemini is presently under contract with the NFDC, which needed a theatre for its films after Lotus was demolished to make way for a high-rise on the same property. Unfortunately, the NFDC has been able to procure the Gemini theatre only at a very exorbitant price. A 200-seat capacity at Gemini gives only Rs 800 per day to the film producer if all the four shows are full. As Mirza put it, that was the main theatre available to him when he decided to release his film and he had to accept it. Now that the film has been successful, he is still wary of taking *Albert Pinto* out of the Gemini because it is houseful for days in advance. The other theatre at which Saeed Mirza premiered the film was Liberty, generally known for showing trashy films.

'We have broken the myth that a good film will run only at certain classy theatres,' explained Mirza. He had been warned by friends to stay off Liberty and wait till he could get Metro, which is not very far from Liberty. Metro has built such a reputation for showing sophisticated films that for *Junoon*, producer Shashi Kapoor waited and waited for the theatre to become available.

Getting the right theatres is key for the marketing of new films. Shashi Kapoor, on this question, shares the opinion of the commercial film industry. But things are changing so dramatically at the box-office windows in the big cities that Saeed Mirza was emboldened to take *Albert Pinto* to a 450-seat theatre in Kurla in the last week of February. He was also thinking of getting a theatre in Bombay's industrial belt north of the city.

Before *Albert Pinto* became so fashionably acceptable, its maker had cautiously predicted a four-week run for the film at Gemini and two weeks at Liberty, at the very most. Now, of course, Mirza says, 'I have no idea how long it will run in Bombay.'

What has been most helpful to the new film-makers and their movement has been the fact that their films—*Junoon, Aakrosh,* and *Albert Pinto*—have done well at a time when other Hindi films were doing badly. In 1979–80 *Junoon,* directed by Shyam Benegal and produced by Shashi Kapoor, ran in one theatre after another in each city, extending its run and holding fort at a time when the commercial Hindi film was failing. The year 1980 was disastrous for conventional Hindi cinema as one multi-starrer after another crashed, creating a vacuum at the box office which the film industry had no readymade formula to fill with.

This had two significant consequences. First, the big producers, their financiers and their distributors realized that they could not any longer bewitch the film audience just by spending a lot of money and by cramming in a number of expensive stars. The glamour of big money was seriously eroded. Second, as many distributors and producers began to realize, most of the smaller producers and distributors were facing a dead end because of big budget films. This section, which makes for a very large segment of the film industry's population, was on the point of going out of business if it could not come up with an alternative to the multistarrer.

Some of the bigger producers also contributed to the new thinking in this direction. They made small-budget films that had a different idiom and cinematic language. For example, B.R. Chopra made *Choti si Baat* with Basu Chatterji, and then made two quickies himself, *Pati Patni aur Woh* and *Insaf ka Tarazu.* Yash Chopra made *Noorie,* one of the big hits of the year, and the *Sholay* Sippys produced *Ahsaas* with newcomers and a new director. Of course, almost the first man among Bombay's movie moguls to make the best of this new possibility was Tarachand Barjatya of Rajshri Pictures. A distributor of *Sholay* and other big-budget circuit movies, he began producing and distributing his own low-cost films. Risking little in his small investments and making a tidy profit on each of his films, Barjatya did well enough to turn the minds of other big producers towards the same direction.

Along with the sheer temptation of this profitable, low-cost venture, a personal element has also been operating within the film industry, gradually making commercial film-makers less and less hostile to the so-called art film. The movie moguls have always suffered, in their hearts, from the fact that they have seldom been acknowledged as creative artists. They have seldom been winners of national film awards and nobody worth his salt has granted them any intellectual status. Over the years, as new film-makers like Shyam Benegal, Basu Chatterji, Muzaffar Ali, Govind Nihalani, and Saeed Mirza began to narrow down the gap between 'art' and box office, the better directors among the movie tycoons have begun to have second thoughts about the new cinema. According to Shashi Kapoor,

the genuine film-makers in the commercial cinema are only too glad that these new kind of films are acceptable to people. Raj Kapoor, for instance, is very happy about the new trend. I remember when we released *Junoon* in Delhi, Raj Kapoor and Shyam Benegal spent a very long night discussing things with each other. The genuine film-makers in the industry look upon these films as a strong competition that they must personally face. It is only the synthetic film-makers who howl.

Selling a small film is even more difficult than producing one. Big films are never made by the producer with his own money; the situation is exactly the reverse for the small film, which has no financiers in the market. As a result, most of the money invested in small films is either through loans from the NFDC or investments made by new producers who come into the film line with profits made in other businesses.

The search for money is always a difficult one for the directors of the new cinema. At the same time, the small film does make it easier for a businessman with a comparatively smaller sum to spare, of say five to ten lakh of rupees, to enter into film production without having to learn the knotty ropes of the regular film industry.

Producing a small film may be easy for a producer with a few lakh of rupees to spare, but selling it is extremely difficult. Most small films lie in the cans for months, and even years, before they find a distributor to release them at even one centre in the country. For instance, producer Suresh Jindal had to release his first film *Rajnigandha* on his own. It was his good fortune that the film went on to become a silver jubilee success and made Amol Palekar and Vidya Sinha stars.

Even a successful film like *Gharaonda*, which did not depart too much from the commercial film's format, was released only a long time after it was ready. According to its producer-director, Bhim Sain, it was

only after the completion of the film that I came to know the hardship that goes into selling it. It took me six months to complete *Gharaonda* and ten months to sell its distribution rights for one territory. If *Gharaonda* had not clicked in Bombay, it would not have been released anywhere else. This can be the story of any newcomer making his first film. Film-making, by itself is incomplete unless you have a total distribution and exhibition chain. Till then film-making is only half the job.

Nor, for that matter, do most film-makers make profits with their first films, even if they are quite popular with the audience. That is the price for learning the intricacies of the dubious business of 'exploiting' a film in the market. All that a new film-maker can hope for, or so it seems, is to learn on one distribution circuit and then make some money from the other circuits where the film is released after a while.

According to Bhim Sain, the commercial set-up establishes a chain of financial investments between the big producers, the big distributors, and the theatre exhibitors. Since theatre owners give advance money to the distributors of big films, and the distributors give production money to the producers while the film is being made, a financial arrangement is developed between the three sectors, and even if one film flops, there is enough of an involvement between the three to ensure that the producer and director of the flop get a chance to make another film and recoup the existing with the expected profits of the next venture. A small film producer cannot afford a flop; he gets wiped out.

Sunday, 29 March 1981.

* * *

Films and Critical Theories

The limitations of popular Indian cinema are only too well known. But even the sharpest of analysts have not been able to explain the reason for the persistence of its problems. Whether the analysis of the minds of a paying audience will unravel their real needs in terms of cinema is a core question that needs to be addressed.

During the last four years there has been a growing realization among the elite that the magic of commercial films does not evaporate at being treated with intellectual opprobrium. It is now granted that while popular Indian films may be irrelevant as films, they are relevant as pegs on which the social psyche from time to time hangs the clothes of its fantasies.

However, most critiques and analyses into 'Bombay films' display a lack of direction. The analysts hardly seem to realize that analysis should lead to more stable intellectual and critical propositions that go beyond such limited questions as why a film clicks. Their analysis is no more than an extension of the analysis game played within the film industry itself (occasionally by film fans).

It is, therefore, necessary to confront two questions that arise once the analysis game is extended outside the film industry, into journalism. First, will an analysis of the popular film lead to perceptions into the audience's mind? That is, will it lead to a greater

understanding of those sections of our society that depend emotionally and intellectually on popular cinema? Second, does
popular Hindustani cinema belong to a genre in itself? Does it have
a form that, in spite of the plagiarism, is peculiarly native to the
conditions in which the popular Hindustani film operates? Is it,
therefore, the indigenous form of the popular Hindustani film?

A serious consideration of these two questions shall be found
necessary if any in-depth analysis of popular cinema is to establish
its own relevance and provide film-makers with a sense of direction
even as the criticism acquires its own sense of direction. It would
be meaningless to conduct an analysis into popular cinema if it is
going to be simply another means of attacking it. For one thing,
the failures of popular Indian cinema are only too well known.
Not even the sharpest of analysts has been able to come up with
new points.

In one idiom or another, those who wish to uproot popular
cinema come up with the same points again and again. Second,
popular cinema is a 'desecrated cow' that thrives on desecration,
contempt irreverence, and caricature.

And this brings us to the first of the two questions mentioned
above. Popular Hindustani cinema has a message and a format that
is actually attuned to the broad masses of the people. Its films are
for them and not for narrow, bigoted classicists. To grumble, as most
recent analysts do, that the framework of popular Indian films
is stereotyped, or that there is little more than a riot of sex and
violence in popular film today, is to begin with a 'classicist'
approach on a subject that belongs to 'folklore'.

Critical analysis can serve a sociological purpose by considering
popular film not from the point of view of film-makers—as most
film critics and analysts do—but from that of the people. It is only
too easy to say that a popular Hindustani film is atrocious because
of its contrast with a popular foreign film. Western film-makers and
critics have built up a tremendous academic body, which is very
useful for attacks on films that are not made in the Western tradition.

What is not so easy is to try and find the connections between films and the collective psyche of their audience and, simultaneously, to accept the premise that the people are their best judges. This leads us to the second question. If the people are able to relate popular films and elements in them with their lives, their dreams, their problems, their solutions, their fantasies, and their sense of their future, a sociological analysis of the films is bound to lead to an analysis of the form and structure of popular Hindustani films, primarily within the context of the tradition of popular films here and abroad and secondarily in the context of the classicist aesthetics of cinema.

This, in turn, should lead to a realization that, despite the eclecticism and the plagiarism, popular Hindustani films are made in a peculiar genre that derives from other genres but which is, ultimately, an entity in itself. A critical assessment of this genre will give, in the first instance, the intellectual self-awareness that the makers of popular Hindustani films do not adequately have. This will give serious Indian film-makers source material for study and for drastic modification, so that they may be able to extricate their own work from the confines of the European and American tradition, and make films that communicate, with a sense of urgency, with the broad masses of the Indian people and that are stylistical originally also.

This is not as far-fetched as the Indian cineaste has been brainwashed to believe. After all, both Jean-Luc Godard and Francois Truffaut are on record saying that many of their innovations were inspired by B-grade stunt films from Hollywood. Moreover, the New Wave in Italy, France, Poland, Czechoslovakia, and elsewhere grew because serious film-makers gave their audiences the films the audience, wanted and not, as in India, New Wave films thrust on the people without any faith in the people's judgement.

Everyman's, *published early-1970s. This magazine has since ceased publication.*

* * *

Between Fact and a Film-maker's Intention

Film buffs often analyse a film-maker's intentions rather than what he has actually achieved. This needs to be changed and the critical approach must focus more on the outcome than on the intention.

One particular reason can, perhaps, be singled out for our intellectuals' habit of confusing the aesthetics of the cinema with its intrinsic quality as medium. The intellectual sets greater store by the intentions of the film-maker, overlooking the craft of film-making. The loftier the intentions, this reasoning goes, the more deserving it is of serious consideration.

No wonder, thus, that most of our critical discussion on the cinema is in terms of the film-makers and not of films. It is easy—and falsely elevating—to evaluate cinema in the European intellectual tradition. From this tradition we, as have other societies, borrowed the critical premise of the 'auteur (author) theory', that the director of a film should be evaluated like a literary author.

While there is no denying that the auteur theory is one established approach for critical appraisal, what has happened in contemporary Indian criticism is that we have forgotten our very fluid Indian situation and the absence of powerful creative personalities in the world of contemporary Indian art. It is not a world that calls for evaluation in terms of an individual's work over the years. It calls for an insightful understanding of various works indicating a certain direction in terms of our social process.

What happens in critical debates about both commercial and non-commercial fillm-makers, is that the critics look superficially at the films, harbouring too many preconceptions about the artistic endeavour they represent, rather than what they have actually achieved.

The audience, however, doesn't think in critical terms. It gives no latitude, as an academic study may, to a film-maker with respectable intentions. It insists that the first criterion of a film—

which it shares with journalism—be maintained, that it make an immediate impact, no matter what its subject or social relevance. That is also why it is simplistic to say that a film is essentially visual; for there are films whose impact is totally through its arguments or dialogues. It is equally simplistic to castigate a film merely because it has songs and dances.

The film is an extremely complex and dynamic form of expression. And because the production of a single film involves far greater organization and sustenance of creativity over a far longer period of time than any other work, in all honesty we should evaluate a film only by the end product that emerges on the screen. Anything can go wrong, from the original spark of an idea for a film to its final editing, showing the limitations of a film-maker.

There is another argument for not accepting the auteur theory. Most Indian film-makers rely heavily on their team and to attribute all the credit to particular individuals rather than to the team as a whole would be to invest them with false glamour. This is equally true of the intellectual Indian film-maker. Though Satyajit Ray seems the lone exception to this rule, there are arguments that tend to include him also in it. For when Ray makes a film on a less cohesive script—as in *Sonar Kella* or *Jana Aranya*—the total quality of his film slips sharply from that of his best films.

All these thoughts come to mind as one compares two recent Hindi films—Hrishikesh Mukherjee's *Kotwal Saab* and Mohan Segal's *Ek Hi Raasta*. Given Hrishikesh Mukherjee's image as an offbeat commercial film-maker and Mohan Segal's reputation as an out and out commercial producer-director, we are surprised to find that on a very basic level Hrishikesh Mukherjee, for all the respectable intentions behind *Kotwal Saab*, is highly insincere to the cinematic medium. On the other hand, through the glamorous songs and dances, the sensational twists in the not very deep moral drama, and the obvious emotionalism of the basic conflict in the film, Mohan Segal's *Ek Hi Raasta* is far more genuine stuff. The limitations arising from its box-office orientation and its focus on the common audience get neutralized. Despite the cabaret-style dances of the typical Hindi film with which Mohan Segal crams the first half of the film or the predictable storyline or transparent characterizations, the totality of Ek Hi Raasta is closer to the soul of cinema. Cunning and wit, the sense of a visual and narrative rhythm from sequence to sequence, the construction of a particular effect, and the sensibility of cinema as a whole—the film is loyal to all these.

It is only in India that decade after decade criticism of popular elements of commercial cinema holds that a sexy dance or slapstick comedy is beneath cinema. In Europe and America the fact that even very sensationalist or seemingly superficial popular films can and do touch the soul of film as a medium is recognized only too well now. But we in India are still thirty years behind that very scholarly American poet-novelist and film critic Parker Tyler (whose film criticism is much more original than the Indian intellectual's favourite, James Agee who was a fad among American intellectuals thirty years ago). Tyler was the first to dissect the popular fantasy film in terms of its sociological and psychological relevance. He saw behind the glamorous facades of the dream factory film to the structural endeavour of the film-makers.

Mohan Segal is one of our slickest directors when it comes to song-and-dance picturizations, though critics have not for some reason given him credit for this. He is also extremely competent in Ek Hi Raasta with the old style of film-making—telling a story through characters rather than through visual images and symbols. He blends these two virtues in Ek Hi Raasta, giving it both an extremely racy and sensational structure and at the same time extracting very competent performances from all the members of his cast. He makes Jeetendra, Asha Sachdev, and Vinod Mehra perform much more impressively than they do otherwise, uses accomplished character artistes like Om Shivpuri, Jagdeep, and Indrani Rehman to the best cinematic impact, and gets very fine performances from Utpal Dutt and Shabana Azmi, the two really talented artistes in the cast.

I don't think Utpal Dutt has used his wide range and control over the actor's craft as cleverly in any other Hindi film as he does in *Ek Hi Raasta*—a performance that one should compare with the best of Sanjeev Kumar's. Similarly, Shabana provides a much more powerful image of the sacrificing woman than Raakhee did in *Tapasya*, with which *Ek Hi Raasta* shares something in approach and in totality of impact. Shabana's performance matches the best she has done yet—in *Ankur* and *Nishant*.

The striking quality of Mohan Segal's conception of the film is that he has gone in for the emotional catharsis that can be had from conflict in human life rather than the more conventional cinematic way of depicting a cathartic experience from tragedy or near-tragedy. In this, Mohan Segal's direction and editing and the acting of his cast are well served by Nabendu Ghosh's screenplay.

The only real flaw in the film is that the process of drama that leads to its conclusion—Jeetendra's return from his second wife to his first—ought to have been more original in conception. But then if that were so, *Ek Hi Raasta* would not have been essentially a box-office film. It would have been outside the purview of Mohan Segal's ambition to make a commercial film more intelligently, sophisticatedly, and movingly, no matter how great a sense of film structure his film might contain.

Hrishikesh Mukherjee's *Kotwal Saab*, on the other hand, emerges as a thoroughly confused film though it has the good intentions of being a clean entertainer with a serious note. The confusion is mainly because the film constantly raises expectations which the film-maker too cleverly tries to avoid satisfying. It is also a very verbal film, though Shatrughan Sinha and Aparna Sen, who play the lead roles, are impressive. But the director and scriptwriter (Dr Rahi Masoom Raza) are so confused in their intention that they realize very little of the film's potential.

The Fortnight, *published mid-1970s. This magazine has since ceased publication.*

* * *

The Glorification of Bhagat Singh

A passionately-argued piece on The Legend of Bhagat Singh *directed by Raj Kumar Santoshi. Santoshi's dismissal of Gandhi as an ineffectual leader in comparison to Bhagat Singh lacks conviction. The film offers no arguments to justify this belief, especially with several historians insisting that the twenty-four-year-old revolutionary Bhagat Singh's hanging in 1931 could not have been averted even if Gandhi had interceded on his behalf with the British.*

Even as time marches on, there is an air of intellectual stasis in our analysis and assessment of several critical questions pertaining to India's freedom movement. The differences between Gandhi and Netaji Subhas Chandra Bose, Gandhi and Bhagat Singh, Gandhi and Veer Savarkar, Gandhi and Babasaheb Ambedkar have only now begun to be discussed outside academic cloisters and political seminars.

Thanks to the series of feature films that have now been made on protagonists critical of the leadership of Mohandas Karamchand Gandhi, we have begun to return to these historical questions in a broader area of debate than in the past fifty years.

Yet this is only the beginning of the re-evaluation of personalities and issues. Consequently, the arguments put forth on behalf of protagonists such as Bhagat Singh, Veer Savarkar, and Dr Ambedkar, and against M.K. Gandhi, are still imbued with the political folklore of the first half of the twentieth century.

The contempt with which Raj Kumar Santoshi's film *The Legend of Bhagat Singh* dismisses Gandhi—as a weak, ineffectual leader—is an attitude that has been maintained by Gandhi's critics ever since he took over leadership of the freedom movement led by the Congress. Over the last seventy-five years, Gandhi has been derided by the Communists, by Veer Savarkar and the Hindu Mahasabha, by the RSS and the Jana Sangh, by armed revolutionaries such as Bhagat Singh, and by certain Dalit ideologues. As late as 1970, the Marxist film-maker Ritwik Ghatak described him as a '*suarr ka bachha'*. Raj Kumar Santoshi is not, therefore, being particularly courageous in his denunciation!

Gandhi aroused these fulminations for two reasons. First, he believed that only a long, protracted struggle that was an 'unarmed' political protest could overthrow the British India government. His politics was the politics of a centrist and so attracted the condemnation of all those who believed in extremist and militant politics.

Second, Gandhi refused to offer lip-sympathy to peers who disagreed with his political strategy. He was perhaps as bluntly honest as any extremist leader—a quality not generally appreciated in a centrist politician by educated Indians, who prefer that the right noises are made publicly, even if hypocritical.

Fifty-four years after Gandhi's death, fifty-four years after urban Indian society turned its back on Gandhi's ideas of economic development in village India, a half century after we dumped his concept of public morality and simple living, Gandhi's critics have kept Gandhi alive as a man, political leader, and social commentator. Ironically, this is something that Gandhians and Gandhites were reluctant to undertake after 1948, except when it was politically expedient for them.

Santoshi's film *The Legend of Bhagat Singh* blames Gandhi for not saving Bhagat Singh, Sukhdev, and Rajguru from death by hanging. The film categorically states that if Gandhi had not signed the Gandhi–Irwin Pact of 1931, the British India government would not have carried out the death sentence against the three great revolutionaries. However, it offers no arguments to justify this belief. Nor does it offer any reason to show us why Gandhi did not move heaven and earth to prevent these executions.

The Legend of Bhagat Singh tells us that Bhagat Singh was consistently derisive of Gandhi's political beliefs and strategies. Indeed, as far as the revolutionaries of the Hindustan Socialist Republican Association (HSRA) were concerned, Gandhi's *satyagraha*s and non-violent protest would never win Mother India its freedom from British rule.

Santoshi's film also declares that in the opinion of the HSRA revolutionaries, the freedom struggle led by Gandhi was little more than a 'stooge' movement, a placatory device suiting to the British Indian government. Yet Santoshi's film complains Gandhi did not do enough to save Bhagat Singh's life. Is that logical? If Gandhi and the movement he led were but convenient devices for the British rulers, would the British India government have set aside the three death sentences at the behest of its own political stooge?

The emotionalism of Santoshi's film is understandable. It is a mere reflection of many common Indian's 'folklore' that Gandhi could have 'saved' Bhagat Singh if he had wanted to. This is presuming that there was nothing that Gandhi could not achieve; which again is illogical.

Film-maker Santoshi has done a disservice to the historical re-evaluation of the Gandhi–Bhagat Singh difference of opinion by simplistically projecting Gandhi as a convenient stooge of British India. Evidently, Santoshi has not read enough historical data in this connection. He seems ignorant of the fact that many a critic of Gandhi was supported in oblique ways by the British India government to be publicly critical of Gandhi.

The more important question is whether Bhagat Singh and the HSRA revolutionaries were correct in believing that only an armed revolution could free India or whether this was merely a passionate belief held by young revolutionaries? The facts are that the First War of Freedom in 1857, led by Jhansi Ki Rani, Tantia Tope, and others, was crushed by the East India Company; and armed revolts in various parts of the country were repeatedly put down by the British. After 1947, the communist armed struggle in Telengana did not succeed either. The insurgencies in Nagaland and the north-east have not won the secessionists the 'independence' they sought. Nor have General Musharraf's 'freedom fighters' made substantial headway towards their goal of '*azadi*' in Jammu and Kashmir.

Modern Indian history is replete with armed revolts that failed. It is simplistic, therefore, to believe that if Bhagat Singh had not been hanged by the British rulers, he would have been proved right in believing that only an armed revolt could have won India its freedom.

www.chowk.com, 2004.

* * *

Three Films about Gandhi

A critique of three films made about Mahatma Gandhi in the last decade. The most nuanced portrait of Gandhi to emerge on the film screen is an indirect one, in a film on the great Dalit leader B.R. Ambedkar, directed by Jabbar Patel. Richard Attenborough's Gandhi proffers a heroic Gandhi and Kamal Haasan's Hey Ram shows Gandhi only as a concept rather than as the dynamic man he really was.

Three recent films in India have attempted a reconsideration and review of the personality of Mohandas Karamchand Gandhi— Jabbar Patel's *Dr Balasaheb Ambedkar* which has been running in theatres across India in 2001; Shyam Benegal's *The Making of the Mahatma*, an Indo-South African co-production of a couple of years earlier; and Kamal Haasan's *Hey Ram* which has been the focus of media attention for well over a year now.

Not just in contemporary Indian cinema but across the intellectual landscape of the country (if not the subcontinent), there seems to be a compulsion to come to grips with the political profile of an enigmatic man whose memory, some fifty years after his death, still seems to haunt the Indian intellect.

Perhaps the fourth and final draft of Sir Richard Attenborough and John Briley's script for the big-budget, Oscar-winning *Gandhi* (1982) was the opening of the floodgates. Attenborough descended out of the blue as it were in 1979–80 upon an India which had by then almost forgotten M.K. Gandhi, though official doles and stipends were still being regularly collected by a mute but populous tribe of so-called Gandhites. And on the other side of the ideological fence, a hostility to Gandhi's supposedly soft stance towards Muslims (and Pakistan) still rankled in the heart of traditionalist Hindu ideologues.

It took close to twenty years after the international success of the Attenborough *Gandhi* before serious Indian film-makers could muster the pecuniary nerve to bring to celluloid some of their own perceptions about the man who had dominated the freedom struggle, whom the Indian political establishment then treated as a mythic figure who ought to remain above for critical review.

Indian film financiers and entrepreneurs were no doubt hesitant to invest in a subject which, in real terms, they felt was probably not within the scope of our film-makers. The Hindi version of the Attenborough *Gandhi* had a contorted, un-colloquial translation of the film's original dialogues and much of it was so abstruse as to quite escape the intelligence of those who went to see the dubbed Hindi version. The film did not have impressive grosses and this must have frightened off any thoughts about a fresh venture concerning M.K. Gandhi.

Not surprisingly, of the three recent films in which Gandhi's historical personality features, only one, Shyam Benegal's *The Making of the Mahatma*, relates primarily to Gandhi. Both Jabbar Patel's *Dr Balasaheb Ambedkar* and Kamal Haasan's *Hey Ram* focus on other aspects and personalities of recent Indian history. They touch upon Gandhi obliquely, on the sidelines of their primary subject.

In my opinion, as one individual filmgoer, perhaps the one that most effectively states its point of view on Gandhi is *Dr Balasaheb Ambedkar*. Gandhi figures briefly in the film, in the context of Dr Ambedkar's meetings with him and in the brief comment Amebdkar makes about Gandhi. As a bio-pic on the great Dalit intellectual and leader, Jabbar Patel's film has the commendable cinematic merit of brilliant simplicity. It sets out to lucidly re-enact the life story of Dr Ambedkar with a plausible ring of authenticity.

The history of the man's life and thoughts and his political activities is retold with conceptual finesse, dramatic alertness, detailed and impressive production values, and marvellous portraitures by Mammooty (as Dr Ambedkar) and other members of the cast.

First-rate research on the subject and a finely tuned script by Sooni Taraporewala, Arun Sadhu, and other subject consultants enabled the director—along with his team of production advisers and consultants (including Shyam Benegal) and his lead players— to tell the story of Dr Ambedkar's life with some of the power of the man's own journey from a humble origin to his emergence as a national leader of substance and considerable achievement.

The sweep of the film's precisely structured narrative is complemented in terms of its cinematic drama by the fact that for most members of India's intelligentsia, the film also brings home unknown aspects of the history of our freedom struggle. It thus unveils aspects of events and people of which many of us were ignorant heretofore.

Dr Ambedkar's and Gandhi's conflict, their world views and political strategies, come across in the film as pitting two powerful, evenly matched public personalities representing diverse political forces against each other. It is for historians to evaluate the authenticity of this brief but meaningful confrontation between the two Indian leaders; but as a filmgoer one may say that there were shades to Gandhi's personality which we were generally not aware of till this film came to us.

The most telling lines in the film come from Gandhi himself, when he irascibly asks his aides, after his first encounter with Dr Ambedkar, 'Why didn't somebody tell me that Ambedkar is a Dalit?' It is a line in the script which opens much up to speculation— How would Gandhi have handled Ambedkar in that first meeting if he had known better his visitor's social identity? Then we have Ambedkar's ambiguous reaction on being told of Gandhi's death—revealing Ambedkar's instinctive realization that with the death of Gandhi, he, Ambedkar, had lost the one upper caste Hindu leader with whom he could have argued in the hope of persuading him to concede his own point of view: Gandhi had the courage no other upper caste Indian leader had, of taking a stand when convinced against mainstream opinion.

On the other hand, Kamal Haasan's film *Hey Ram* would, in my opinion, have been more cohesive if Kamal, as its scriptwriter, had wholly avoided bringing in Gandhi as a character in the film. Kamal Haasan's Gandhi is extremely one-dimensional, though the script intends its Gandhi figure to provoke the climatic turnabout in its protagonist, Saket Ram, the would-be assassin, who is intellectually overwhelmed by the sheer presence of his potential target.

Hey Ram would have stood out as a coherent statement and a dramatically integrated film if it had limited itself to the transmutation of an educated, Westernized archaeologist into a person haunted by a personal tragedy and sucked therefore into the vortex of revenge. There are sequences in the film that are outstanding in the repository of Indian political cinema. There is the depiction of the communal riot in Kolkata during which Saket Ram's first wife (played by Rani Mukherjee) is massacred, of Saket Ram's encounter and continuing dialogue with his new mentor, and his disturbing, tortuous transition into a would-be assassin.

Regrettably, this, the longer and predominant content of the film is set against a fleeting and rather inexplicable turnaround which is supposedly set off by the narrative device of the Gandhi figure. But why does Gandhi—or, rather the concept of Gandhi held in 1948 by the majority of the Indian people—prevail upon Saket Ram at the ostensible climax of his mission? This is a question that the film raises but does not analyse or answer. In terms of narrative drama, for over two hours the film's protagonist moves convincingly down the anti-Gandhi path. Then suddenly a generalization about the Gandhi of 1948 is thrown in and this is to be accepted as the pivot for the narrative's miraculous catharsis.

Kamal Haasan's *Hey Ram* ought to have eschewed the Gandhi character altogether, in my opinion. Or it should have developed the Gandhi characterization with the fullness which would justify why one of Gandhi's would-be assassins turned finally into an obsequious clone of the man he wanted to gun down. Kamal Haasan is unable to do any better than prop up a clichéd Gandhi as defined by jaded Gandhites. That, as modern Indian historians attest, and as Sir Richard Attenborough and John Briley's script so clearly delineates, was not the Gandhi who could inspire the greater number of the Indian masses participating in the freedom struggle. The Gandhi of the effete Gandhites, and of Kamal Haasan's script, could not have been the man capable of heading the freedom movement! Kamal Haasan's screenplay uses some of Gandhi's political statements in isolation, without being able to elaborate or suggest Gandhi's motives or the thought processes involved in the taking up of his political stances during that frenzied era of the subcontinent's Partition and its Independence.

In the post-Gandhi era, Gandhites have refused to analytically explain Gandhi's concepts and public stances and Kamal Haasan's screenplay errs in not being one better than them, seeking out its own comprehension of the man. In twentieth-century Indian history, Gandhi was too important a political personality to be represented sweepingly by a cliché in a film focusing largely on his intellectual opponents.

Shyam Benegal's *The Making of the Mahatma* has the merit of being the first public endeavour to scrutinize the complex, often antagonistic relations between Mohandas Karamchand and his eldest son, as well as to dwell on the all too human differences that occasionally erupted in the course of their marriage, between Gandhi and Kasturba.

The quintessence of Benegal's film, its subject, was and is extremely relevant to the contemporary Indian scene. Not just because it demystifies the personality of a man who has all too often been the victim of pseudo-intellectual deification by Gandhites but also because in contemporary Indian society the theme of antagonism between a public figure and his progeny is in itself a theme of import and relevance. It is a social phenomenon which we need to understand for our own reasons, too.

Unfortunately, as has happened with some other Benegal films in recent times, *The Making of the Mahatma* does not quite achieve the dramatic impact it intends to. We are therefore left with only a partial and not wholly convincing denouement of the whys and wherefores of the very human conflict within the family of a public person, who is lauded by his followers in the outside world as an idealistic figure.

For what the opinion of a little man is worth, I would say that there will be other times and other films, when we may perhaps arrive at a fuller, more credible comprehension of what made Mohandas Karamchand Gandhi.

www.chowk.com, 2004.

* * *

What Went Wrong with Bhansali's *Devdas*?

A level-headed criticism of Sanjay Leela Bhansali's screen version of Devdas *based on the novel written by Sarat Chandra Chatterjee in 1915. The piece was written days after the film's release and reveals doubts about it ever becoming a popular success. The doubts were unfounded.* Devdas *did roaring business despite its dodgy aesthetics.*

There is an axiom of literary criticism, expounded by the American scholar Yvon Winters, that should be posted at every film school in the world. Winters insisted that all poetry should make sense in terms of the living experience; even a poem written by T.S. Eliot or Gerald Manley Hopkins.

Since the serious Indian film-maker always aspires to create 'poetry on celluloid', it is imperative that Yvon Winter's advice be brought into reckoning in all Indian film-production companies and film schools. For they do aspire to take cinema beyond the boundaries of storytelling into the realm of poetry.

Sanjay Leela Bhansali's interpretation of Sarat Chandra's *Devdas* too thus emanates from his obvious desire to transform the novel into a cinematic narrative poem. Yet, as so often happens in Indian cinema when the director aims to create 'a poem on celluloid', the basic premises of aesthetic communication become blurred.

Understandably, Bhansali's *Devdas* also has several precedents within the commercial cinema itself. The most notable and famous of these is Guru Dutt's *Kaagaz ke Phool*. Waheeda Rehman was to say, in the course of an interview in the mid-1980s, that Guru Dutt and his team knew, before the film's theatrical release, that *Kaagaz ke Phool* was not going to do well at the box office because it had become 'overtechnical'.

Nobody can deny a director as gifted as Sanjay Leela Bhansali the right to interpret or reinterpret a novel. The best film and theatre productions of great novels and plays are the ones that offer their own interpretation of the writer's work. Just as Shakespeare's plays have been reinterpreted by stage and film directors down the ages, great novels too tend to gain from the creativity of film directors who have the courage to appropriately adapt the novel for the film medium. One has only to compare the engaging Hollywood production of Leo Tolstoy's *War and Peace*, starring Audrey Hepburn and Mel Ferrer, with the ponderous, unendurable Sovexportfilm production of the same novel to immediately concede the right of interpretation to a director.

What Bhansali attempts in *Devdas* is not an interpretation of Sarat Chandra's novel, but a transcreation of the novel into a 'pure film', which Indian film intellectuals believe is something that is closer to poetry than to storytelling. However, Indian notions about what constitutes poetry, inclusive of 'poetry on celluloid', are wholly misplaced and misdirected. Most of our film directors and actors believe that poetry is mood, ambiguity, and an extreme of emotion. They are unaware that since the mid-twentieth century, poetry is being defined by such precepts as Ezra Pound's that 'poetry is written with brains' not emotions and T.S. Eliot's exposition of 'the idea as a sensation'. Nor are they aware of Albert Camus's recommendation to the modern artist that it is a requirement of the times that the artist articulate the most complex of ideas in the simplest of ways.

What almost invariably happens when an Indian film director wants to create 'poetry on celluloid' is that he wishes to make every single moment in his film a great moment—of high emotion, grand gestures, extraordinary feelings—hoping to convey thereby that every single strand of life in the film is nothing short of the exceptional and the incomparable. This level of intensity creates its own one-dimensionality; a monotony that, within half an hour of the film's opening, destroys the dramatic rhythm that is so essential in both literature and the performing arts for the creation of dramatic surprise.

The desire to make every split second in a film a great moment in itself tends to become something that is as bland and non-dramatic as the eulogies we hear at public functions commemorating the great on winning an award or on their seventy-fifth birthday.

One has to go back again to the counsel of the world's most influential poet-critic of the last hundred years, T.S. Eliot, for the secret of what creativity is all about. Poetry, said Eliot, 'transcends from the ridiculous to the sublime'. That is, from the commonplace it rises up to the sublime thanks to the imagination of the poet.

The great films, even the popular classics, instinctively follow Eliot's recommendation. In its essence cinema is a medium that incorporates the simplicity of everyday life within the cinematic masterpiece—the way a person walks and sits, moves his hands about, nods his head, shrugs his shoulder, speaks and laughs, turns sad, listens to another, etc. It is against the backdrop of the simple, everydayness of human behaviour that a great film sets its dramatic surprises, narrative twists, and its heart-wrenching moments.

These controlled pendulum-like swings of moods between the ordinary and the extraordinary are what give a film its dramatic rhythm and imbue with a three-dimensional depth, its emotional content. But if a film-maker ignores this juxtaposition of the commonplace with the exceptional and focuses every second of the edited film only on the grandiose and the extraordinary, then there is a very great risk that he might violate the first rule of film-making—Thou Shall Not Be Boring.

Unfortunately, contemporary Indian film directors are so obsessed with the belief that art can be created within a feature film only if the film is closer to poetry than to storytelling, that they are constantly trying to deny the basic truth of the feature film, that it must be structured and made as a story if it is to have half a chance of coming close to 'poetry'.

In the case of Bhansali's *Devdas*, which is a product of the commercial cinema circuit, what the film industry has begun to ask is why Bhansali had to make such an exorbitant film.

The economics of mainstream cinema is such that at the time of a film's release, it involves a chain of financial investments stretching from the film financier and producer to the film's distributor and the various theatres that are booked for the film's screening. If a big-budget film fails to deliver, it hurts the pockets of several people along this financial chain.

The moment a big, big budget film is produced, it raises the financial risks of all those who invest in its production or release. Its colossal budget requires, ipso facto, that the film run long enough to make a profit for each investor. These days there is a school of thought at Mumbai that is becoming more and more influential within the film industry, that it is safer to make an average-budget film and go in for smaller returns than make a titanic of a film which could sink half the industry. Therefore, it is for its own sake that the film industry is praying these days that Bhansali's *Devdas* runs long enough all over the country to recover the costs and price.

www.chowk.com, 2004.

The Makers of
Popular Cinema

The Evergreen Troika

The three great stars, Dilip Kumar, Dev Anand, and Raj Kapoor, ruled Hindi cinema during the 1950s and 1960s. Each had carved a niche for himself and evolved a distinct acting style. Each had a large following well into middle age and after.

India's Independence in 1947 coincided with the emergence of three actors in the cinema world who were to dominate Hindi film for nearly twenty-five years. It was the year in which Dilip Kumar, Raj Kapoor, and Dev Anand came into their own as leading men in films.

They became the ruling troika of the box office. Their cultivated images turned them into institutions. Within the film industry itself, nobody dared challenge their status or authority till age finally began to take its inevitable toll. But so charismatic are their legends and so deep their influence in the cinema world that even today nobody in the film world dare write them off.

Dilip Kumar was the first of the three to make his debut as a leading man in *Jwar Bhata* (1944). By 1946 Dilip, Dev Anand, and Raj Kapoor had established themselves as the actors to watch. In 1947–8, they assumed command of the box office. During these two years they starred in eighteen films amongst them; most of these films became major box-office hits—*Jugnu, Mela, Shaheed, Aag, Dil ki Rani, Neel Kamal, Ziddi, Vidya,* and *Mohan.*

Their advent coincided with the disintegration of the studio system in India. Immediately after Independence, a horde of financiers—a large number of them Sindhis—moved into the film business. The freelance system in film production was thus born. Artistes and technicians now moved from one producer to another without the constraint of working as staff members of a big film studio. The freelance system, which still prevails, skyrocketed and quadrupled star 'prices' immediately, as an increasing number of film financiers competed with one another to sign on the biggest stars of the day. Dilip Kumar, Dev Anand, and Raj Kapoor led the queue to the bank. In 1970, industry sources say, Dilip Kumar received Rs 1.7 million for B.R. Chopra's *Dastaan*— record fee that has been surpassed only recently by Amitabh Bachchan who, according to Bombay rumours, has touched the Rs 3 million figure.

Dastaan, however, went down as one of the biggest flops in Hindi cinema. Its failure at the beginning of the 1970s was to signal the end of the living legend that was Dilip Kumar. Nor did failure come to Dilip alone. In 1970, Raj Kapoor's autobiographical magnum opus, *Mera Naam Joker*, collapsed at the box office. Time seemed to have pulled the carpet from under the feet of Hindi film's biggest showman. An entirely new, and even brash, set of filmgoers had come of age by then. The legends of Dilip Kumar and Raj Kapoor could not quite stand up to their iconoclasm. The new filmgoer began to evaluate each film on its merits. Moreover, this new filmgoer initiated a process of adulation in which no matinee idol lasts at the very top for more than four or five years. The 1970s, for instance, have seen three crazes—Rajesh Khanna, Dharmendra, and Amitabh Bachchan.

In 1970, Dev Anand alone stood firm among the Big Three. His *Johnny Mera Naam*—a title that obviously parodied Raj Kapoor's *Mera Naam Joker* became the biggest success in years. It also revived the trend for action films. This turned out, however, to be a swansong, the last flicker of the dying flame. Soon after, Dev Anand also fell to the axe of time.

Despite the blows they have suffered, the Big Three have managed to hold on at the top. Raj Kapoor fought back with *Bobby* (1973). Dev Anand finally turned the tide with *Des Pardes* (1978). And now Dilip Kumar has got down once again to the serious business of acting successfully. He plays the pivotal role in Manoj Kumar's *Kranti* and other big-budget films now under production.

There was a time when it was easy to pick a quarrel simply by declaring that Dilip Kumar was a bad actor. Until *Dastaan*, Dilip Kumar was the acknowledged king of tragedy, an actor par excellence; the only actor in Hindi cinema who could be described as a method actor, a label that Hollywood gave to Marlon Brando, Montgomery Clift, and James Dean because they followed the Lee Strasbourg approach to action.

Dilip Kumar's studied, restrained style and his calculated control over gestures and movements is most noticeable in *Ganga Jamuna*, where it stands in sharp counterpoint to the vivacious spontaneity of Vyjayanthimala. One reason for Dilip Kumar's phenomenal popularity from 1947 to 1970 was the fact that his intense emotionalism provided filmgoers with a cinematic correspondence to the intense personalities of such national leaders as Gandhi and Nehru. Like them, Dilip Kumar combined in his roles a passionate concern for the poor with an ultrasensitive temperament.

Dilip Kumar's undoing in later years was his inability to handle high comedy with the spontaneity and the nonchalance with which Sanjeev Kumar began to woo audiences. In *Ram aur Shyam* and *Sagina Mahato*, Dilip Kumar's attempt to replace the 'out of fashion' emotionalism of the past with a comic dimension (perhaps inspired by Jack Lemmon) did not quite click at the box office.

These days a single male star tends to stand out over and above his compatriots. But for over two decades Dilip Kumar, Raj Kapoor, and Dev Anand held their own against one another. This was partly because of the completely distinct screen images that they cultivated for themselves.

Dilip Kumar was the first Angry Young Man of Hindi film. He was always fighting for the common man's cause, often playing a villager or a worker. Dev Anand and Raj Kapoor, on the other hand, became lone wolves, personifying two separate romantic images of modern urban life.

Dev Anand was a taxi driver, a pickpocket, a CID inspector, a gambler, a secret agent, a tourist guide, a cinema ticket black-marketeer, and a paying guest—a playboy of the technological city, dressed in striped shirts and a leather jacket, a scarf round the neck, a cap perched jauntily on his head; a huge, six-inch puff jutting out of the cap like a standing wave of black hair over his forehead. During the 1950s, there was no urban bazaar in the country where one did not run into a young local who had a puff of hair as high as Dev Anand's and who did not walk with a slouch, one shoulder higher than the other, all imitative of the matinee idol.

Raj Kapoor provided a perfect counterpoint to Dev Anand's image of the urban city slicker. Where Dev was smart and fashionably dressed, like an Indian Gregory Peck, Raj Kapoor moved around his own films in loose, shabby garb derivative of Charlie Chaplin's tramp. With the help of radical colleagues such as writer-director K.A. Abbas, Raj Kapoor adapted Chaplin's tramp into a very Indian mould. His easy-going tramp cocked a thumb at the worldly-wise. He became an extension of the bohemian immortalized in Urdu poetry by Ghalib's romanticism about *phaaka-masti* and the 'pleasures' of bankruptcy.

Raj Kapoor confined his simpleton tramp image to films he himself made but other film producers developed variations of the the tramp's innocence. He was an '*anari*' for Hrishikesh Mukherjee, a naive cart-driver in Basu Bhattacharya's *Teesri Kasam* and the yokel *chhalia* for Manmohan Desai. A man whose simplicity tempted smart alecs to dupe him but who always ended up on the right side of Dame Fortune.

2003, Unpublished.

* * *

Golden Girls of a Golden Era

A tribute to the actress-stars of Hindi cinema from the 1950s. Actresses like Nargis, Meena Kumari, Madhubala, Geeta Bali, Waheeda Rehman, and Nutan performed with no less intensity than their successors such as Jaya Bhaduri, Shabana Azmi, and Smita Patil. The actresses from earlier times mirrored the often abject social conditions that the average middle-class Indian woman was forced to accept.

Nobody quite expected that the new age of Independence would unveil new facets of the Indian woman in cinema. An amazing depth of personality from a bevy of talented actresses was soon to wow the audience.

It was as if these new female icons of the cinema were gradually liberating Indian women and leading them beyond the restrictions of domesticity and the cocoons of *ghunghat* and purdah.

India's Independence in 1947 was followed by two decades of social upheaval. Daily life was defined by the clash of tradition and modernity. Domestic, household values were pitted against the new mores of business, the joint-family structure began to break up, and the Indian nuclear family began to find an identity in the social fabric.

In an Indian world still divided by gender segregation, the soft malancholy look in the dark eyes of actresses like Suraiya, Meena Kumari, Waheeda Rehman, and Nutan released an ocean of suppressed emotions among men, and unveiled a mirror reflection of what women wanted to be.

The warmth of Nargis' smile and the protective embrace of her companionship conjured up the ideal portrait of an educated women as partner-cum wife. The uninhibited openness of Madhubala's laugh, the teasing abandon of her smile, the sensuous toss of the locks of hair around her high cheekbones, her slim hourglass figure, all made her into our sublime sexy goddess.

Indian film dramas of the late 1940s and 1950s were sagas that mixed the joys of youth with the sadness of the adult world. These films gave a generation of actresses the perfect platform from which to cast a spell over the audience's heart. When Suraiya sang 'Na tadapne ki ijaazat hai, na faryaad ki/ Dil to rota ho, magar hoton par faryaad na ho' (in A.R. Kardar's Dard, 1947) she tugged at the heart strings. Meena Kumari's oval face, with its near-perfect classical features, glowed like a gentle diya when the hurt of her sad, sad scenes seemed to blow across it like monsoon clouds.

Waheeda Rehman's glances of vulnerable girlhood, Nutan's magical ability to silently swallow her tears, Nargis's sublime portrayals of the pain of her passion... these are some of the unforgettable memories of free India's years of adolescence.

Even Madhubala's tragic defiance in 'Pyar kiya to darna kya' (Mughal-e-Azam, 1960) rose above all the moments of fun, frolic, and playfulness that had given her elfin romantic charm in other films. Madhubala, born in 1933, started as a child artiste at the age of 10; at 14 she was the lead in Kidar Sharma's Neel Kamal and of another four films by director Mohan Sinha, who gave her the name Madhubala, 'the honey vine'.

Nutan, born on 4 June 1936, started a little older. She was launched in mother Shobhana Samarth's production Hamari Beti (Our Daughter, 1951), although she had already faced the camera at the age of 9, for her director father Kumar Sen Samarth's Nal Damyanti (1952), which starred her mother and Prithviraj Kapoor. However, it sould be pointed out that statistical records from Bombay's film world tend to somewhat misrepresent reality. On average, an actress's age is stated to be three to four years lower than it actually is. The records say that Suraiya was born on 15 June 1929 at Lahore, began her film career in 1941, at the age of 12, and played her first lead role in Ishara, which was released in 1943, when she was just 14 years old! Nargis, born on 1 June 1929, was launched as a child star at the age of 5 in her mother's production *Talashe Haq* and first played a romantic lead at 14 years in Mehboob's *Taqdeer* (1943).

Nargis, Meena Kumari, Waheeda Rehman, Nutan, and the now seemingly forgotten but unique Geeta Bali often came up with acting performances that match the internationally acclaimed roles of Jaya Bhaduri Bachchan, Shabana Azmi, and the late Smita Patil. The status of these actresses has not diminished to this day. Contemporary actresses aspire to achieve the same class.

The question is still asked why Suraiya so suddenly terminated her career after her great musicals *Khubsurat* (music director Madan Mohan, 1952) and *Mashuqa* (music director, Roshan; singer Mukesh her co-star; 1953). Was it because she could never co-star with Dev Anand again?

Meena Kumari's career as a leading lady took nearly four years to take off. It was *Magroor* (1950), directed by R.D. Mathur, the legendary cinematographer of *Mughal-e-Azam*, who was also the first cameraman in the movies to use bounce lighting, who alerted the big directors to the talent behind her beautiful face. In 1952 she charmed the nation with her pensive look in *Baiju Bawra* and *Tamasha*. In the latter, her co-stars were Ashok Kumar and Dev Anand. After Bimal Roy's *Parineeta* (1953), she became the perfect foil for Ashok Kumar. Her heavy dramatic presence bounced off his style of casual naturalism. He provided the flow, she the depth to the drama of *Parineeta*, based on a Sarat Chandra story. She was to star in more movies with him than with anyone else—fourteen in all.

Meena Kumari's films with Dilip Kumar—Zia Sarhady's celebrated *Footpath* (1953; with Balraj Sahni, Nutan and the latter-day editor of *Seminar*, Romesh Thapar), the romantic comedy *Azad* (1955), Bimal Roy's *Yahudi* (1957), Hrishikesh Mukherjee's *Musafir* (1957), and the film *Kohinoor* (1960)—provided glimpses of her as an art film actress or in comic roles. But it was with Raj Kapoor in L.V. Prasad's *Sharda* (1956) that she gave what many believe was her finest performance then. Of Meena Kumari's seventy films as leading lady, the ones that are rated most highly in artistic terms are Prasad's *Sharda*, Kamal Amrohi's *Daaera* (1953), B.R. Chopra's *Ek Hi Raasta* (1956), Guru Dutt's *Sahib Bibi aur Ghulam* (1962), and Amrohi's *Pakeezah* (1972).

It is said that her own favourite was Guru Dutt's heart-wrenching saga. As the neglected and latterly alcoholic wife on a debilitating feudal estate, Meena Kumari came closest to her own loneliness. '*Na jaao saeeyaan churha ke baeenyaan*' was the essence of her own life song.

'She was an artist with a rare talent,' said the poet Sahir Ludhianvi, 'with the soul of a poet which she had to sacrifice. Her youth was spent in depicting the various tragedies that befall Indian women, with no time to think of her personal tragedy.'

At first sight, Nargis did not appear glamorous. She was not the kind of actress who would stun the audience with a dramatic entry. As a matter of fact, she used to be criticized for her 'horsy face'. But that was before she appeared before the camera and became a superstar with a series of super-hits, starting in 1943 with *Taqdeer* and *Kismet*, followed by *Mela* (1948), *Andaz* and *Barsaat* (1949), and *Jogan* (1950). The magic of Nargis lay in her ability to avoid theatrical flourish and to understate her natural presence on the screen. In this her great successors were to be Waheeda Rehman and Nutan.

If Meena Kumari was the perfect face of Hindi cinema, Nargis personified all the hopes of modern India. She sailed through romantic comedies, especially in her films opposite Raj Kapoor, with her bobbed hair, bare shoulders, and songs in the rain. She was modern yet unassuming, a free woman but modest of presence, charming but also intense. She was a strange amalgam of the delicate and the strong, the romantic and the persevering.

On her death in May 1981, V.P. Sathe, co-scriptwriter of many of Abbas' scripts for Raj Kapoor, said that Nargis stood out among her peers because she brought to her love scenes the same intensity that other actresses gave to a tragic sequence. There is a scene in

Awara (1951) in which Raj Kapoor says, '*Agar kishti doob jayegi to?*' (If our boat sinks?), and Nargis replies, '*Doob jaane do!*' (Let it!). That phrase, according to Sathe, conveys the essence of her expressive intensity. It was this same intensity of feeling that made it possible for her to convince the audience that the only solution to the problems of the village in Mehboob Khan's *Mother India* (1957) lay in her shooting down her son, played by Sunil Dutt.

Sunil Dutt had been a fan of Nargis even before he began working in films. Their relationship developed in sensational circumstances when he saved her from a fire on the outdoor set of *Mother India*. After they married, she returned his devotion by dedicating herself to their family. But she also persuaded him to make three art films—*Mujhe Jeene Do* (1963), *Yaadein* (1964), and *Reshma aur Shera* (1972). The failure of these films at the box office then led her to sever all links with film-making, until Sunil Dutt began preparations for *Rocky* (1981), which launched the career of their son Sanjay Dutt.

Waheeda Rehman and Nutan were the angels of black-and-white cinema, their faces so eloquently expressive, their eyes so full of depth in the play of light and shade. But what if they had been born twenty years later? Would Waheeda Rehman have looked as irresistible in colour as she did in Guru Dutt's extraordinary films, *Pyaasa* (1957), *Kaagaz ke Phool* (1959), *Chaudhvin ka Chand* (1960), and *Sahib Bibi aur Ghulam* (1962))? Would Nutan have conveyed the silent tragedy of the untouchable *Sujata* (1959) or the subdued tension of the prisoner in *Bandini* (1963) as effectively in colour?

Nutan (1936–91) grew up under the arc lights, often accompanying her actress mother Shobhana Samarth to the studio. But she also inherited from her writer father, Kumar Sen Samarth, a love for Sanskrit and for writing. Nutan was a self-critical actress, always studying her performances, trying to remove possible flaws. She would prepare intensively so as to reach the film's set with a very clear idea of what her role demanded. She grew so accomplished at her craft that she appeared to act intuitively and without deliberation.

The range of Nutan's talent is perhaps unmatched. She may never have played coy glamorous roles like Asha Parekh in *Dil Deke Dekho* or Sadhana in *Inteqam*, but no other Indian actress could play both high drama and light comedy with equal flair. Remember, for every *Sujata* she also has a *Paying Guest* or an *Anari* to her credit! Nor did she have any qualms about taking on negative roles, as she made clear with her playing of the older, demanding wife to Amitabh Bachchan in Sudhendu Roy's art film *Saudagar*.

Nutan was extremely proud of the longevity of her career, which spanned forty-nine years and included among its highlights: *Hum Log* (1951), *Seema* (1955), *Paying Guest* (1957), *Dilli ka Thug*, *Anari*, (1958), *Sujata*, *Chhalia* (1960), *Bandini*, *Tere Ghar ke Samne* (1963), *Milan* (1967), *Saraswatichandra* and *Saudagar* (1973), *Main Tulsi Tere Angan ki* (1978), *Karma* (1986), and *Kanoon Apna Apna* (1989).

Waheeda Rehman, it is fair to say, was the favourite of the 1960s generation of intellectuals in India. For academics, journalists, writers, painters, theatre workers, musicians, young actors and actresses, she was a muse of the dramatic arts!

Waheeda's secret was that she looked like a goddess in black and white. Trained as a dancer, she took to acting as if born to it, instinctively. When she looked at the camera she could stun viewers with an indescribable photogenic magic and yet appear to be nothing other than her natural self. This was a quality she shared with Nutan—with one difference. Waheeda Rehman's natural look was intensely sensuous. She combined this with a grace and dignity and never needed to overplay her feminine identity, whether in a street song sequence in *CID* (1956) or *Pyaasa* (1957), or in an open display of sensuousness in '*Aaj phir jeene ki tamanna hai*' (*Guide*, 1965).

And she has played a mind-boggling range of roles; a nautch girl in *Teesri Kasam* (1966), an upper class actress in *Kaagaz ke Phool*, a glamorous danseuse in Vijay Anand's *Guide*, an average young woman in *Ram aur Shyam* (1967), or a woman with a secret past in *Kabhi Kabhie* (1974). In all these roles, she mesmerized us because she never sought to create an effect.

Guru Dutt discovered her quite by chance. On a brief visit to Hyderabad he was persuaded to attend the premiere of a Telugu film in which the 16-year-old Waheeda was making her debut. He was so impressed by her screen presence that he invited her over to Bombay and immediately cast her in *CID*, directed by his chief assistant, Raj Khosla, and co-starring his friend Dev Anand. During the six years of her association with Guru Dutt, Waheeda Rehman made only five films for his production company, but it is in these films—all masterpieces—that her legend is rooted.

She was the leading lady of some thirty-seven films. Apart from Guru Dutt's films, the most notable were: *Solva Saal* (1956), *Dil Apna Preet Paraya*, *Kala Bazar* (1960), *Bees Saal Baad* (1962), *Mujhe Jeene Do* (1962), *Kohraa* (1964), *Dil Diya Dard Liya*, *Teesri Kasam* (1966), *Ram aur Shyam* (1967), *Aadmi* (1968), *Reshma aur Shera* (1971), and her last film as a leading lady *Kabhi Kabhie* (1974). She also acted in *Jaisingh* (1958), a Hindi film with N.T. Ramarao, the legendary Telugu star who in the 1980s went on to become a charismatic political leader in the state of Andhra Pradesh.

Madhubala was one of Ashok Kumar's three favourite co-stars. 'Her smile was simply superb. She moved with the muses and the graces,' he would say. Dev Anand thought she was the most beautiful actress he had worked with and had a face 'which looked attractive from all angles'. Dilip Kumar declared in an open courtroom, 'I shall always love her until the day she dies.' They might have married but for the disapproval of her father, Ataullah Khan, who, to stop them from being together on an outdoor location for *Naya Daur* (1957), went to court against film-maker B.R. Chopra. Thanks to the court's hearings, the great love story of Dilip Kumar and Madhubala became public, even as Vyjayanthimala took over Madhubala's role in *Naya Daur*. Madhubala was eventually permitted to marry Kishore Kumar in the 1970s. By this time, she was grievously ill. Madhubala had never been strong—she was born with a hole in her heart—but the demands of filming took their toll. For *Mughal-e-Azam* she was weighed down with heavy chains and never quite recovered.

Sparkling in her beauty, infectious in her laughter, sincere, but also irreverent even to producers and directors, Madhubala was the siren of Bombay cinema 1947 onwards. The film world itself was in love with her, though it could have done without her father who managed her affairs and controlled her life till she escaped into matrimony.

Most of the money that Madhubala earned was dissipated by her father, through ill-conceived film ventures, and she did not have much of a bank balance when illness overtook her at the apogee of her career. During her last years, the care and consideration that her husband, Kishore Kumar, showered on her made up for much of her private grief. Kishore Kumar took a furlough from his own career and spared no effort for her treatment and care.

Over the years, as an actress Madhubala teamed up with Ashok Kumar for the unprecedented hit of 1949, *Mahal*. She was the exquisite lady-love in Guru Dutt's exceptional comedy *Mr and Mrs 55* (1955); and the heart-throb in *Chalti Ka Naam Gaadi* (1958), the all-time comedy classic of Indian cinema. Then she became the immortal Anarkali who defied a Mughal emperor in *Mughal-e-Azam* (1960), watched on the sets by her great love, Dilip Kumar.

2003, Unpublished.

* * *

Johnny Walker—A Comedian of the Machine Age

Johnny Walker is the most popular Funny Man in the history of Hindi films, probably because of the charm with which he disturbed the status quo. Johnny Walker dominated Hindi films in the 1950s through sheer ingenuity and held his own well into the 1960s, even when the more aggressive Mehmood made his presence felt.

Despite the pats we give ourselves on our backs about having one of the biggest and most vibrant cinemas in the world, film studies in India are in such a sorry state that I cannot tell you, with any degree of authenticity, whether Johnny Walker was born in 1924 or 1925. Both versions have been reported in the media at Mumbai! It is a situation that may have amused Badruddin Sahib himself.

Born to a mill worker at Indore, it took Johnny Walker, alias Badruddin, some twenty-five years to discover that cinema is one of the most democratic economies of the modern era; that there one could metamorphosize a bus conductor into a comic star—provided one met the wizard in time. In Johnny's case the wizard was director Guru Dutt.

He was luckier than many others in that he was born at the right time and came to maturity in the 1950s. The 1950s was the glorious decade that gave birth to the hitherto undefined world of pop culture, and not just in India. Across the seas, rock-n-roll music exploded as a sensational new genre in the early years of the same decade through the likes of Bill Haley and Elvis Presley. If Elvis Presley's wriggle shocked old-world prudes in the USA and Europe, in India Johnny Walker's personification of street culture sent conservative aesthetics halter skelter!

He was a born contortionist and didn't have a straight bone in his body. He only had to shrug a shoulder or bend a knee while taking a stroll to create a slow-motion distortion of respectable middle class society. He was, I tend to believe, the first modern-day comic star of Hindi cinema. At the very first instance he was a breakaway from the style of comedy that preceded him in Indian cinema and urban theatre.

Let us just juxtapose the uncontrollable dance of contortions sketched out by Johnny Walker with the satirical profile of Master Vinayak in films such as *Brahmachari*, or the rhythmic grace of Bhagwan. We see straightaway that Johnny Walker was the denizen of the new social landscape and soundscape where machines and

mechanics, the jangle of bicycle bells and the screeching tyres of
buses had taken over from the hoof-beat cadence of tongas and
bullock carts.

Much as Charlie Chaplin wove his 'boogie ballets' around the
artefacts of new machines in the 1930s and the 1940s, Johnny
Walker helped us recognize and readjust to our confusions and
vulnerabilities in the big city—vulnerabilities such as crossing a
road in the frightening face of roaring motorcars, trucks and lorries,
public transport buses and tramways. He turned our traumatic
confrontations with the new machines into a philosophic teaser—
'Main, main, main' he sang in 1958, 'Main Qaartoon! Bajjh raha
hai baar baar, dil ka telephoon!....' He would, and so therefore
could we, adapt the new gizmos to the emotional content of our
everyday lives.

To truly understand Johnny Walker's phenomenal difference
from his predecessors, to understand why the then 'gen next' representatives, Guru Dutt and Dev Anand, took to him immediately,
we have to remember that he entered the film world at a time
when a fairly large number of old-style comedians held centre
stage. Both Bhagwan and Master Vinayak were lead players with
tremendous comic flair. Then there was Yakub, albeit at the fag
end of his career, and Gope, Kanhaiyalal, Agha, and Dhumal, all
of whom had statures of no small measure as comedians.

It was because Johnny Walker's innate, overelastic personality
was in such a different mould from that of his predecessors that
he was able to quickly establish a new line of comedy in films. Its
influence spanned the decades to come, right down to Asrani and
Johny Lever. Nor should we forget that he thrived in an era when
comedy blossomed like a thousand flowers on the Mumbai film
scene. The seeds of the legend that Johny Walker became were
first sown at a time when he had such formidable contenders to
reckon with as I.S. Johar and Kishore Kumar; even as Mehmood
lurked in the wings. Let us not forget that these were the years
when two of the Hindi cinema's greatest comedies, Chalti Ka Naam

Gaadi and *Bewaqoof*, were made. During the mid-1950s there were, therefore, three comic superstars coexisting in the pantheon.

Despite the brevity of his debut in *Baazi* in 1951, within the next two years he was accepted as a major comic star and by 1956 he became a veritable superstar—telling us, much like Shakespeare's Fool: 'Ai dil, hai mushkil, jeena yahan....'

The Raj Khosla-directed *CID* (1956) and Guru Dutt's *Pyaasa* (1957) featured two of his most unforgettable appearances. As Guru Dutt's extraordinary scriptwriter Abrar Alvi once pointed out, what we admire as 'a Guru Dutt film' was in fact a cinema co-created by the brilliance of a small, core group of creative minds.

I had asked Abrar Alvi whether there was any truth to the popular belief that while his name was credited as the director of the film *Sahib Bibi aur Ghulam*, it had been directed, secretly, by Guru Dutt himself?

According to Alvi Sahib, Guru Dutt was so conscious of this unfounded accusation that he would not even turn up on the sets if he was not required to shoot for his role in the film.

He then added that by the time *Sahib Bibi aur Ghulam* was made, the key members of the unit had become so fused into a creative groove that the film would have had, more or less, the same lighting and camera placements, acting and performances, musical sequences and editing style, no matter who directed it on the sets. It would have been difficult for the unit to shoot the film in any other way.

Alvi Sahib then counter-questioned us in the media why we did not realize his personal contribution to the evolution of what we call 'the Guru Dutt film'. Was there, he asked, any social comments in the films Guru Dutt directed before he, that is Abrar Alvi sahib, joined the unit as scriptwriter? That, said Abrar Alvi, was 'my contribution to what you call "a Guru Dutt film".'

This core creative group evolved within the unit of the Guru Dutt Films production company in the early 1950s. As we can see in Johnny Walker's accompaniment to Guru Dutt's rendering of the song 'Dil par hua aisa jaadu' in the film Mr and Mrs 55, they are as one on screen, in the same way as a singer and a tabla player are one during a music concert. Johnny Walker seems here to be the perfect satirical foil for Guru Dutt. It is a chemistry rarely seen in cinema; perhaps because, as is hinted by Guru Dutt's acting performances in Aar Paar and Mr and Mrs 55, there was a Johnny Walker inside Guru Dutt himself. As a film-maker, Guru Dutt needed a Johnny Walker to best express his world view.

What stands out for me about Johnny Walker's role in Kaagaz ke Phool (1967) is the ease with which he slips into the sardonic character of a young man from the upper crust of society. In sharp contrast to earlier personifications of the street-smart, urchin-style city dweller, in Kaagaz ke Phool, Johnny Walker turned his image around, and became a member of a snooty and stiff-upper lip family that looks down on such low people as those who work in films.

The major song that picturized him in Kaagaz ke Phool goes a step further in deviating from the archetypal Johnny Walker image. It's a sad song. Moreover, it is a song in which Johnny Walker shies away from marriage—which is a bit of a shock, because in every other film he had done till then, his character was always in a hurry to get the girl to say yes to him. To highlight this parody of the Johnny Walker archetype, Guru Dutt picturized the song to a semi-classical, Westernized tune—at a complete remove from the 'Tell maalish' number in Pyaasa.

In 1956, Johnny Walker also presented a marvellous parody of the by-now overfamiliar character of the political agitator. The film Chori Chori offered one of the many hilarious 'item numbers' that we associate with the legend of Johnny Walker as he leads his enormous family squad to the beat of 'Left, right, dhibree tight—All line kil-lear!'

There is no doubt that as a social iconoclast in cinema, as a satirist, a revue artiste, a master of parody, and a comic philosopher, Johnny Walker was particularly lucky to be working in an era when the film world at Mumbai was also home to some of the great poets of the modern era—Sahir Ludhianvi, Hasrat Jaipuri, Shailendra, Kaifi Azmi, and Majrooh Sultanpuri, to name a few. These were poets who revelled in the excitement of transforming street slang. They took it to the transcendental ambiguity of great poetry—as T.S. Eliot put it, transcending from the ridiculous to the sublime. They were all sombre, often melancholic, poets in the literary world. But they also revelled in the 'rejuvenation of language' and they revealed a talent quite removed from their literary seriousness when they wrote film songs and lyrics. These may be best delineated as T.S. Eliot's category of nonsense verse. To this unexpected realm of literary playfulness, Johnny Walker provided the appropriate caricature. He gave it flesh and bone because there is a satirical musical rhythm to his comic expressions and his comic timing. Something that is so clearly illustrated by the song sequence for 'Sar jo tera chakraaye' (Pyaasa), the masseur's fingers drumming on his victim's scalp with the nonchalance of a tabla player.

Guru Dutt was not the only one among the socially aware film-makers of the era who found Johnny Walker irresistible. As one scans the early years of his film career, one comes across Aandhian (1952), Taxi Driver (1954), and Joroo ka Bhai (1955) directed by Chetan Anand, Munna (1954) directed by K.A. Abbas, Railway Platform (1955) directed by Ramesh Saigal, Paigham (1959) by S.S. Vasan, Naya Daur (1957) directed by B.R. Chopra, and Sitaron se Aage (1958) by Satyen Bose.

There were few directors in the top echelons of Mumbai's film studios those days, who did not cast Johnny Walker in a film or two. K. Asif included him in a small cameo in his magnum opus Mughal-e-Azam. We saw him in Roop K. Shorey's Aag Ka Dariya (1953), Devendra Goel's Ek Saal (1957), in P.L. Santoshi's Peheli Raat (1959), and in Kamal Amrohi's Dil Diya Dard Liya (1966). He even had a role in the 1954 production of Shaheed-e-Azam Bhagat Singh. Hrishikesh Mukherjee had cast him as far back as 1961 in *Aashiq*; and Johnny Walker was there in Bimal Roy's great popular classics *Devdas* (1955) and *Madhumati* (1958).

One can say that after Guru Dutt it was Dilip Kumar who saw in Johnny Walker the requisite foil for his occasionally ponderous demeanour. We know that Dilip Kumar's comedy style was, like much of his acting, both deliberate and cultivated. Perhaps, as with Guru Dutt, there was a Johnny Walker lurking within Dilip Kumar and he needed to be articulated through a foil. Among the top leading men of his time, after Guru Dutt, it was with Dilip Kumar that Johnny Walker featured in more films than he did with anybody else; and that includes Dev Anand, though Dev sahib was very much in the same group as Guru Dutt in the early 1950s.

As one scans the list of Johnny Walker's more outstanding films, one discovers that he was the leading man, the hero, of as many as nine films—at the very least. I don't know of any other comic star of Hindi cinema, after Bhagwan, who played the hero in as many films as Johnny Walker did.

The first of these *Chhoo Mantar* was made as early as 1956. His leading ladies were Shyama and Amita Guha. Shyama was the actress he was most faithful to as a leading man, for they were at cross-purpose in most of these nine films. Director M. Sadiq's *Duniya Rang Rangili* and *Johnny Walker*—yes, a film dedicated to his screen name—followed immediately after, in 1957. In 1958, he broke all box-office records, not just with *Mr Qartoon MA* directed by Ved-Madan but with two others 'solo lead' films—M. Sadiq's *Khota Paisa* and *Naya Paisa*. The year 1959 saw two more films with Johnny Walker in the lead—Inder's *Mr John* and N.A. Ansari's *Zara Bachke*; in 1960 we have his swansong as a leading man, in director Shanker Mehta's *Rikshavala*, with Amita Guha as his leading lady.

He continued to act as the comic in character roles long after his days as a leading man came to an end. We all remember with pleasure that he was very much there in Hrishikesh Mukherjee's *Anand*, in the company of more recent superstars. The Kamal

Haasan starrer *Chachi 420* marked his very last appearance on the silver screen.

The 1950s was truly a golden era in Indian cinema, commemorating India's Independence and sovereignty. And this golden period was brought about by the likes of Johnny Walker. Long live the Johnny Walkers of the creative world.

www.chowk.com, 2004.

* * *

A *Chela* Salutes Guru Dutt

Guru Dutt's (1925–64) films are in the same class as the novels of Jean-Paul Sartre, the poems of T.S. Eliot, and the iconoclastic world of new political ideas that held sway in the 1950s and 1960s. A perceptive tribute to the maker of Pyaasa, Kaagaz ke Phool, and Sahib Bibi aur Ghulam—three films that have withstood the vagaries of changing public tastes.

Perhaps Waheeda Rehman, writer Abrar Alvi, cinematographer Murthy, and other close associates of the great film-maker did not even suspect our existence. But I am sure that like me there were hundreds and thousands of young filmgoers in the 1950s and the 1960s who soon realized, as they began to take stock of their own coming of age, that one of the most important gurus and mentors in our lives was a film-maker we had never met expect through his frames on the silver screen.

There have been so many of the student generations of the 1950s and 1960s, into whose lives Guru Dutt's films came as a shaping influence, moulding their intellectual sensibility, inculcating in them a philosophy of life along with poets, novelists, and thinkers.

For me, more than any other film-maker, Guru Dutt's films co-existed in a kaleidoscopic precipitation of ideas along with the novels of Jean-Paul Sartre, the poetry of T.S. Eliot, and the iconoclastic world of new political ideas that were arising in Indian society.

Guru Dutt was the film-maker who, in this filmgoer's opinion, kept alive an important intellectual tradition at a time when the Indian value system was being overwhelmed by ideas from abroad. The very cultural moorings of the Indian lifestyle were being replaced—by the beat of rock 'n' roll music and Elvis Presley, by the gadgets of Western technology, and by the modernistic, scientific socialist ideology championed by Pandit Jawaharlal Nehru and his vision of a new India. Industrialization was beginning to change the very face of India by the late 1950s.

Though the films of Guru Dutt, like those of V. Shantaram, Bimal Roy, and Raj Kapoor, were children of this new industrial era, there was something in the vision of Guru Dutt's films that went beyond the contemporary mood. Suddenly in *Pyaasa* (1957) we were confronted with the crass avarice and opportunism that was eating into the entrails of modern Indian society. There was no other film in the late 1950s that was as critical of the new commercialized values of our society as the indictment of it that Guru Dutt, Sahir Ludhianvi, and Abrar Alvi made in *Pyaasa*—'*Jinhe naaz hai Hind ab woh kahan hain*'. It was a song that tried to temper the heady, gushy euphoria that the mere fact of Independence had brought. In 1957 it was a song that expressed the evaluation by the masses of the first decade of Indian Independence, of what remained to be done in creating a new India; at the same time it was a song that represented a catharsis of emotions for the individual in the audience.

But perhaps more significantly, the essential tone of *Pyaasa* and the film's theme was typified by '*Ye duniya agar mil bhi jaaye to kya hai*'—Even if you attain the world what's its worth? In its philosophic iconoclasm of the material world, the song and the sequence in the film atavistically echoed the great Indian principle of renunciation. It is a song whose emotional soul goes back directly to Kabir and the poetry of the Bhakti movement; and to the essence of the Indian approach to the illusory world of *maya*.

It was this very Indian philosophical streak in *Pyaasa* that was to shade the films Guru Dutt made immediately after—*Kaagaz ke Phool, Chaudhvin ka Chand*, and *Sahib Bibi aur Ghulam*. These three films also reflected the sensibility of a film-maker who had once said with conviction—'*Ye duniya agar mil bhi jaaye to kya hai*'.

Whereas the Shantaram, the Bimal Roy, and the Raj Kapoor of the 1950s and early 1960s projected a vision that was primarily shaped by sociological factors and situations. Guru Dutt alone among his peers was expressing a deep philosophical concern, indirectly asking us whether life itself had any real meaning or purpose, beyond the problems of day-to-day existence. The poet of *Pyaasa* is ignored by both his publisher and his relatives. An idealistic love becomes irrelevant in the context of the great friendship such as the one between the characters portrayed by Guru Dutt and Rehman in *Chaudhvin ka Chand*. In *Sahib Bibi aur Ghulam* what disturbed us most was not the extinction of the feudal order, but that a woman as complex, beautiful, and sensitive as Chhoti Bahu should be so ill-fated as to be killed and buried simply because she had spoken to a man other than her husband.

The tragedy of Chhoti Bahu's existence in *Sahib Bibi aur Ghulam* seems to be as important in itself as the entire story of the disintegration of a feudal family (and an obsolete social system). Similarly, in *Chaudhvin ka Chand* every single character in the romantic triangle becomes a notable tragic victim in his/her own right. It is difficult to come out of this 1960 release and say, as we filmgoers are apt to do so often—'if only so-and-so had done this, or not done that'. In *Pyaasa* the story of an individual poet never becomes more important than the philosophical reality about our world, in which the original voice of feeling will always be crushed, generation after generation, by the greed and the materialistic opportunism that is unavoidable in human society.

By confronting us with the very essence of the human dilemma in some of its myriad forms, Guru Dutt the film-maker achieved a rare, near-impossible, objective as an artist—showing his audience the pessimistic truth about life, the inexorable and unavoidable tragedies that the human soul endures through history. And yet he so enchants and enwraps us in an ecstasy of cinematic style that we revel in a dance of tears within the mind and applaud the mere expression of the tragic truth of our existence.

What became irresistible for Guru Dutt's audience was the simple juxtaposition his personality expressed between the tragedy and the comedy of life. Though his later films enveloped such a pessimistic culmination of human existence, he handled the tragic and the joyous aspects of life with the same verve, vitality, and creative feeling. Life may be essentially tragic, but Johnny Walker was not going to let anybody die without the sound of laughter.

The rising graph of Johnny Walker's screen persona in Guru Dutt's films, starting with the restrained comic cameo in *Baazi* (1951), revealed a film-maker revelling in a combination of the ludicrous and the sublime. In his films of the Guru Dutt era, Johnny Walker epitomized the philosophical nonsense that life is made of. In *Pyaasa*, Johnny Walker's street-smart clown is almost comparable to the Fool of Shakespeare's plays.

Perhaps the weakest characterization that Guru Dutt made in his later films was through Johnny Walker's satirical broadside at the upper class, English-speaking Indian in *Kaagaz ke Phool*. Here Guru Dutt made a directly satirical statement on a certain social type—the upper class Indian obsessed with the British way of life, infatuated by a heightened sense of social respectability, and looking down on everybody else. There is no philosophical streak to Johnny Walker's nonsense in *Kaagaz ke Phool*; but these satirical sequence show quite clearly how much contempt Guru Dutt had for the falsehoods of respectability and etiquette that the upper classes preach.

I have always believed that *Kaagaz ke Phool* is the Guru Dutt film with the weakest content, because Guru Dutt's sense of judgment about the script became caught in an Indian trap typical of the literary period starting with Saratbabu and extending to the late 1960s and the early 1970s. During this period, modern Indian culture was too sentimentally preoccupied with the definition of the artist as a person too sensitive to fit into this cruel world. The artist was considered some kind of a superperson—too virtuous and good to be considered a normal human being, though such is, in truth, never the case. The artist is but another human being blessed with a certain talent—no different from others blessed otherwise.

Whereas in *Pyaasa* the poet never presumed any inherent superiority, *Kaagaz ke Phool* gave too much value to the cultural belief of a particular era—that a good artist's work would not be accepted by a commercial society.

This sentimentality in its content, however, should not detract from the fact that it was in *Kaagaz ke Phool* that Guru Dutt revealed in passages that he was as much a master of the cinematic craft as anybody else in the world—Jean Renoir, Roberto Rossellini, Vittorio De Sica, Robert Bresson or Frederico Fellini. There is one shot in *Kaagaz ke Phool* which, I think, is unique in the history of the cinema—the camera moving in an arc above a mob of people crowding around Guru Dutt and Waheeda Rehman at the landing of the palatial movie house. But, as Waheeda Rehman said to this writer, during the course of a newspaper interview in February 1986,

The fact is that we were not shocked that *Kaagaz ke Phool* did not run. Though it was very artistic, the photography overpowering, and the effect of each scene so strong visually, all of us knew *Kaagaz ke Phool* was going to be a catastrophic flop. At the same time we were also quite clear in our mind that technically the film was superb.

However, it is not as if Guru Dutt's technical brilliance and his creativity as a film-maker are to be found only in the later films of his career—as most serious students of Indian cinema have been led to believe. Most of the serious writing on Guru Dutt has revolved around *Pyaasa* and the other films of the second phase. We only have to take a second look at *Baazi*, *Aar Paar*, and *Mr and Mrs 55* to realize how ingeniously he used film grammar to create the mood for each scene in the two detective stories and in the light comedy *Mr and Mrs 55*.

I remember seeing *Mr and Mrs 55* years and years ago, to discover that of the countless number of close-ups of Madhubala that the film has, no two close-ups are alike. Even within one sequence, each close-up had a different angle, different lighting, and a different expression from the actress. Each close-up is a complete cinematic portrait in itself, quite different from the other portraits he constructed for the other close-ups.

This is but one example of Guru Dutt's imaginative range in the use of the medium. The reason why we still fall in love with his films, viewing them more than a quarter century after they were first made, is because as a film technician he was as brilliant and imaginative as the best in the world. For me personally, Guru Dutt is one of the greatest craftsmen in the history of Indian cinema. And a young Indian director ought to measure his own talent by comparing his work with that of Guru Dutt. I believe firmly that he is among the three greatest geniuses of Indian cinema.

Hindustan Times, *7 August 1988.*

* * *

A Tribute to Raj Kapoor

Raj Kapoor's popularity at home, the Soviet Union, and even Latin America was due to his mastery of the craft of film-making. The songs and music in his films also played a key role in his success. All through his life, the businessman in Raj Kapoor was at odds with the artist in him.

MOSCOW 1954: The inaugural ceremony of the film festival is coming to an end. Raj Kapoor turns to K.A. Abbas and asks,

'*Hamara kya hoga?*' Another Indian film has been screened that evening. A full house had risen in applause for Bimal Roy's *Do Bigha Zamin*. It was a film Raj Kapoor had liked immensely. But through the deafening animation of the applause he could not but ask of himself and his scriptwriter, what about my film?

'Patience,' advised Abbas, 'wait till tomorrow when *Awara* is shown. The applause you hear today is the response of intellectuals and critics. Let us see how the public reacts tomorrow.'

Thus, in a way, was the legend born—from the Volga to the Ganges.

Nearly a decade later an Indian businessman visiting Istanbul happened to be sitting in the office of the film's distributor for Turkey. A huge portrait of Raj Kapoor adorned the room. The distributor rang up his theatre and gave instructions that *Awara* should be screened on Sunday morning. 'Does it still run?' asked the Indian. 'Yes, it does,' replied his host, who went on to explain that he needed ready-cash on Monday morning and that he could always depend on *Awara* to solve his short-term financial problems.

In Peru, a film distributor by the name of Fernandez became a millionaire after he bought the Latin American rights for *Mera Naam Joker*. Indeed, said Radhu Karmakar, Raj Kapoor's cinematographer from December 1949, the film's popularity in Latin America helped Raj Kapoor pay off his debts—*Joker* had put him in the red for Rs 67 lakh.

Despite the collapse of *Mera Naam Joker*, Raj Kapoor went back to the same team of writers—K.A. Abbas and V.P. Sathe. Temperamentally he was not given to changing friends and partners easily. He simply could not adapt himself to all and sundry. He had chosen his team with care. He believed in each man he chose and he gave him all his time and all his cooperation. His sound-recordist since *Aag*, Allauddin Qureshi says, 'The most important department of the unit was the one which was at work. It was even bigger than Raj Kapoor. That was the way he worked.'

Nevertheless, *Joker* shook him up a bit. He told Abbas that their next film together had to be a hit, and that it would be a love story.

When Abbas and Sathe took the script of *Bobby* to Raj Kapoor at his farm in Loni near Pune, K.A. Narayan had already met him. Narayan was the writer of that stupendous 1970 blockbuster, *Johny Mera Naam*, the film that had eclipsed *Joker* at the box office. Raj Kapoor had met him, heard his story, but decided that it was not to his temperament to make Narayan's *dishoom-dishoom* kind of film.

Once *Bobby* began to roll, Raj Kapoor changed the scenario. In Abbas's version, on their first date the boy and the girl see a movie in the cheapest stalls, eating chana in the interval. 'He made Bobby's father a rich man, so that they could go swimming at the club. If he had made it the way I had envisaged, perhaps the film would have flopped,' confessed Abbas.

There was considerable indecision about the film's ending, too. Raj Kapoor wanted *Bobby* to be a tragedy, but Sathe and actor and brother-in-law Premnath insisted that the film end on a happy note. Despite *Joker*, Raj Kapoor still wanted to defy the conventions of the box office. Even after the film was ready he would fret that he had been forced by his distributors to incorporate a fight sequence. It was something he abhorred. But by 1973, he had learnt many harsh lessons as a businessman.

Mera Naam Joker was not the first financial crisis in the career of the movie mogul. After *Aah* (1953) had done poorly, an attempt had been made by his financier, V.V. Puri of the All India Film Finance Corporation, to take over Raj Kapoor's studio, says cinematographer Radhu Karmakar.

Yet he never did worry about the financial implications of his style of film-making. His films always went over the budget and depended on an overflow of profit to redeem the company.

As a film-maker, he was notorious for the extensive footage of raw film he exposed, shooting take after take, till he was satisfied that the shot was perfect. He took thirty-five takes of one shot for *Awara*, came back dissatisfied, the next day and proceeded to take the shot all over again. He had exposed over 3000 feet of film negative the previous day, unmindful of the cost. But, after he had got what he wanted the next day, he ordered that money should not be wasted in getting the previous day's footage processed!

For *Sangam*, he had shot a song at Venice, a Lata Mangeshkar-Mukesh duet that began with the *mukhra* 'Kabhi na kabhi, koyi na koyi'. But before the film's release, he discovered that the opening line had been used for a song in another film. He scrapped the song from the soundtrack, though he managed to retain the scene in which Vyjayanthimala and Rajendra Kumar float down a canal in a gondola.

The films that Raj Kapoor did not make provide for equally interesting filmography. The film he wanted to make after *Awara* was *Ajanta*. It was to be shot in technicolour and he sent cinematographer Karmakar to learn the process under Jack Cardiff in London. He also had plans to ask Cardiff to come over and help shoot *Ajanta*. A multitude of designs for the sets and the costumes and hairstyles of the film had been commissioned. Then he learnt that his artist had shown some of the sketches to another producer who had immediately plagiarized some of the designs. *Ajanta* was shelved!

A complete script for *Param Veer Chakra* was worked out recently by Abbas and Sathe, based on an idea given by a member of the R.K. Studio staff, Major Kaul. Conceived as a young soldier's story, it would have been Raj Kapoor's first war film and the film-maker's personal tribute to the Indian Army, Navy, and Airforce. Raj Kapoor and his scriptwriters had driven down to the National Defence Academy at Khadakvasla a number of times to study the Academy's mode of living and Raj Kapoor had even talked to the press about *Param Veer Chakra*, when he decided to return to another old obsession—*Henna*.

Joker was originally conceived as a film in six episodes. One of the unfilmed episodes was to deal with the Joker's marriage and his wife. But Raj Kapoor's showmanship had so inflated the first three episodes that he decided to shelve the rest of the script. Recently, it was suggested to him that he should make a sequel to *Joker*. Raj

Kapoor tried to dismiss the suggestion, saying that he didn't know of the actor who could play the role today. But he did have in mind a sequel to *Joker*, with Rishi Kapoor the most likely contender for the lead role.

It is scriptwriter Sathe's belief that Raj Kapoor's conception of his films was guided by only one thing, the songs, and that the film's script would be worked and moulded so that the songs could be an intrinsic part of the story. The script for *Ram Teri Ganga Maili*, for example, was developed backwards so that it could lead to the film's emotional climax symbolized by the song 'Ek Radha, ek Meera', picturized on Mandakini and Divya Rana. The title of the film, incidentally, came from a pronouncement made by Sant Totapuri, Swami Ramakrishna's guru.

What makes the songs of Raj Kapoor's films unique is the ease with which the poetry of the songs was blended with the tunes conceived for them, say his associates. He would play around in his mind for years with melodies and mukhras (opening-lines) before he worked out the symbiosis that would be picturized in a film. Anand Bakshi's mukhra *'Jhoot bole kauva kaate'* was in his mind for ten years.

Then there was the song *'Main kaa karoon Ram mujhe buddha mil gaya'*. Raj Kapoor first heard it in 1957, at a party given at Delhi by Chhotubhai Desai, his local distributor. He finally used the song in *Sangam* (1964), set in a hotel room in Paris. The melodious strains of *'Jane kahan gaye woh din'* can be heard as part of the background score of *Aah*, made almost twenty years before *Mera Naam Joker*.

He interwove the songs and the story so skilfully that to miss a song sequence would also mean missing a part of the story. He was able to achieve this only by being singularly obsessed with his work. His films always came before his family, but it grew to understand his obsession with his work.

He was constantly discussing his concept of the film, his *mise-en-scene* and the script, his picturizations for scenes and songs. He was always open to suggestions and rediscovered his own ideas through these discussions. Forcing friends and associates to respond to his ideas was his way of sizing up and anticipating the impact they were likely to make on the multitudes waiting inside the darkened movie halls with their capacity to love or destroy a film. He would listen quietly to criticism, controlling his temper even when provoked, as this writer once observed in 1973. During the making of *Jis Desh Mein Ganga Behti Hai*, music directors Shankar and Jaikishan were sceptical whether they could make any contribution at all to a dacoit film, blissfully unaware that it would become one of the biggest musical hits of their career.

It is the opinion of at least one of Raj Kapoor's closest associates that it was he who had created the outstanding duo of music directors, Shankar and Jaikishan. They were drawn into Raj's team from Prithvi Theatres where Jaikishan played the harmonium and Shankar the tabla.

Another splendid illustration of his uncanny musical sense, a testimony to his belief that music meant the box office, was epitomized in the making of *Boot Polish* (1954), directed by his assistant Prakash Arora. Arora had made a seventy-minute-long film without any songs, but Raj Kapoor took a look at the film and wondered how it would run. He then decided to make his own contribution to the movie and incorporated eight songs in the film, including such everlastingly popular numbers as '*Nanhe munhe bachche teri mutthi mein kya hai?*' and so ensured that Prakash Arora's film became a success.

But then Raj Kapoor had been both actor and singer, at least to start with. He had sung his own songs in his first few films, films like *Chittor*, *Vijay*, and *Dil Ki Rani*, and recalled on S.D. Burman's death that he had sung for Burman Da, too.

During filming, because of the intensity of his own work ethic, says audiographer Allauddin Qureshi, 'Raj Kapoor would create a certain amount of tension on the set. But this would help everybody to become even more alert. Those who were naive would become nervous, but the others would understand that this way they would be working at a sharper level.'

He had taught himself all aspects of film-making and often said that a film was made on two tables—the writing table and the editing table. Even when he failed, he would ensure that it was the failure of a grand effort, and not because he had not worked hard enough at giving his audience something new and different from the rut.

Hindustan Times, 8 May 1988.

* * *

The Ageless Pran

Pran Sikand, beloved character actor of Hindi films, started his career as a villain in the 1950s. He rose to the top and is admired for having lasted for fifty years in the business and for maintaining his unique style.

What Shakespeare said of Cleopatra is equally true of Pran Krishan Sikand. For neither changing trends nor the ravages of time have lessened even a wee bit the popular acclaim that Pran, the film actor, has enjoyed over the last fifty years.

The number one villain of the silver screen, a charismatic character actor and one of the most dignified gentlemen in the film jungle, Pran enters the new year after completing five glorious decades in cinema. He began his film career accidentally, with a lead role in the Punjabi film *Yamla Jat* released in 1940. It was at a paan shop in Lahore that he was cornered one inebriated evening by Wali Mohammed Wali, a prolific film-writer. To his surprise and amusement, he was invited to the film studios next morning to be considered for the villain's role in *Yamla Jat.*

Pran never turned up for that appointment presuming that since both Wali Mohammed and he himself had had a drink too many the previous evening, the offer was nothing more than loose talk. So Pran let the offer slip by till he ran into Wali Mohammed at a Lahore cinema hall some days later. Wali was extremely offended at Pran's nonchalance and swore at the young man for ditching him. However, the role was still open and Pran finally made his way into the film.

It was not smooth sailing, however. Within a week after shooting had commenced, the director wanted to sack Pran because he couldn't speak Punjabi properly. Pran himself confesses that though a Punjabi by birth, he had spent most of his school days at Delhi and UP and couldn't speak the language the way it is spoken in the Punjab. However, he promised to improve and was given a short period of time to do so, and thus began Pran's lifelong demonstration of his amazing talent for rising to the occasion no matter what the role's demand.

He is one of those who will prepare for every nuance of the get-up and the make-up that he is to wear for a particular role, no matter how small it is. To a group of film journalists at Delhi last fortnight over lunch he declared, somewhat to their surprise that he did not particularly care for author-backed roles. Instead, what he enjoyed was the challenge of bringing alive a role that was not author-backed. 'It must have depth' for him to tap, said Pran by way of explanation, even if the scriptwriter had not bothered to spell it out. 'It is the quality of the role and not its length that is important for me.'

Therefore, when he was asked about the roles he had liked most in his fifty years as actor, he said that the ones he personally 'remembered most' were the ones in Dil Diya Dard Liya, Shaheed, and Majboor. Everybody else said, though, that he was best in Halaku, Jis Desh Mein Ganga Behti Hai, Madhumati, Upkar, Zanjeer, and, of course, Shaheed.

For Pran there is no personal challenge in an author-backed role and it is his constant search for challenges within the stereotyped characterizations of mainstream cinema that has kept his creativity alive. He insisted that he had never felt 'bored' in the over 300 films he has acted in—even though a multi-starrer does not quite justify the presence of three heroes, three heroines, and three villains. 'With so many people around, very few characters are justified.' The only multi-starrer that achieved the impossible in his opinion was *Amar Akbar Anthony*.

He no longer cares for film awards either. In the early 1970s he refused to accept a Filmfare Award for his performance in *Be-Imaan* because he felt that the award for music direction should have gone to the late Ghulam Mohammed's score in *Pakeezah* rather than to the composer of *Be-Imaan*. 'That would have been my third Filmfare Award. I refused it because I felt strongly about Ghulam Mohammed. After that the Filmfare Award was never again offered to me.' Not even questions about the National Film Awards roused his interest and he shrugged them off saying simply that even they were subject to controversies

He is prouder of the fact that in the early 1970s a group of college students at Bombay rang him up and asked for an appointment— to tell him that they had done a survey in all the schools and colleges in Maharashtra and discovered that after he had become a film villain, nobody had been named Pran by his parents. 'They did not come across a single schoolboy or a college student named Pran in the whole of Maharashtra,' he said with the quiet air of a man stating a unique personal achievement. (But Pran is not a Maharashtrian name!)

Similarly, he is also proud that late in life he got over his personal awkwardness about singing songs in front of the camera. Though he was a villain in *Yamla Jat*, two years later he came on the screen as a hero in *Khandaan* (1942). Nur Jehan sang all the songs of *Khandaan* and Pran was spared the ordeal of going through motions he had come to dislike. After two or three films as hero, he decided that since he couldn't run around trees, he didn't want to do the hero's role at all. It was some thirty years later in films like *Upkar* and *Zanjeer* that he finally got over his diffidence and now admits that he actually likes song sequences, especially if the songs are in-built into the story.

Looking back over the years the single biggest change he has seen as a film actor is in terms of social respectability, because 'when we started working in films people did not even want to rent us their houses and films were considered a bad line of work'. Today, fortuitously, things have changed.

Hindustan Times, *24 December 1989.*

* * *

The Amazingly Talented Sanjeev Kumar

Sanjeev Kumar was a talented and versatile actor with a penchant for comedy. He was not without predecessors, prominent amongst whom was Marathi writer-director and actor-comedian, Master Vinayak, who worked in the 1930s and 1940s.

None of the senior journalists ever let us into Sanjeev Kumar's secret. All through the years Sanjeev seemed to be a loner and a pioneer, not caring a damn for his uncontrollable waistline and combining a tremendous talent for serious drama with an astounding ability to parody some of the sacred conventions of young love in Hindi cinema.

For the post-Independence generations, Sanjeev was the first of the matinee idols who defied all the characteristics of conventional glamour. Yet this unusual film star is not without predecessor in Indian cinema.

In terms of artistic tradition, Sanjeev's obvious ancestor in the cinema would be Master Vinayak, who was equally roly-poly and equally adept at conjuring up a fast-moving series of the most fantastic expressions. Like Sanjeev, a master of parody and of visual and cinematic repartee, Master Vinayak's performance in

Brahmachari, one of the six old classics being shown at a festival here, demonstrated a sense of timing superb in its reflex, its variety of expressions, and its depth. One wonders why, when serious writing on cinema is coming more and more into fashion, the older generation of film journalists has not compared the ebullient brilliance of Sanjeev Kumar with Asrani at his best, why they have not compared his talent with that of Master Vinayak, which the years have not deemed and who is so genuinely modern. Indeed, it would be difficult to choose even today, if one was asked to make the choice, between Master Vinayak in *Brahmachari* and Sanjeev Kumar in *Manoranjan* or *Manchali*.

Brahmachari (made in 1938) was one of the six classics shown at a festival organized in the capital by the Delhi Film Society. The other films being shown were V. Shantaram's Marathi classics *Adodhya Che Raja* and *Maya Machindra* (1932), Mehboob Khan's *Aurat* (1940), Osten and Himanshu Rai's *The Light of Asia* (1926), the Marathi film *Shejari* (1941), and a film made on D.G. Phalke by the National Film Archives, which incorporates sequences from Phalke's *Raja Harishchandra* and other films.

Towering among these vintage gems is undoubtedly Master Vinayak's *Brahmachari*, with one of the most perspicacious and effective scripts ever written for the cinema, by the legendary playwright and journalist P.K. Atre.

According to senior cineastes, *Brahmachari* secured its release only after a lot of trouble with the censors. Quite apart from its devastating satirical approach, *Brahmachari* had woven so cleverly into its script so many aspects of the national freedom struggle that one can imagine the film censors of the British Indian government being shocked out of their complacency. The masterstroke of Atre and Vinayak was that, in an extremely modernist way, they were projecting their message of Gandhi's leadership and of the national cause even as they seemed to satirize the loud manifestations of hollow Gandhists. They thereby made the film much more complex than film censors are habituated to experiencing.

For instance, the entire community of the self-help ashram is shown with a slant that attacks those who made a caricature of Gandhi's ideas. It makes, thereby, a clear suggestion to the film audience as to the real nature of Gandhian ideals. Thereby, *Brahmachari* also poses a serious challenge to the ambitious writer or film director who would like to make a film on the theme of family planning. It is the film that today's film-makers should compare their own work with, if they wish to use comedy as the instrument for taking social messages to the masses.

Incidentally, the planting of trees and afforestation is also savagely satirized through the cameo of the character of the heroine's father. This is said to be a parody of a luminary of the British Indian government who was a great advocate of afforestation as the solution to the problems of India.

In the late 1930s and the early 1940s, *Brahmachari* was a sensational topic of social conversation and divided people on opposing sides. Educated girls were instructed by their parents not to see the film because of its bathing scenes, featuring the mischievous Meenakshi and Master Vinayak, and because Meenakshi bared her calves for the magnifying vision of the motion picture camera. That surely should be the culminating testimony of *Brahmachari* as a film classic! For if we look at the history of international cinema, the greatest films have always raised the most intense controversies. It almost begins to appear now that a relevant film must, of necessity, stir a hornet's nest in the complacency that society loves so dearly and so unconsciously. The ability to provoke a sharp and widespread social debate is a film's most powerful function, its best gift to society.

The parallel between Master Vinayak and Sanjeev Kumar is not the only parallel this festival of film classics provided. For Sardar Akhtar's personality in Mehboob Khan's *Aurat* brings out the acute resemblance that Zeenat Aman shares with Mehboob's leading lady. They have the same kind of face and figure. Sardar Akhtar seems, despite the emphatically rural atmosphere of Mehboob's film and all its characterizations, unable to really hide a Westernized and upper class background. Zeenat may do well to study and compare Sardar Akhtar's ability to blend her Westernized personality with the local environment.

Though it might seem far-fetched to filmgoers of an earlier generation, there is, to my mind, some kind of a parallel that may be drawn between Yakub (in *Aurat*) and Shatrughan Sinha. Yakub had perfected a particular and effective screen personality that enabled him to juxtapose the more common features of the other artistes with the individualized air of violence in his own personality. Every gesture he made in *Aurat* seemed to be his own. And considering the promise that Shatrughan showed as a highly individualized stylist, it may be that he realizes the depths of his own talent in taking Yakub not just as his model but as his inspiration—not to imitate but to learn from, so that he can make discoveries into his own self as an actor.

A study of the early films made by V. Shantaram should open the eyes of those film intellectuals who are always making the same points of criticism against popular cinema. For it is strange that these critics applaud Shantaram's early films on the one hand and, on the other, criticize today's film-makers for many of the things they derived from Shantaram. For instance, the huge set of the queen's throne in Shantaram's *Maya Machindra* (1932). A massive lion's head, it opens automatically when the queen (played by Durga Khote in her prime) approaches it and reveals her throne. In *Maya Machindra*, Shantaram included a leopard as the queen's personal pet to suggest the Amazonian queen's strength and sternness. The leopard, of course, raises another question. Why is it that animal trainers in India are not able to make the big cats behave naturally for a film sequence? There were moments in *Maya Machindra* when the leopard seemed to be more conscious of its trainer (outside the camera's field) than of its supposed mistress, the queen. Though forty-five years have passed since

Shantaram included a leopard in *Maya Machindra*, we cannot yet say that our animal trainers have been able to come up with scenes where big cats of the lion family have 'acted' well in a film. To an extent, many of the trends in Hindi cinema in the 1950s derived inspiration from other aspects of Shantaram's films. Yet only too often we have come across the discordant argument that praises Prabhat Films and criticizes a later use of many of the same elements. Is the objective analyst to presume then that popular cinema, since it is intrinsically controversial, can be praised only by posterity but not by the present?

Hindustan Times, *11 November 1985*.

* * *

Analysing a Stylist—Mani Ratnam

Mani Ratnam's grasp of film technique and social concerns has made him one of Tamil and Hindi cinemas' most respected and imitated film-makers. Ratnam's cinema revolves around filial relationships and the centre of his cinematic universe is the family pitted against society.

Power and family—in recent years these have been the main thematic concerns of director Mani Ratnam's films. After *Nayakan*, everybody even at Bombay, began to acknowledge that he is the most creative director within the framework of the so-called commercial cinema. And since *Nayakan*, only on one occasion has a Mani Ratnam film strayed from the emotionalism of a family drama. That was *Thiruda Thiruda*, which won critical acclaim but which flopped with Mani Ratnam's own audience.

The struggle for power and the search for happiness within the family—these are the two quintessential characteristics of the contemporary mood. Popular cinema too perhaps stresses that which seems most absent in the social environment and that which seems most desired by the many. The search for strong family ties has thus become one of the pivots in the fantasies of cinema, along with the struggle for power with self-respect. This becomes most evident in Mani Ratnam's *Dala-Pati*, recently released in a dubbed Hindi version.

The most popular action films in the Hindi cinema have, almost as a rule, combined the seemingly far-removed elements of individual bravura with a strong emotional content. To see *Sholay* again is to realize that this magnificent action drama is in many ways an intensely emotional film too. In the 1970s, big hits like *Mera Gaon Mera Desh, Johny Mera Naam, Deewar, Zanjeer, Jugnu,* and *Roti Kapda aur Makaan* provide us with splendid examples of this combination of action and sentiment. In recent years, almost as a cliché, all action films—the good, the dull, and the boring— seek to remix the potion in a bid to give a new touch of old glory to young actors who wish to claim a slice of the legacy of *Zanjeer*.

Seen against the current crop of mainstream action films, Mani Ratnam's *Dala-Pati* assumes a completely different look. But, in fact, is that all that different in its content? Is it not yet another stylistic, technical wonder that in fact adds to the mainstream tradition while seeming to break away from it?

There is no doubt that in his use of cinema's technical impro- visations, Mani Ratnam is one of the major innovators of our time. He was one of the first directors in India to shoot dance sequences against the light. In *Geetanjali*, a love story that seemed to be an updated version of Hrishikesh Mukherjee's *Mili*, glamour and glitz exploded on the screen as the lead pair went break-dancing on the street in the full glow of car headlights staring through a diffused lens at the camera. This brilliant improvisation can be seen again in several Hindi movies made in the last five years. The most effective development in this direction has been the use of mov- ing lights for the *Mast mast* number in director Rajiv Rai's *Mohra*. The true film buff could well mark out the two song-sequences for comparison. That is how striking the street dance number was in *Geetanjali* about eight years ago.

However, with the exception of *Roja* that set its action against a backdrop of the Kashmiri terrorist movement, which had never previously been picturized effectively on Indian screen, most of Mani Ratnam's recent films conform to the traditional framework of the 'story' in mainstream Indian cinema.

In this writer's opinion, *Dala-Pati* can be seen as a sequel of sorts to Yash Chopra's *Deewar*, reinforcing the traumatically intense drama of estrangement between mother and son. (And, as they say, *Deewar* itself seemed like the 'urbanization' of the theme of *Mother India* and *Aurat*.) Of course, no two films are wholly alike. *Dala-Pati* offers a perspective of its own to the thematic denouement of the mother-son relationship in *Deewar*.

What is striking, however, are two characteristics of Mani Ratnam's oeuvre. First, his stylistic rebrews of old wine in dazzlingly new bottles. This enables him to stay within the essential framework of mainstream Indian cinema, while at the same time his visual treatment ensures that the film has an original look.

Second, in the delineation of the emotional content of themes, Mani Ratnam constantly expresses an extremely contemporary sensitivity to the way people evaluate social values. In their nuances, his films touch upon social values that are only newly emerging within the social framework of the family; and these new values Mani Ratnam drives home with great power.

In *Dala-Pati*, for instance, we see the husband supporting his wife in her grief, and in her search for the illegitimate child she had abandoned at an orphange at the immature age of 15 years. It is a social comment quite remarkable in its ramifications, and absolutely in tune with the doubts and debates taking place in contemporary India about what is 'correct' and what is 'pardonable' in the human condition.

The full impact of Mani Ratnam's creativity on the Indian film scene will take some time to be realized. But to give credit where it is due we must underline the fact that it was Ratnam's *Roja*—and not Spielberg's *Jurassic Park*—which was the pathbreaker as the first dubbed film to storm the box office of the Hindi film industry.

Of course, *Dala-Pati* has not started with the resounding box-office collections that *Roja* engineered, but the cause of good mainstream cinema will be strongly served if word-of-mouth publicity helps *Dala-Pati* garner a wider audience.

It does, of course, suffer from the fact that the success of *Roja* has led to an inflationary price range. *Dala-Pati* is the most expensive dubbed film to be marketed in India, at over Rs 17 lakh for the distribution rights of each major territory. It is a price that is much, much more than the distributors paid for either *Roja* or *Jurassic Park*.

At the same time, Mani Ratnam himself would do well to reconsider that his more unusual film, *Roja*, became a bigger national success than his films with more conventional themes. This is a question he will have to face in the days ahead.

Published in Hindustan Times.

* * *

3956/31.12.08

O U P

90585344

21.6.11